# THE PRESIDENT'S TEAM

# THE PRESIDENT'S TEAM

*The 1963 Army–Navy Game
and the Assassination of JFK*

Michael Connelly

Foreword by
Senator Edward M. Kennedy

Afterword by
Roger Staubach and Admiral Tom Lynch

MVP
BOOKS

This book is dedicated to the members of the 1963 football programs at the United States Naval Academy and the United States Military Academy at West Point who made the ultimate sacrifice in defense of freedom and democracy, exemplifying the courage, honor, and valor of our military services: From Army, Mike Berdy, Gary Kadetz, and Bill Sipos; and from Navy, Michael Burns, Tom Holden, and Douglas McCarty.

To my beautiful wife, Noreen, whose smile still lights up a room; my son, Ryan, whom I thank God for every day; my mom and dad, who raised six children the old-fashioned way—with love and accountability; my brother and sisters, who aren't just my siblings but my friends and are always there for me as I will be for them.

First published in 2009 by MVP Books, an imprint of
MBI Publishing Company and the Quayside Publishing Group,
400 First Avenue North, Suite 300, Minneapolis, MN 55401 USA

MVP Books are also available at discounts in bulk quantity for industrial
or sales-promotional use. For details write to Special Sales Manager at Quayside
Publishing Group, 400 First Avenue North, Suite 300, Minneapolis, MN 55401 USA.

To find out more about our books, visit us online at www.mvpbooks.com.

**Library of Congress Cataloging-in-Publication Data**

Connelly, Michael (Michael P.)
 The president's team : the 1963 Army-Navy game and the assassination
 of JFK / Michael Connelly ; foreword by Senator Edward M. Kennedy ;
 afterword by Roger Staubach.
  p.  cm.
 Includes index.
 ISBN 978-0-7603-3762-2 (hb w/ jkt)
 1. United States Naval Academy—Football—History. 2. United States
 Military Academy—Football—History. 3. Kennedy, John F. (John Fitzgerald),
 1917–1963—Assassination. 4. Football—United States—History.  I. Title.
 GV958.U512C66 2009
 796.332—dc22                                             2009029021

**Edited by** Josh Leventhal and Chad Caruthers **Designed by** Diana Boger
Printed in the United States of America

# Contents

# Foreword

by Senator Edward M. Kennedy

WE ALL LOVED TO PLAY TOUCH FOOTBALL GROWING UP. From the time I could walk, we were playing football together—and that included my sisters as well. We loved it, and some of my earliest memories are of those early games. Sports are such an important part of childhood, and in my family, we took it seriously. Nothing could equal the competition of some of our games of touch football on the Cape.

Jack and Bobby used to captain opposing teams. Neither liked to lose, let me tell you! The games were supposed to be touch, but I remember getting tackled in a lot of them.

My brothers Joe and Bobby played football at Harvard, and from the first game I saw them play, I knew I wanted to follow in their footsteps. Jack didn't play football at Harvard because of his back. He did play at Choate School and loved to be part of the touch football games we played on the Cape.

Bobby was an amazing player. He was terrific, and he lettered. Although he was smaller than a lot of the other players, he practiced harder, hit harder, and was more tenacious than any two other teammates put together. He would stay after practice and continue to work with Kennedy O'Donnell, running plays until they became second nature to him. In his senior year Bobby started the first game and scored the only touchdown. A few days later he fractured his leg in practice but told no one. He kept on trying to play until he collapsed on the field. The injury knocked him out for the rest of the season, but the coach sent him in for his letter during the last moments of the Yale game even though his leg was in a cast. He was involved in the last play and fortunately didn't injure himself any further. After he graduated, he used to play on weekends with a semi-pro team on the Cape, just for the fun of it. He was sensational.

My brother Joe played for the varsity as well. He was an end, but not a starter. He was smaller than many of the other players, and although he was tough and agile, he was prone to injuries. He had to have his knee operated on as a result of one injury. Unfortunately, he was one of the seniors who did not get to play in the final Yale game, so he didn't get a letter. Harvard was ahead in the game, but because the coach, Dick Harlow, was afraid of a possible loss, he kept the starters in. This disappointed the team, who all wanted the nineteen seniors to get in the game, even if only for one play, to qualify for their letter. It was a tough day for all of them.

I played left end at Harvard, and I tell people that's where I learned my professional philosophy. I made many great friends on the team. The one memory that stands out for me is catching a touchdown pass in the Yale game. That was a real thrill—especially since my father and brothers were in the stands watching. It doesn't get any better than that!

Unfortunately, we didn't win the game. But Dad took us out to dinner, and we had a wonderful time catching up with each other and remembering our time at Harvard and other great games. It was a memorable day in so many ways.

❨ ❨ ❨

My brother Jack was proud of his Navy service and certainly felt a great loyalty to the Navy and the lifelong friends he made there. He was always especially delighted to accept invitations to speak at the Naval Academy, and he always felt a special tie to the students who were soon to be officers under his command during the Cold War. I often think of his beautiful words to the new class of midshipmen at the ceremony in front of Bancroft Hall in the summer of 1963, when he told them,

"I can imagine no more rewarding career. And any man who may be asked in this century what he did to make his life worthwhile, I think can respond with a good deal of pride and satisfaction: 'I served in the United States Navy.'"

He loved to joke with them as well. At the end of that speech, Jack told them the story of the admiral who'd pull out a piece of paper from his desk drawer every morning before he started his work. The paper said, "Left-port; right-starboard." Jack told the young men, "If you can remember that, your careers are assured."

My brother always admired excellence in any field, and athletics was no exception. He greatly enjoyed meeting Navy football stars Joe Bellino and Roger Staubach and Tom Lynch, and talking with them about football and their future as officers in the Navy. It was an enjoyable break in his otherwise busy day dealing with the needs of the nation.

As president, Jack had to remain neutral during the Army–Navy games, since he was commander in chief of all the armed services. Traditionally, the president changes sides at halftime so he won't be seen as favoring one team over the other. I remember one year he was on the Army side for the first half and then walked across the field and was met at the 50-yard line by the Navy brass. He shook hands with the Army generals and West Point cadets who had accompanied him and then turned to walk with the Navy escort to his seat on the Navy side. A roar went up from the Midshipmen and the Navy supporters because they knew, as a former navy man, he was coming home, so to speak. He got an especially loud and warm welcome, and flashed a particularly big smile.

I served in the Army, so Jack always gave me a good-natured kidding whenever Navy won over the years, and I paid him back in kind when Army won.

I remember the 1963 game being on in the background and that it was more subdued than usual. I believe there was a tribute to the president, but it was a difficult time, and we really couldn't give the game our full attention. Navy won that year. My brother would have liked that.

# Preface

THE SEEDS OF A BOOK ARE SOMETIMES SOWN over a period of years. Such was the case with the story of *The President's Team*. A decade ago, I was working on a separate project and had the honor of interviewing Navy great Roger Staubach. During that interview, he recounted the story of the 1963 Army–Navy game, which was played two weeks after President John F. Kennedy's death. The story was fascinating, and what really struck me was the genuine sentiment behind his words. It was apparent that moment in the country's history and that specific game greatly impacted Staubach as a football player and person.

Staubach told me of the feeling of running onto that field at Municipal Stadium in Philadelphia (just days removed from accepting the Heisman Trophy) and being overcome by emotion. Fans in the bleachers, viewers at home, and players on the field all looked to the game as a remedy for the ills that enveloped the country and its people. The death of Kennedy, a member of the Navy family, cast an indefinite pall over the nation. The Army–Navy game offered fans and players alike a chance to escape the horror of November 1963. Staubach has never again realized the palpable emotion of that moment in time, not even while playing in Super Bowls as the star quarterback of the Dallas Cowboys.

"Where were you when President Kennedy was shot?" is a question every American of cognizant age at that time can answer in precise detail. From the moment the shots rang out on that sunny Dallas day, the country was suffocated by the shock of quashed promise and an extinguished life. Consequently, the nation was desperate to escape the melancholy. On December 7, 1963, the country was allowed a brief moment to exhale when the service academies faced off in their annual football game, which was only played at the request of the president's family.

Originally, I intended to limit the scope of this book to the two weeks that began with the president's death on November 22, 1963, concluding with the Army–Navy game. But when I finally rolled up my sleeves and dove into the essence of research and interviews, I discovered that the story was so much more. Not only did I come to realize that the relationship between the Navy football team and President Kennedy was profound, but I also found that the kinship shared among the players wearing the blue and gold of Navy was strong. Suddenly, I couldn't help but widen the scope of the story.

With each article I read and interview I conducted, I became closer to the 1963 Navy team. I recognized that there was something unique and worthy of greater exploration. Sent back in time, I sat at my computer or at the microfiche machine vicariously living through that amazing season as if I were actually a participant in the program. I held my breath with every story of touchdown passes, laughed at accounts of pranks, smirked at sources of nicknames, and smiled at genuine moments of comradeship.

The nature of the bond that still exists among members of the team half a century later is so special that to define them collectively as teammates would grossly undervalue the strength of the connection that links one to the other. These men were brothers, young men who met in Annapolis and were destined to play football at the highest level but who never allowed football to define them, though it was a big part of them. It is within this brotherhood that grown men are unabashed in their love for one another and pledge to be there for each other always.

The 1963 Navy football team is a team like no other. To this day, it remains winched together like a square knot tied at sea, one rope dependent upon the other. The master of the knot is still their captain, Tom Lynch, a man possessing a gene of leadership that allowed him to inspire his peers in a noble but firm manner. After graduation, Lynch rose to the rank of admiral before returning to the Naval Academy as superintendent. He will always be the captain of the 1963 Navy football team.

> O Captain! my Captain! our fearful trip is done.
> The ship has weather'd every rack, the prize we sought is won,
> The port is near, the bells I hear, the people all exulting.
> —Walt Whitman

Ultimately, *The President's Team* is a blended story about a charismatic commander in chief and the team that fascinated him.

# Acknowledgments

DURING THIS SPORTSWRITING ADVENTURE, I was honored to interview twelve Heisman Trophy winners, multiple members of the College Football Hall of Fame, and countless all-American athletes. I stood on the sideline of a University of Wisconsin football game next to Elroy "Crazy Legs" Hirsh, who pointed at the regalia of Camp Randall Stadium and remarked that this is what is special about college football. Former Northwestern University and Purdue University assistant football coach George Steinbrenner (yes, that George Steinbrenner) talked with me on the phone about how special Saturday afternoons in autumn are. All-American Teddy Bruschi tried his best to articulate to me the essence of the rivalry between his University of Arizona team and Arizona State University, finally trading decorum for sincerity: "When I think of those Sun Devils, I want to vomit!"

I have been fortunate in my writing to have visited more than thirty college football stadiums. I stood at midfield while Peyton Manning was introduced to an adoring Tennessee crowd for the last time. I was a guest of the Downtown Athletic Club and watched Ricky Williams accept the 1998 Heisman Trophy. I partied in Baton Rouge, Louisiana, and marveled at the native obsession, known as LSU football. But there was no greater indoctrination to the great sport of college football than sitting in my den watching games on the family Zenith TV with my father as he shared stories of his playing days at Boston College, while Chris Schenkel read scores (including those from the Slippery Rock game) during the Prudential post-game show.

It was in my father's stories, which he gladly shared with his three boys, that I heard my first anecdote relevant to the United States Naval Academy's football team. As the story went, it was a game in which Navy had long decided the outcome of the contest, and the final seconds were ticking off the clock. It was then that a midshipman by the name of Anthony A. Anthony picked up a loose ball and began to run. Never having scored a touchdown in college, he couldn't believe his eyes when he saw only grass between him and the end zone. With six points and a special college football moment within Anthony's grasp, he was suddenly tackled by my father, who had run him down from behind just yards shy of the pylon. Months later when my father arrived at boot camp in Quantico, Virginia, he was greeted by his platoon leader, one Anthony A. Anthony.

In 1997, I invited my father to join me while I was on assignment at the Army–Navy game in East Rutherford, New Jersey, at Giants Stadium in the Meadowlands. During that game, we stood on the sideline or in the press box in awe of what was the Army–Navy game. As the final moments of the game fell off the clock, Navy leading 39–7, my father became incensed when Navy Coach Charlie Weatherbie refused to empty his bench, thus failing to allow his reserve players the chance to create a lifelong memory of participating in the classic rivalry. At Weatherbie's post-game press conference, I had to restrain my father from grilling the coach on his failure to be an advocate for all of his players.

Despite my father's justified irritation with the Navy coach, that Saturday was a special father-and-son moment that will forever be shared: The march on by the midshipmen and cadets, the pageantry of the game, and the genuine effort by all who participated, from fan to player, were inspiring. It was the reason, in President John F. Kennedy's eyes, that Navy football represents all that is good about this country.

There are many to acknowledge, and I must start with my father, John "Boots" Connelly. Despite my chance meetings with Heisman winners and all-Americans, the greatest football player I've been blessed to know is my father, who ran down a midshipman and later paid the price in the form of pushups and long marches. I also thank my mother, Marilyn, who continues to be a proofreader, editor, and supporter of my writing, which she is convinced surpasses Hemingway, Twain, and Steinbeck; my wife, Noreen, who not only reads and lovingly makes suggestions but also tolerates a husband who spends too much time at the keyboard; my son, Ryan, who is my life's blessing and sacrifices so I can realize satisfaction in this sometimes selfish pursuit of writing; my editor-extraordinaire, Josh Leventhal, who patiently guided me word by word; my friend Steve Alperin, a constant source of encouragement and suggestions; my pastor, Monsignor William Helmick, for his support and guidance; cousin Sarah Kenny, who brought Washington to Boston; Betty Maas, who brought Annapolis to Boston; and Tom Lynch, who allowed me the honor of entering the special world of the 1963 Navy football team. Admiral Lynch, the team's center, joined forces with quarterback Roger Staubach to pen the afterword, while Senator Edward M. Kennedy graced my book with his generous words in the foreword. Heisman Trophy winner Joe Bellino; Bill Belichick, legendary football coach and son of Navy assistant coach Steve Belichick; and college football historian and writer Dan Jenkins contributed kind words for the back cover of the book. Scott Strasemeier, sports information director at the Naval Academy, was helpful in providing photos and information on the 1963 team.

To those who volunteered their time to share memories of glorious days past, I thank you:

Jack Clary, Navy football historian; Ted Sorensen, President Kennedy's adviser and special counsel; Kathy Townsend Kennedy, daughter of Robert Kennedy and former governor of New Jersey; James Cheevers, senior curator of the United States Naval Academy Museum; Phil Marwill, College Football Hall of Fame; and Tony Verna of CBS television and producer of the 1963 Army–Navy game.

In addition, I would like to acknowledge numerous college football representatives: Rollie Stichweh, Pete Dawkins, Coach Paul Dietzel, and the "Lonely End" Bill Carpenter of the United States Military Academy; Darryl Hill, University of Maryland; Beano Cook, University of Pittsburgh and ESPN college football analyst; Johnny Roderick, Tom Caughran, Mac White, and Gerry York of Southern Methodist University; and David McWilliams, University of Texas.

# Introduction

IN 1890, THE U.S. NAVAL ACADEMY FOOTBALL TEAM WALKED UP THE HILL on the banks of the Hudson River and onto the plains of West Point to answer the challenge of the newly formed Army Cadet team. In the years since, the gridiron match-up between these two academies has been a bloody and passionate example of the power of sport and its capacity to galvanize, inspire, and devastate. The Army–Navy football game has induced a spirit of both respect and hatred, deference and disdain. From kickoff to the sound of the final gun, the energy of competition that emanates from the field is what makes this rivalry so special. It's genuine. It's the essence of sport.

When John F. Kennedy assumed the office of President of the United States in 1961, he represented the promise of a new frontier that roused the country and filled its people with a spirit of hope and anticipation. A young and vibrant leader resided in the White House, prepared and ready to transport the nation from the stagnancy of black-and-white into a world of Technicolor—a world where all was possible. From his rocking chair in the Oval Office or behind a microphone in the rose garden, the sandy-haired president urged and prodded Americans to join him on a journey where the only limits were those that the citizens of the nation placed upon themselves. He would serve as the country's compass, hoping to lead its people on an exploration across the universe. His mission was to inspire the nation, to embrace the ideal by which he and his family lived: "Other people see things and say, why? But I dream things that never were and say, why not?"

It was on the 50-yard line of the football field at Rice University that the president personified this relentless quest for discovery. It was his wish to lead the nation on a course that would travel beyond the borders of man's earthly confines to the moon. It was this cosmic ambition that he posed to his audience that day: "But why, some say, the moon? Why choose this as our goal? And they may well ask, why climb the highest mountain? Why, thirty-five years ago, fly the Atlantic? Why does Rice play Texas?"

By the conclusion of the speech, all who questioned the probability now believed in the possibility. "Space is there, and we're going to climb it, and the moon and the planets are there, and new hopes for knowledge and peace are there. And, therefore, as we set sail we ask God's blessing on the most hazardous and dangerous and greatest adventure on which man has ever embarked."

President Kennedy possessed a spirit that was devoid of boundaries. He inspired Americans to recognize that all was possible. His vision and sense of hope helped to invigorate a country and its people to act, not just speculate.

In Annapolis, Maryland, just north of Washington, D.C., there was a collection of forty-four young men who embodied the very essence of the president's vision for a new America. They came from every corner of the country to the Naval Academy, where they were fused together as one to form the Navy football team. As individuals they were undersized and consequently undervalued by college coaches across the nation. But what these so-called evaluators of talent failed to understand was that any perceived physical deficiency these young men might have possessed was mitigated by a passion to achieve on the field, in the classroom, and later, on the high seas of battle.

The fact that they were not only football players but also midshipmen, and eventually U.S. Navy officers, served to link one team member to the other. They shared experiences and vulnerabilities that extended beyond the gridiron. They all wore the white uniform of the Naval Academy; they survived plebe year; and they carried with them the same communal concern with the unknown, as active duty and a volatile Southeast Asia lay beyond graduation. It was a bond that made them so much more than teammates. They were brothers.

The 1963 Navy football team transcended athletics. Its members used the sport as a catalyst to cast them forward into the future to serve each other and the nation. They traveled to the Naval Academy as individuals but departed as one, leaving their mark upon the great school and the country.

Early November 1963, less than two weeks away from meeting its rival from West Point, the Navy Midshipmen football team was preparing to lay claim to service academy pride and earn an invitation to the Cotton Bowl. Situated throughout the dining room of King Hall, the brigade members sat at attention with eyes forward as they waited to be addressed over the loudspeaker system. In eleven days, the school's second-ranked football team, and in extension the entire brigade, would travel to Municipal Stadium in Philadelphia to wage "war" with the Army Cadets. The game would be attended by 102,000 fans, among them navy hero and ardent fan of the Midshipmen, President John F. Kennedy. The president had attended the 1961 and 1962 Army–Navy games, and while protocol demanded that the head of all selective services remain neutral and refrain from showing favor toward either academy, there was no question in the minds of all in attendance who the one-time lieutenant of the PT 109 was cheering for.

In anticipation of the 1963 game, the president penned a note to the midshipmen, which was read to plebes and first classmen alike: "I look forward to sitting on the winning side in the second half. Signed, President John F. Kennedy."

The note drew a roar from the midshipmen. Just months previous, the commander in chief had flown to Annapolis, Maryland, to greet the incoming class of the brigade and mark the twentieth anniversary of his service as skipper of the PT 109. Each member of the academy could relate to the man who sat in the Oval Office, and vice versa. Each felt a special bond with the president, and it was a bond that was formed before and during his presidency. The president was a navy man himself, earning hero status during his service in World War II. He looked at the Navy football team and saw what was good about America and its prospects for the future. It was under the gold helmet that the leaders of tomorrow forged ahead seeking to win, not only for themselves and the Naval Academy, but also for their biggest fan, John F. Kennedy. He was one of them.

The 1963 Army–Navy game would be televised to a national audience on CBS. Lindsey Nelson would announce the game, in which the new technology of instant replay would be introduced to America. The innovation was being rushed to television for this game to allow America to enjoy the artistry of the Navy team's brilliant quarterback, Roger Staubach. Known as Roger the Dodger and the Jolly Roger, Staubach was the number-one sports story in the country, thrilling America with his running and passing.

Several days prior to the game, a spokesperson from *Life* magazine had called Navy sports information director Budd Thalman and informed him that Staubach would be featured on the cover of the magazine that week. An excited Thalman asked, "Is there anything that could derail it?" The magazine spokesperson replied, "Only some kind of catastrophe."

Three days after the commander in chief's note was read to the Navy students, the president was dead.

Word of the tragedy spread across the campus like an electric current from midshipman to midshipman. From windows where banners hung imploring the team to "Beat Army," classmate yelled to classmate the fateful news. On televisions across the country, Walter Cronkite took off his glasses as if he couldn't believe what he was reading and announced, "From Dallas, Texas, the flash apparently official, President Kennedy died at 1:00 p.m. Central Standard Time." The "Voice of America" then paused, trying to compose himself. Putting his black-rimmed glasses back on, the veteran newsman's voice wavered in distress, for he knew what all America knew at that very moment: The nation was changed forever.

As good midshipmen, the students still made their way to classes and took their seats while whispering the latest rumors as they waited for their professors to arrive. In their minds, the horror couldn't be true. Kennedy had seemed immortal. Sadly, their proctors eventually took their places behind their desks or classroom podiums, shaken and ashen. Most teachers were too distraught to teach and elected to cancel class and allow students (and themselves) the opportunity to process the tragic news.

Most of the midshipmen returned to their rooms to reflect. Members of the football team reported to the locker room for the scheduled practice. Somber and confused, they sat in front of the lockers quiet and reflective. When Coach Wayne Hardin came into the room, his players stared at him in desperate need of guidance. With a tremble in his voice and eyes red from crying, Hardin asked the team to take a knee on the cement floor of the locker room and say a prayer for their friend, the president.

Practice was cancelled, and players were left to their own means. Some made their way to the campus chapel while others sat in their company room listening intently to the latest news reports. The campus and the country were paralyzed by shock and uncertainty. For the last three years, it was President Kennedy who stared down Cuba and Russia; it was he who told the country that it could reach the stars; it was he who instilled in Americans a spirit of confidence and promise.

But now the force of idealism was replaced with a cloud of vulnerability. In New York, the stock market was closed. Around the perimeter of the country, borders were locked down as the nation and its armed forces were placed on high alert.

At Annapolis, the midshipmen felt the loss personally. Just three months earlier, the president had visited the campus to greet the incoming class of plebes. At the end of his speech, President Kennedy departed the dais to the sound of wild cheers. The president was so taken by the spirit of kinship shown to him by the plebes that he made his way back to the podium and added, "In view of that warm cheer I'd like to . . . using my powers of the Office, to grant amnesty to whoever needs it, whoever deserves it." The midshipmen roared in approval. He was their president.

Following Kennedy's appearance at Bancroft Hall, the superintendent of the Naval Academy wrote to the president in thanks for his visit.

8/2/1963

Dear Mr. President,

Your visit yesterday gave a tremendous lift to our young gentlemen of the plebe class. Your remarks were perfectly chosen, and could not have been more appropriate.

All of us at the Naval Academy were greatly honored and privileged to meet you here and we hope that during your visit you were able to sense some of the enthusiasm and dedication of the fine young men of the Brigade and Midshipmen. Many thanks for your kindness in sharing one of your very busy days with us.

From,

Superintendent Rear Admiral Charles C. Kirkpatrick

Throughout the coming fall, the president followed the progress of the Navy football team with great interest. Navy had one of the greatest players in college football history playing quarterback, and the team was ranked second in the nation. At the end of November, his plan was to leave the Thanksgiving gathering at the Kennedy compound to fly to Philadelphia and watch his favorite team play its most ardent rival. In anticipation, the president had penned the following message to be included in the game-day program:

To the Corps of Cadets and Brigade of Midshipmen:

It is a pleasure to once again send my best wishes to the Cadets and the Midshipmen on the occasion of the annual Army–Navy game in Philadelphia.

Our service academies in this game, which has become traditional, always field spirited teams. This inter-academy rivalry is intense but at the same time is a standard of good sportsmanship and a mark of keen competition.

Most of all, we have an opportunity to see fine young men who are preparing to be future military leaders of our nation. Good luck to both teams, and my warm regards.

The president never made it to the Thanksgiving gathering or the game that he so looked forward to attending. His death shocked the nation. The Pentagon suspended all federal activities (including the Army–Navy game) to observe a month's mourning period. The spirit of exploration that had enveloped the country was now replaced with the power of the unknown. The beacon of hope and promise had been dimmed, casting a pall of darkness across the nation that left a people searching for the light that had once shined so brightly, now extinguished.

# CHAPTER 1

# John Fitzgerald Kennedy, From Navy Hero to President

THE KENNEDY BOYS WERE GROOMED FOR SUCCESS, from the family dining room in Hyannisport, Massachusetts, to the classrooms of the most exclusive schools in the country. Originally, elder son Joseph Kennedy Jr. was the chosen one. His death while flying missions in World War II passed the baton to the next son, John, in the tradition of Irish succession.

Massachusetts senator John Fitzgerald Kennedy's decision to run for president began a long, arduous journey for him, one that Kennedy family members viewed as an odyssey to fulfill what family patriarch Joseph Kennedy felt was the family's destiny. John F. Kennedy's presidential candidacy was an amazing step for the family, which had landed in America aboard an Irish-immigrant ship.

During the presidential campaign of 1960, Kennedy spoke of the responsibility he was undertaking. "Just as I went into politics because Joe died," then Senator Kennedy said, "if anything happened to me tomorrow, my brother Bobby would run for my seat in the senate, and if Bobby died, Teddy would take over for him."

The Kennedy family dream could not and would not be quashed. Issues and crises that presented themselves were handled with steely resolve. Across the country, questions of his youth, of his Catholic religion, and of his father's ability to manipulate and influence with his money were unrelentingly discussed and debated.

When opponents pointed to the forty-three-year-old senator's age and perceived lack of experience, the Democratic presidential candidate created an image of a fighter who would not be denied. He aligned himself with aging baseball great Stan Musial. The St. Louis all-star was a well-respected national figure who was also facing the tendency of people to correlate ability with age. The Cardinals lefty was hearing whispers that he should retire as he approached forty, but he was resolute. Musial asked to be judged by performance and not age.

At a baseball game in Milwaukee, Kennedy summoned over the sweet-swinging Musial before the first pitch and encouraged, for all to hear (including the press), the future Hall of Fame player by saying, "Stan, they say you're too old to play ball and I'm too young to be president, but I've got an idea we'll prove them wrong." One year later, Kennedy was in the White House, and Musial, with his .330 batting average, was elected to baseball's annual all-star game.

Efforts to ostracize the Kennedy family dated back two generations, to the early 1900s, when John "Honey Fitz" Fitzgerald (John F.'s grandfather) faced similar encumbrances in his effort to penetrate the walls of Boston's established political realm. During his campaign against Henry Cabot Lodge, Fitzgerald's opponents attempted to sway voters by suggesting that his politics were affected by his religion. Consequently, Fitzgerald delivered an impassioned speech on the campaign trail that brought people to their feet as he addressed what he perceived to be the core of American values:

> The time has gone by when religious prejudice or racial bigotry can be successfully appealed into political warfare. The citizens of the United States have learned that America is the child of no single European nation, and that American sympathies are not circumscribed by class or creed, by race or sect. The mother country of America can hardly be said even to be Europe because here the

Arian and the Semite, the Jew and the Christian, dwell together, whatever diversity there may be in their respective racial origins or religious beliefs, bound together by the cement of common humanity and by a tie of the American brotherhood which makes Americans free and equal before the law. I am an American citizen and as such I have only contempt for the man who would seek to drag his race, or his creed, or any other citizen's race or creed into politics as a stepping stone to personal success.

As much as the country had changed in the half century following this speech, it had remained the same in many ways. As his grandfather had to overcome ethnic and religious biases, presidential candidate John F. Kennedy also had to fight eloquently with those who attempted to confine the hallways of political power to the established.

Kennedy addressed such concerns in what was in many ways the epicenter of Catholic disdain, at a gathering of the Greater Houston Ministerial Association. He made clear that neither his religion nor its leaders would interfere with his ability to represent people from all walks of life:

But because I am a Catholic, and no Catholic has ever been elected president, the real issues in this campaign have been obscured— perhaps deliberately, in some quarters less responsible than this . . . . I am not the Catholic candidate for president. I am the Democratic Party's candidate for president, who happens also to be a Catholic. I do not speak for my church on public matters, and the church does not speak for me. . . . I do not intend to apologize for these views to my critics of either Catholic or Protestant faith, nor do I intend to disavow either my views or my church in order to win this election. . . . If this election is decided on the basis that forty million Americans lost their chance of being president on the day they were baptized, then it is the whole nation that will be the loser.

Kennedy's eloquence, good looks, and boundless energy intimidated his opponents and roused a nation that was set on change. With his family's backing, Kennedy was a political machine, impelling rivals to blur issues with personal attacks.

In West Virginia, Kennedy's rival for the nomination, Hubert Humphrey, not only pointed to Kennedy's unfair financial backing but spoke in code about the ultimate destination of that money when he said that Kennedy had the advantage of "a little black bag and checkbook." Quick to dilute and anxious not to allow such issues to gain momentum, Kennedy stood in front of a microphone and extracted a piece of paper from his coat pocket. "I received a telegram from my father that said, 'Don't buy a single vote more than necessary. I'll be damned if I'm going to pay for a landslide.'" Kennedy successfully mitigated fallout from Humphrey's comments by pointing out its very absurdity.

❨ ❨ ❨

John F. Kennedy graduated from Harvard University in the spring of 1940. While the nation pursued its policy of isolationism, war ravaged across Europe and soon spread to other continents. In the fall following his graduation, the young Kennedy enrolled at Stanford Business School for postgraduate studies. Disturbed by the state of the world, he eventually chose to enlist in the military.

A first attempt to sign on with the army was rebuked because of the effects of a debilitating back ailment, which resulted from an injury suffered as a Harvard football player. Undeterred, as was his nature, Kennedy worked out, exercised, and added weight before exploiting family connections to convince navy personnel to accept a physical conducted by Kennedy's personal physician. His enlistment application was accepted, and he was subsequently appointed ensign and assigned a desk job in the Office of Naval Intelligence in October 1941. Two months later, Japan attacked Pearl Harbor, and the United States was thrust full-on into the global conflict.

As America's involvement in the war escalated through 1942, Ensign Kennedy was unsatisfied with his desk job and was determined to have a more direct role in the war effort. In February 1943, he sent the following memo to navy personnel:

From: John F. Kennedy
To: Chief of Personnel
Subject: Change of Assignment
It is requested that I be reassigned to a motor torpedo boat squadron now operating in the South Pacific.

In April 1943, Kennedy received his transfer. Before assignment, he was sent to Melville, Rhode Island, for training on PT (patrol torpedo) boats. There he joined the camp's football team, which subsequently traveled to West Point to scrimmage against Earl Blaik's great Army team, featuring Doc Blanchard and Glenn Davis. In the game, the upset-minded campers from Melville took an early 13–0 lead against the favored Army squad. The lead would be short lived, however, as the stampeding Cadets scored 55 straight points. Years later in the Oval Office, President Kennedy teased Coach Blaik by reminding him that they had led the game at one point. Blaik responded by reminding him, in turn, of the game's final score, 55–13, which drew a great laugh from the president.

After completing his PT training at Melville, Kennedy was assigned to the Solomon Islands in the Pacific, where he was placed in command of PT 109. On August 1, 1943, PT 109 and its crew of thirteen were sent out on patrol, along with fourteen other American ships, into the black of night. An official report noted overcast conditions with poor visibility. Their task was to tour the Blanket Strait, where Japanese vessels were known to run supplies back and forth to island strongholds. On this night, a skirmish forced the American vessels, including the radar-less PT 109, to separate.

A shadowy image appeared approximately 250 yards off the starboard side of PT 109. A brother boat, PT 162, was nearly hit and was able to identify the vessel by its pair of raked stacks and pair of turrets, and possibly a third turret. It was the Japanese destroyer *Amagiri*. What occurred in the next ten seconds was chronicled in an article written for Japanese newspapers by the commander of the *Amagiri*, Lieutenant Colonel Kohei Hanami:

> August 1 was a starless night with a touch of squall. On the bridge I saw an object stirring up white waves that was 1,000 meters on right stern. My judgment immediately was that it was a torpedo boat and I cried out, "Ten degree turn full speed." Strategy to negate torpedo boats was head on crash. The boat was sliced in two, a thunderous roar.

Executive officer Ted Robinson, stationed on another vessel, heard the explosion and looked back and thought the worst. "We figured no one could live through that blast." The PT 109 had been split in two, severing gas lines and igniting the water's surface. An official report that night read, "PT 109 was seen to collide with warship, followed by an explosion and a large flame that died down a little but continued to burn for 10 or 15 minutes."

Two shipmates on the PT 109 were immediately lost and perished. Some survivors were thrown into the water, while others, including Lieutenant Kennedy, were thrown onto the floor of the floating remains of the PT 109. As Kennedy lay there in pain, he said to himself, "This is how it feels to be killed."

The surviving crew took refuge on the boat's carcass, hoping that rescuers would find them before the Japanese did. As dawn broke the following morning, Kennedy, as commander of the ship, decided it would be safer to seek asylum on a neighboring island. Shipmate Patrick McMahon was badly injured and unable to swim, so Lieutenant Kennedy towed him along with the strap of McMahon's life jacket in his mouth. For five hours, Kennedy swam the breaststroke with his comrade behind him.

When they arrived at Bird Island, Kennedy's feet were bleeding from the coral reef that protected the island, and he was violently ill from the water he took in while swimming. He collapsed on the sandy beach, exhausted and with his back aching.

Over the ensuing days, Kennedy would leave the sanctuary of Bird Island and swim out into the passage between islands, searching for a potential rescue party. Although rescue efforts were conducted from the Allied base on Rendova Island, the parties did not cross paths. Officials at the base gave up hope and concluded that the men from PT 109 were gone. Further searches were terminated.

The camp held funeral ceremonies for the crew of PT 109. The chaplain's words seemed inadequate to reconcile the horror of war. Following the services, families of the deceased were contacted. At Hyannisport, Ambassador Joseph Kennedy was notified that his son was missing in action and that all searches had failed. The family patriarch decided to keep this information to himself until it was conclusive.

Meanwhile, on the islands, Lieutenant Kennedy and shipmates, alive but hungry and thirsty, finally encountered two island locals named Biuku and Eroni. The friendly natives provided the men with food and agreed to transport a message carved into a coconut that read, "11 alive. native knows posit & reef Nauru Island Kennedy." Biuku and Eroni delivered the message and soon returned with a response from Australian scout Lieutenant Arthur Reginald Evans, who requested that Kennedy travel with the natives to the Rendova camp.

Kennedy was placed in a canoe and covered with ferns to avoid detection by the Japanese. At one point during the journey, a Japanese fighter plane flew overhead, close enough for the natives to see the pilots inside and to wave to them. The canoe finally arrived at camp, and Kennedy led an American rescue party back to the island, where the ten other survivors were saved.

Kennedy served in the navy for several months after his dramatic rescue in the Solomon Islands and skippered the PT 59. During this time, he led a daring rescue of about sixty Marines who were trapped aboard a sinking vessel while being subjected to constant gunfire from the Japanese. Eventually, the injuries and illness he suffered during the ordeal of the PT 109 led the navy to force Kennedy's transfer back to the United States. His combat days were over, but not before he had contributed valiantly to the war effort, as he had desired. Lieutenant John F. Kennedy was later awarded the Purple Heart and the Navy and Marine Corps Medal. The accompanying citation read:

> For extremely heroic conduct as commanding officer of Motor Torpedo Boat 109 following the collision and sinking of that vessel in the Pacific war area on Aug 1–2. Unmindful of personal danger, Lieutenant Kennedy unhesitatingly braved the difficulties and hazards of darkness to direct rescue operations, swimming many hours to secure aid and food after he had succeeded in getting his crew ashore. His outstanding courage, endurance, and leadership contributed to the saving of several lives and were in keeping with the highest traditions of the United States Naval Services.

The official navy report of the PT 109 incident had been written and submitted by Byron White, an officer stationed in the Pacific. White, who was known as "Whizzer" in his college days, had been an all-American football star at the University of Colorado. In 1937, he led his team to the Cotton Bowl with an 8–0 record and placed second in the Heisman Trophy voting, finishing behind Yale's Clint Frank.

After college, White was awarded a Rhodes Scholarship to study in Oxford, England. While in England, he toured Europe with John F. Kennedy, son of the then American ambassador to England. Years later, Byron White would be named to the U.S. Supreme Court by President Kennedy.

❰ ❰ ❰

Seventeen years after John Fitzgerald Kennedy barely escaped with his life from an attack by a Japanese destroyer in the Pacific Ocean, Joseph

Kennedy's vision of his family's destiny came to fruition. In the smallest margin of popular vote in the history of presidential elections, John F. Kennedy defeated Richard M. Nixon by a mere 0.01 percent, 34,220,984 to 34,108,157. President Eisenhower's putting green was being sized up for a touch football field.

Beginning as a U.S. representative for Massachusetts' 11th District and then serving as a U.S. senator, John F. Kennedy had reached the ultimate pinnacle of president. He became the youngest man to be elected to the highest office in the land.

On the eve of the inauguration on January 20, 1961, eight inches of snow blanketed the city of Washington. Blizzard conditions shut down the city and the airport, causing former president Herbert Hoover's plane to be turned away. On the parade route, some 3,000 workers labored through the night and morning shoveling and removing snow, as record crowds were anticipated to welcome John Kennedy to the White House.

When Mr. and Mrs. Kennedy awoke in their Georgetown home, the soon-to-be first lady was presented with a dozen roses, compliments of Lieutenant Arthur Reginald Evans of Australia, who nearly eighteen years before had helped save her shipwrecked husband in the Solomon Islands. The president-elect himself was reminded of those days when a note of congratulations was delivered from Lieutenant Colonel Kohei Hanami, commander of the Japanese destroyer *Amagiri* that had rammed the PT 109 that fateful August night.

For the day's events, the Naval Academy Brigade was selected to lead the inauguration parade, and the Navy Choir was chosen to sing at the ceremony. In southeast Washington, 3,500 midshipmen marshaled as one, waiting to march through the frigid temperatures. Dressed in their blue wool parkas, they were handed government-issued overshoes to protect their leather shoes from the slush that covered the streets.

Led by battalion sub-commander Joe Bellino, the brigade marched with pride. The order was "eyes forward" when brigade members approached the reviewing stand, but many risked demerits and snuck a glance at the new president and his beautiful wife. At the end of the parade route, the midshipmen had a memory to last a lifetime. They also had frozen hands from holding their steel rifle butts, and their feet were soaked, since nearly every midshipman had marched right out of his overshoes, leaving them on the parade route as a memento of the brigade's presence.

Despite the cold, it was a day of great promise. The inauguration signaled the rebirth of a nation. On the steps of the Capitol, the president urged American citizens to "ask not what your country can do for you; ask what you can do for your country." This spirit of inclusion and obligation inspired millions with a desire to participate in the process of democracy.

# CHAPTER 2

# John F. Kennedy, Sportsman and Devoted Fan

ON DECEMBER 26, 1960, PRESIDENT-ELECT JOHN F. KENNEDY and his wife, Jacqueline Lee Bouvier Kennedy, appeared on the cover of *Sports Illustrated*, depicted sailing on Nantucket Sound offshore of the family compound in Hyannisport, Massachusetts. In the cover article, Kennedy expounded on his love of sports and sailing, sharing a secret ambition to someday race sailboats to Bermuda. At the six-acre family homestead on Cape Cod, the Kennedys filled their days with a never-ending schedule of sports activities. The estate was equipped with a tennis court, boathouse, and pool and featured a large, rolling backyard, where the family staged their famous touch football games.

Sports were a staple of the Kennedy family. Patriarch Joseph Kennedy had been captain of his Boston Latin High School baseball team and played first base for Harvard College. The one-time ambassador to England saw sports as a tool to help shape a balanced life while sharpening the competitive spirit, for which the family would become renowned in the arenas of both athletics and politics.

The senior Kennedy was followed to Harvard by eldest son Joe Kennedy Jr., who also wore the Harvard uniform as a football player. Son number two, John, suited up for the Crimson from Cambridge but not before struggling to establish himself as a football player at Choate

School in Connecticut. His coach at Choate, Earl Leinbach, wrote in his year-end evaluation in the fall of 1933 about the frail, underweight, but determined player: "Tackle on first team. Aggressive, alert and interested—Jack [John] was a tower of strength on the line." At Harvard he played freshman football but saw limited action. In a 34–6 loss to Dartmouth, he played at left end. Against Yale, he played right end in a 26–14 loss. Following the season, he was awarded the minor "H" for participating in football. John also swam and played freshman golf. As a sophomore, he played on the 2-1-1 junior varsity football team, though during the season he suffered a back injury that would haunt him the rest of his life. His teammates were later quoted in the *Boston Globe* as saying that Kennedy "lacked size and speed, but would have found a way to make varsity if not for his back."

The two sports that John was most successful in were activities that he refined at Hyannisport. As a swimmer for Harvard's varsity squad, he finished top three in several meets in the discipline of backstroke. In the *Harvard College Clipping Sheet*, Coach Harold Ulen said that Kennedy "always gave it everything he had." Sailing, though, produced his greatest sport success, as he won the 1938 Intercollegiate Championship, earning Harvard the McMillan Cup. John was the skipper of the team and was joined by his older brother, Joe, whom he cherished and competed against in sports and in life. The two were posthumously voted into the Harvard College Hall of Fame for their accomplishments. In 1965, the nation's oldest collegiate sailing event was renamed the Kennedy Cup in honor of the president.

Following John, brothers Bobby and Ted Kennedy continued the family legacy in Cambridge, joining the ranks of Harvard men. Both would letter in football, with Ted catching a touchdown pass in the big Yale game.

Lloyd Johnson, who coached the Kennedy boys at Harvard, described the family's competitive spirit: "Hard nosed; capable of magnificent second effort. They never quit. The harder you played against them, the harder they played against you."

These same characteristics were evident in the family's touch football games. Kennedy Touch Football has been a staple activity for generations. In these games, brothers and sisters alike competed and participated in the family tradition. They played the sport as if it were a rite of passage, playing to win as if protecting a valuable Kennedy heirloom. Over time, the game evolved and was altered to allow for more offense and exertion. In a wide-open game, the family could exploit those less inclined to run and block and touch. The format of the game was detailed by family friend Lawrence Leamer in his book *The Kennedy Men*. "They didn't play the game as you normally play it," Leamer wrote. "They could throw the ball all over the field. You could throw it behind the line of scrimmage, . . . and if you caught it you could throw it again. The offensive team could keep passing the ball forward beyond the line of scrimmage until the player holding the ball was finally touched."

In the biography by Michael O'Brien entitled *John F. Kennedy*, navy mate and lifetime friend Paul "Red" Fay spoke of the first time he was introduced to touch football by Kennedy, after their torpedo classes in Melville, Rhode Island. "Jack helped organize the touch football game," Fay recalled, "the kind where players could pass anywhere on the field. Jack called all of the plays." Fay "saw nothing but elbows, shoulders, and knees, and acquired a collection of bumps and bruises."

Years later, at an event honoring President Kennedy, comedian Bob Hope joked about the Kennedy love of touch football. "I never dreamed that I'd be sitting here with all these wonderful players and also the quarterback of the Hyannisport All Stars," Hope quipped. "It's just wonderful. And anybody that thinks touch football is a sissy game is wrong because up there roughing the passer is a federal rap."

The Kennedys played the game with a coarseness that could occasionally depreciate to the edge of uncivil. According to Randy Taraborrelli's book, *Jackie, Ethel and Joan*, "that family had the meanest football players ever put together—the girls were worse than the men. They'd claw, scratch, and bite when they played touch football. Playing to win was a family characteristic." Bumps and bruises were common. The most notable injury was suffered by Jacqueline Kennedy, who broke her ankle attempting to conform to her in-laws' game.

In sports and especially touch football, the members of the Kennedy family honed their competitive drive, which they applied in the arena of politics as well. Indeed, sports and politics were weaved together almost as one quilt in the Kennedy home. This was never more apparent than in the family's weekly game against its most intense rival, the prominent Massachusetts Lodge family.

The Kennedys and the Lodges had been primary political protagonists since the early 1900s, and on the football field, the families participated in an event that was an extension of that arena. In touch football, they waged battle for a much-coveted trophy; in the political realm, they waged battle for influence and power.

Since the turn of the century, the two families had battled over state and national seats of honor. In 1916, Henry Cabot Lodge Sr. defeated John "Honey Fitz" Fitzgerald in the election for U.S. senator for Massachusetts. Fitzgerald, the father of Rose Kennedy, later served as political adviser to the thirty-five-year-old John Kennedy and literally danced a jig when his grandson upset the incumbent Henry Cabot Lodge Jr. in the 1952 election for the same senate seat. In the family's eyes, this victory avenged his grandfather's loss and set in motion a period of dominance by the Irish-Catholic family over the Boston Brahmins. John F. Kennedy sustained this mantle of superiority in the presidential race; Lodge was the running mate of Republican presidential candidate Richard Nixon in 1960. Two years later, Ted Kennedy defeated George Cabot Lodge II, son of Henry Cabot Lodge Jr., in a runoff election for the Massachusetts Senate seat.

The Lodges and the Cabots were established Boston families who arrived in the "city on the hill" with the earliest settlers. They held positions of power, accumulated great wealth, and went to great lengths to sustain and defend it. When immigrant families such as the Kennedys and Fitzgeralds arrived in the United States, the establishment rallied its brethren to make sure everyone knew that "Irish need not apply." Such efforts were repulsive to John Fitzgerald, who saw this spirit of separatism as contrary to the core beliefs of the country and its constitution. At a political rally in 1916, John Fitzgerald articulated his repulsion and sought to differentiate himself from his opponent Henry Cabot Lodge by reciting a poem that spoke to the Lodges' wealth and elitism:

I dwell 'neath the shades of Harvard
In the State of the Sacred Cod,
Where the Lowells speak only to Cabots
And the Cabots speak only to God.

The Kennedys never forgot the political loss their grandfather suffered to Lodge, and they played in both the political and athletic arenas to avenge the 1916 defeat. To ensure such dominance, Robert Kennedy routinely conducted touch football practices, imploring family members to push and challenge. He chastised dropped passes by siblings or children with the admonition, "If it hits your hands, you should catch the ball."

Such prodding and the will to win were passed from one generation to the next. Joseph Kennedy Sr. once brought a game between brothers to a halt in order to mentor youngest son, Ted. The youngest Kennedy was struggling to get kicks off under the pressure of his older and unrelenting brothers. Walking onto the field, Joseph pulled Ted to the side and suggested, "If you can't kick the ball, kicking one of your brothers on the other team is all right."

The game of touch football served as a metaphor for life, representing the family's thirst to win at almost any cost. It was an obsession articulated by writer Art Buchwald, who was a frequent guest of the family. "The Kennedys always wanted to win first prize," Buchwald said in a 1969 interview. "They never wanted to settle for a second prize ribbon."

Whenever the Kennedys returned victorious from their games with the Lodges, the champion's trophy was immediately placed atop the television, providing evidence of victory for all to see.

Simply put, competition, sports, and football were in John's blood. While at Choate, ignoring requests from his brother Joseph to give up football because of the risk of injury to his thin frame, John pleaded with classmates to throw him passes deep into the night. During his term as senator of Massachusetts, Kennedy would show up at the Harvard locker room and gather current players to work off the stress of political office. He said, in the *Boston Globe*, that such games were a "wonderful tonic relieving the formal pressures of being a congressman." In 1953, while on honeymoon with his new bride, Jacqueline, Kennedy excused himself to attend a San Francisco 49ers game. And while serving as president years later, he would steal away to watch football games during breaks from high-level and often-contentious meetings during the Cuban Missile Crisis.

As president, Kennedy received challenges from around the country for a friendly game of football. The Boston YMCA wrote, "Dear Mr. President: My roommates and I are offering you a friendly challenge. You can name the place and time and rules." A team from Yosemite, California, also wrote with a challenge but "would rescind and please disregard if Justice White [former all-American football player] is on your roster." The president received similar challenges from the Young Republicans of San Francisco; the Kiwanis Club of Stamford, Connecticut; the Jewish Community Center of Kansas City; Princeton University; Ye Old Touch Football Association of Encino, California; Phi Sigma Kappa of Hunter College; the physics department of the University of Georgia; the Livingston Meatgrinder Girls from Huntington College, Indiana; and elsewhere.

The president even got a letter from Lou Saban, coach of the NFL's Boston Patriots, which stated:

Since you were a great pass receiver on the Harvard Touch Football squad, you will be able to assist your favorite pro team the

Patriots on a successful season. We are desperately in need of fine receivers and wonder if you would desire to fill the bill? However we would not want political influence.

Kennedy's involvement in sports as a player, fan, and politician was recognized after he became president. His contributions to sports and society inspired Army coach Earl Blaik and administrators from the National Football Foundation and the College Football Hall of Fame to select Kennedy for the foundation's 1961 Gold Medal award, the highest individual honor bestowed by the National Football Foundation and Hall of Fame. Such an award was given to individuals who have "contributed in a significant manner to college football, and his career shall embody the highest ideals for which the game of football stands." President Kennedy was proud to have his name added to the impressive list of Gold Medal winners, which included legendary coach Alonzo Stagg, Dwight D. Eisenhower, Herbert Hoover, and Douglas MacArthur.

The award ceremony was held on December 5, 1961, at the Waldorf Astoria in New York City. More than 1,500 people paid fifty dollars a ticket, and the audience included such dignitaries as General Douglas MacArthur and General William C. Westmoreland. Following dinner, foundation president Chet Laroche introduced Kennedy to the black-tie crowd:

We are heartened by the knowledge that you learned this discipline on the football fields of Choate and Harvard, learned it in the toughest place of all—on the practice field with the scrubs, week after week, in the battle with varsity.

Such a discipline gives a man more than the will to win. It cultivates in him the ability to pay the price. In any athletic contest you fought with a kind of self determination that is still remembered. You earned a reputation for dedication.

It is the courage we would honor and these values we would hope to instill when we counsel the youth of our country.

Kennedy, in turn, offered the admiring audience the following comments:

> Politics is an amazing profession; it has permitted me to go from an obscure lieutenant, serving under General MacArthur, to commander in chief in fourteen years without any technical competence whatsoever. And it's also enabled me to go from being an obscure member of the junior varsity at Harvard to being an honorary member of the Football Hall of Fame.

Kennedy loved football and was touched by the honor. He saw the event as an opportunity to articulate his ideal of participation instead of simple spectatorship. He called upon the nation to exercise and to be involved in sports, which would help build leaders and teach values that could be applied in all aspects of life. In closing, Kennedy quoted Theodore Roosevelt:

> The credit belongs to the man who is actually in the arena, whose face is marred by dust and sweat and blood, who knows the great enthusiasms, the great devotions and spends himself in a worthy cause, who at best if he wins knows the thrills of high achievement and if fails at least fails while daring greatly so that his place shall never be with those cold and timid souls who know neither victory nor defeat.

# CHAPTER 3

# The Naval Academy and Midshipmen Football

ON THE BANKS WHERE THE WATERS OF THE CHESAPEAKE BAY and the Severn River meet, the United States Naval Academy was founded in 1845 in the seaport town of Annapolis, Maryland. The academy was formed as an undergraduate school with the purpose of training officers for the navy. Candidates for the academy are nominated by their senators, representatives, or congressional delegates, and those appointed at large are nominated by the vice president. *Ex Scientia Tridens* ("From Knowledge, Seapower") is the school's motto, and its mission is, "To develop Midshipmen morally, mentally, and physically and to imbue them with the highest ideals of duty, honor, and loyalty in order to graduate leaders who are dedicated to a career of naval service and have potential for future development in mind and character to assume the highest responsibilities of command, citizenship, and government."

Among the notable graduates of the U.S. Naval Academy are Admiral George Anderson (1927), President Jimmy Carter (1947), William "Bull" Halsey (1904), Admiral John McCain Sr. (1931), Senator John McCain Jr. (1958), Admiral Chester Nimitz (1905), Ross Perot (1953), and astronaut Alan Shepard (1945).

The students at the Naval Academy, like at most other undergraduate schools, attend for four years. Upon graduation, every student is obligated to serve in the selected service of his or her choice for five years.

One particular difference between the academy and other common academic institutions is the school's caste system. First-year students are plebes, a term for a second-class citizen or common person, and not "freshmen." Plebes are subjected to an indoctrination system that filters and weeds out students who are not academy material. Sophomores are known as third classmen or "youngsters." Juniors are second classmen, while seniors are first classmen.

The entire brigade of four thousand midshipmen is separated into twenty-four companies. All are housed in Bancroft Hall, which doesn't have floors but "decks." Situated in front of the dormitory is Tecumseh Court, which is guarded by the statue of Tecumseh, who was the leader of the Shawnee tribe of Native Americans. The statue, which was a gift of the class of 1891, is a replication of the figurehead that was set upon the USS *Delaware*, a seventy-four-gun ship launched in 1820. The statue is the target of many lucky pennies and is called by some the "God of the 2.5"—the Academy's benchmark for passing grades. Also within the court, rallies are held to send the school's football heroes off to games or welcome them home in victory.

❆ ❆ ❆

In the week leading up to the 1960 Army–Navy football game, the cadets from Army paid the ultimate respect to midshipman and football star Joe Bellino, making him the source of high jinks across the West Point campus. From windows of dorm rooms hung effigies of the halfback/defensive back dressed in jerseys bearing the number 27. In the middle of the yard, a battered makeshift boat named the USS *Bellino* received considerable abuse at the hands of students who walked by on their way to class or meals. When game day arrived, those thoughts trained on Bellino during the week were transformed into scrutinizing eyes, from both Army and Navy fans alike.

Game day in 1960 came on November 26. With mere seconds remaining on the clock at Municipal Stadium in Philadelphia, Navy was leading Army, 17–12. Army quarterback Tom Blanda took the snap at the Navy 34-yard line and dropped back to pass. He looked upfield and saw wide receiver Joe Blackgrove uncovered, standing at the edge of the end zone. Instantly, Blanda cocked his arm 90 degrees from his shoulder and slingshot the ball to his ready teammate, poised to score the game-winning touchdown.

Pedaling backward, defensive back Bellino followed the flight of the ball, wrestling with the burden of his earlier fumble that had put Army in position to win the rivalry game. As the ball sailed toward the waiting cadet receiver, myriad conclusions danced through the heads of the 98,616 fans in attendance.

Victory would bring an invitation to a New Year's Day bowl game. More important, it would secure yearlong bragging rights for the men in trenches or on boat decks around the world.

Bellino broke for the ball and traced its path. Blackgrove's eyes were on the ball, his thoughts on being the following morning's headline. Reality followed a different script, though. Almost simultaneously, the ball and the defender converged on the cadet. Through the shadows of the sinking November sun, Bellino snatched the ball just before it landed in Blackgrove's waiting arms. The defender then returned the ball upfield to safe ground, securing victory for the navy community.

"It's a pretty fine line between being a goat and a hero," Bellino said after the game.

When the final seconds ticked off the game clock, fans stormed the field to greet the Navy hero. Bellino's parents and four brothers all hugged at midfield. In his career, Bellino had scored five touchdowns against Army, including a record three in one game. All would have been overshadowed if his fumble in the 1960 game had led to defeat.

In the locker room, Bellino shook his head at the very thought of the fumble. "I died fifty deaths in the last quarter," he said. All was forgiven in victory. Coach Wayne Hardin put his arm around his star back and declared, "He's the greatest player I've ever seen, and I'd marry him if he wasn't going to graduate next June."

As life at the academy went on in the aftermath of victory, the glory of the previous Saturday on the football field was re-injected into the tedium of pre-exam electrical engineering class in Maury Hall when the midshipman officer of the watch entered the classroom and handed a note to the professor, who read the missive. The proctor peered around the paper and called for Joe Bellino to return to his room, change into his dress blues, and report to the superintendent's office immediately.

As ordered, a worried Bellino picked up his books and hustled across the yard to his dorm room, where he changed into his formal uniform and made his way to the administrative offices, curious and anxious about the purpose of the impromptu meeting. He assumed that past struggles in the electrical engineering course—he was now in the bottom half of his class academically—had finally been brought to the attention of his superiors.

Breathing hard from the brisk walk, Bellino arrived at the office of Rear Admiral John F. Davidson, superintendent of the Naval Academy. As he entered, the first classman became aware of a number of high-ranking officers and unfamiliar civilian personnel present. The superintendent came and put his arm around the young midshipman.

"Congratulations, Joe," Davidson said. "You have been chosen as the Heisman Trophy winner."

Bellino was shocked and at a loss for words. Turning to sports information director John Cox, Bellino mouthed, "I can't believe it." He was then swarmed by decorated navy personnel who offered congratulations while slapping his back and shaking hands with the finest college football player in the nation.

The son of Sicilian immigrants, Joe Bellino had chosen the Naval Academy over seventy other colleges that had courted him through high school and preparatory school. A private tour of aircraft carriers docked in Boston Harbor, arranged by a local congressman, won over the three-sport athlete from the bucolic Greater Boston town of Winchester, Massachusetts.

At Annapolis, Bellino's athletic skills shined not only on the gridiron but on the obstacle course, where he set the course record, as well as on the baseball diamond. As a catcher for Navy baseball, he led the team in hitting and stolen bases, and caught the eye of professional scouts. The sport of football, though, is where he found his greatest success. As a senior, he led his team to a number-four national ranking while scoring 18 touchdowns, throwing 2 touchdown passes, and averaging 47 yards a punt as a quick kicker.

Bellino played with an edge and was perfectly willing to run around, through, or over his opponent. Once, with his team tied late in the game against rival Maryland, he fielded a punt on his own 41-yard line. Coach Hardin yelled for him to run out of bounds so that Navy could send in a quarterback as a substitution, since rules dictated that the clock be stopped for such a switch.

As Bellino ran with the ball cradled in his arms, he looked upfield and calculated the prospects of running successfully against the consequences of defying his fiery, red-headed coach. He decided to turn upfield, and he proceeded to run for a 59-yard, game-winning touchdown. When he got to the sideline, Bellino explained his defiance to Coach Hardin: "This is the way I figured it, Coach. If I could go all the way, you wouldn't need a quarterback—except to hold for the point after touchdown."

Joe Bellino appeared on the cover of the November 28, 1960, issue of *Sports Illustrated* wearing his dress-blue uniform and standing in front of a cannon on the Naval Academy campus. In the cover story, Roy Terrell wrote that the five-foot, nine-inch running back "does not look like a Navy hero. In fact, he doesn't look like much of anything except maybe the kid down the block." However, the package set within the five-foot, nine-inch frame was formidable. Boasting eighteen-inch calves that forced him to cut the bottoms of his pants, his legs turned like perpetual pistons, making him virtually impossible to tackle. His low-to-the-ground, compact body, which scouts said moved as fast laterally as forward, enabled Bellino to leave his mark on both Navy football and college football in general.

In the weeks following the Army game, Bellino was presented with the Heisman Trophy and was selected as battalion sub-commander by his classmates because of his outstanding leadership abilities. Across the nation, the sports world was engrossed in the halfback's rise to college football prominence. In Miami, Orange Bowl officials were assured a sellout crowd and strong ratings. *Washington Post* writer Bob Addie penned a poem that included the following:

> To Joe Bellino, number one—
> The Navy's biggest scoring gun.
> Your fame has spread from here to Paris—
> You're Navy's pride (next to Polaris).

In Massachusetts, letters written to Bellino's hometown of Winchester were addressed to the town of "Bellinoville" and were dutifully delivered. Nowhere was the Bellino craze more in full bloom than at the Naval Academy itself. On December 8, 1960, when Joe Bellino was presented with the Heisman Trophy at the Downtown Athletic Club in New York City, Navy brass allowed a thirty-minute suspension of curfew so that the brigade could listen to the proceedings over the public address system.

Bellino, who was the first Navy football player to win the Heisman Trophy, personified the mission of the academy: excellence, life balance, and leadership. During an interview, a reporter listed Bellino's accomplishments, including winning the Heisman Trophy, the Maxwell Award, and all-American honors. The reporter then asked, "What could make this season complete?" Without hesitating, college football's most decorated player responded, "I'd like to be invited to have lunch with another Boston resident who also has had a very good year, President-elect Kennedy."

On December 11, 1960, Pierre Salinger, the president-elect's press secretary, held his daily briefing from Palm Beach, Florida, where John F. Kennedy, his wife, Jacqueline, daughter Caroline, and newborn son John were on vacation at the family's compound. During the briefing, Salinger announced that Joe Bellino and five of his teammates who also resided in Massachusetts—Ronald Bell, Frank Datillo, Sid Driscoll, Ronald Testa, and Dick Fitzgerald—were invited to join the president-elect at his Georgetown home for lunch. The Associated Press report of the event pointed out that although the president-elect had failed in his tryout for the Harvard varsity team, "he still spearheads the wild and wooly touch football games the Kennedy clan engages in."

What Salinger didn't share with the Associated Press or any other reporters at the briefing was that earlier in the day an attempt was made on Kennedy's life. Richard Pavlik, from New Hampshire, had driven to Palm Beach possessed with the idea that the president-elect had "bought" the election, and he felt compelled to right the perceived wrong. When Kennedy's car left the compound's grounds to attend Sunday mass, Pavlik started his engine and prepared to ram Kennedy's transport with his own vehicle, which was wired with dynamite. The would-be assassin put the car in gear before noticing that Jacqueline Kennedy and the couple's two children were also present in the car. He put the gear back to park and aborted his mission. In the book *Live by the Sword*, author Gus Russo states that Kennedy received approximately twenty-five thousand recorded threats against him during his term as president.

Despite being saddled with the stress of final exams, the Navy invitees were thrilled with the opportunity to meet with President-elect Kennedy. It was a lunch that the midshipmen would never forget. Upon being introduced to Kennedy, they presented their host with a signed football inscribed with the score from their recent victory over Army, "17–12." Throughout the lunch, they exchanged stories of football, the navy, and Massachusetts. At the conclusion of the meeting, the players informed Kennedy that the team had named him as the Naval Academy's honorary commander in chief for the upcoming Orange Bowl game against Missouri. Kennedy was pleased by the honor and happily accepted the position, agreeing to attend the game two weeks hence.

Bellino ranked the meeting as a greater thrill than any realized on the football field. "It was very kind to accept us as guests," Bellino said of Kennedy. "Gee, he's a wonderful man." One of Bellino's teammates commented, "I don't know who was more excited to meet who, Joe [Bellino] to meet [Kennedy] or [Kennedy] to meet Joe."

At the Orange Bowl on New Year's Day 1961, the fifth-ranked Missouri Tigers were nine-point favorites over the fourth-ranked Naval Academy. Prior to the game, players from both teams signed a football for the president-elect in honor of his son, John Jr., who was born on November 25, 1960. The ball was presented to Kennedy, who sat on the Navy side in dark sunglasses alongside 71,217 other fans, including friends Senator George Smathers and Grant Stockdale.

During the game, Kennedy made no effort to hide his allegiance to the Navy football team, cheering Navy's successes and frowning at their miscues. With the Midshipmen trailing 14–6 at halftime, he was asked about his team's deficit. "We are looking forward to the second half," replied Kennedy.

Reporters and photographers chronicled the president-elect's day. An Associated Press reporter covering the game wrote, "The president-elect, a Navy veteran of World War II, definitely appeared concerned with the fortunes of the Annapolis eleven. When Missouri connected with a player that brought cheers from the Missouri stands, he smote his forehead and groaned, 'Oh, oh.'"

In the end, Missouri's defense was too much for Navy. The Tigers suffocated Heisman-winner Bellino, holding him to just 4 yards on 8 carries, and Navy was forced to use the star back as a decoy throughout the game. Bellino did, however, have a moment of greatness late in the fourth quarter. With his team trailing 21–6, quarterback Hal Spooner dropped back to pass while Bellino broke into the flat, then down the sidelines toward the end zone. As the pass was thrown, Kennedy rose to his feet and yelled, "Go! Go!" The ball appeared to be overthrown, but Bellino leaped through the air, parallel to the ground, and secured the ball for a touchdown before rolling out of the end zone. College football historian Beano Cook would call it the greatest catch in college football history. Kennedy just shook his head in admiration. "That was a beautiful catch Bellino made," he said.

When the final gun sounded, Navy had lost to Missouri 21–14. As Kennedy left, he commented, "It was a good game. They're both good teams and I enjoyed it very much."

That spring, President Kennedy traveled to Annapolis to honor the Naval Academy's graduating class of 1961. On the morning of graduation day, before the president's arrival, the academy held its annual awards ceremony. Joe Bellino was awarded both the Thompson Trophy and the Naval Academy Athletic Association Sword. He was the first midshipman in forty-two years to be so honored.

After being presented with the awards, Bellino returned to his seat and received a rousing cheer from all in attendance. From the stage, the superintendent of the Naval Academy, Rear Admiral John F. Davidson, announced, "By the request of the brigade of midshipmen, approved by the athletic association and the superintendent, the number 27 will be retired." It was the first time in Navy history that an athlete had been so honored. First Classman Bellino was flabbergasted. "What made it so special," he said, "was that it was suggested by my graduating class, who led the charge."

By early afternoon, President Kennedy's helicopter touched down, and the thirty-third sitting president to visit the Naval Academy was greeted by the superintendent and other Naval Academy officials. After boarding a car, Kennedy was escorted to the field house, where he was greeted by a twenty-one-gun salute and the strains of "Hail to the Chief." As he entered the gym, the president was given a standing ovation by the 11,000 in attendance. When introduced by the superintendent, he received another standing ovation. Kennedy then walked to the podium and addressed the graduates.

> I know that you are constantly warned during your days here not to mix, in your naval career, in politics. I should point out however, on the other side, that my rather rapid rise from a reserve lieutenant, of uncertain standing, to commander in chief, has been because I did not follow that very good advice. . . . Fifty years ago the graduates of the Naval Academy were expected to be seamen and leaders of men. They were reminded of the saying of John Paul Jones, "Give me a fair ship so that I might go into harm's way." . . . What you have chosen to do for your country, by devoting your life to the service of our country, is the greatest contribution that any man could make.

After his commencement speech, President Kennedy helped to hand out 95 of the 785 diplomas. At the conclusion of the ceremony, the graduates conducted the traditional hat-toss ceremony, discarding their hats as they were now officers. Traditionally, after the hats are tossed in the air, graduates find one of their brethren's hats and take it home. At the 1961 graduation, the hat most sought was Joe Bellino's. Seekers of this prized hat were outsmarted by the many graduates who wrote Joe Bellino's name inside their hats. When Bellino finally located his hat, he presented it to Assistant Coach Steve Belichick, who gave it to his son Bill. Nearly half a century later, Bill returned the hat to its original owner.

☾ ☾ ☾

The same week that newspapers reported on the meeting between the Heisman Trophy winner and the president-elect in December 1960, another, minor story in the sports pages noted that a quarterback named Roger Staubach, who played for the New Mexico Military Institute, a feeder school for the Naval Academy, had been named to the Junior College All-American team.

In August 1961, a highly touted plebe class, which included Staubach, arrived at the Naval Academy campus. The Annapolis newspaper the *Capital* wrote, "Plenty of interest is expected when the Navy plebe football team opens its nine-game schedule tomorrow. Quarterbacking the plebes in the 1961 opener will be Roger Staubach."

From 1954 to 1973, the National Collegiate Athletic Association (NCAA) forbade freshman—or plebes at the Naval Academy—from competing at the varsity level. Schools across the country fielded freshman teams that coaches would use as a barometer of future success.

Prior to the 1961 season, Navy bird dogs (unofficial scouts for the football program) and assistant coaches had traveled the country to bring in a strong plebe class. Along with junior college all-American Roger Staubach, also committed to the academy were Southern Methodist University transfer Jim Freeman; halfback Pat Donnelly of Maumee, Ohio; Fred Marlin, direct from service in the navy; and Washington, D.C., track star Darryl Hill.

Assigned the task of molding this team was an old-school Navy athlete, H. Richard "Dick" Duden. Coach Duden was a highly decorated three-sport star at the academy in the mid-1940s. As a senior, he was awarded the "binoculars" by the Navy Athletic Association, which recognizes excellence in general athletics. Duden was captain of the 1945 Navy football team and later selected to the all-American squad. He was also awarded the Knute Rockne Memorial Trophy as outstanding college football lineman in the country.

As a three-year basketball player, Duden played both guard and center, and he led the team to undefeated seasons in 1943 and 1944. In his final sporting event as a Midshipman, his three-run home run sparked the Navy baseball team to victory over an Army team that featured Heisman Trophy winner Glenn Davis.

After graduation, Duden entered the military and was decommissioned in 1948, allowing him to join the New York Giants of the National Football League. In 1951, he was recalled to active duty and assigned the task of coaching the incoming Navy football players. After a period of time as plebe coach, he was elevated to the varsity staff, where he worked for six years. In 1959, he wanted to be named head coach after highly successful coach Ernie Erdelatz abruptly resigned.

The academy instead chose thirty-two-year-old assistant Wayne Hardin as the new head coach, and Duden was reassigned and accepted the task of coaching the plebe team. He was the perfect mentor to groom young men. Roger Staubach later described Duden as a "low-key, determined coach who made football fun." Assisting Duden was previous year's Heisman Trophy winner Joe Bellino, who oversaw the offensive backfield.

Two hundred and fifty plebes reported to the first day of practice. With so many attempting to secure a roster spot, the players were divided into select groups of approximately thirty players. Many of the highly touted recruits were separated from the other candidates and were instructed to report to a side field to play catch. One of the players included in this isolated group was Darryl Hill. Hill stood five feet eleven inches tall and weighed 160 pounds, and his track and football pedigree from Gonzaga High School in Washington, D.C., made it a good bet that he would succeed in his quest to become the first African American to play football for Navy.

As a high school senior, Hill had no intention of attending the academy until his mother casually inquired if he might be interested. He was noncommittal, knowing that the date for congressional assignments had already passed. Much to his surprise, however, a few days later he received a letter of acceptance after being appointed by Congressman William Levi Dawson, who himself had broken color barriers to serve as the third African American elected to congress. What made Hill's appointment unusual was that the congressman represented a district of Chicago in Illinois, while Hill resided in the District of Columbia. Unbeknownst to the midshipman-to-be was the fact that his parents and Dawson had arranged for an "appropriate address," which would read on all his school documents as 123 Peach Street, Chicago, Illinois.

At the first plebe practice, as Hill and the other members of his group played catch among themselves, they began to grow concerned with the lack of attention they were receiving from the coaching staff. Still, the players followed instructions. As they went about their business, Hill noticed one player who was conspicuous for his superior talent. He was a lanky quarterback who threw on the run with great ease and accuracy. His name was Roger Staubach.

Staubach had arrived on the Navy campus with much fanfare after being named a junior college all-American. The previous autumn, Staubach had been quarterback at the New Mexico Military Institute, where he scored nine touchdowns and led his team to a 9–1 record. Amazingly, if not for the indifference of a clerk, Staubach would have never been allowed entrance to the Naval Academy. During a pre-admission eye exam, Staubach was passed despite being color blind. If the malady had been properly identified by the clerk, the midshipman-to-be's assignment would have been immediately revoked.

Eye test passed, Staubach, like the other plebes, was eager to prove his football worth. As they stood around tossing the football, Staubach expressed his concern to Hill: "When are we going to get our chance?"

In Staubach's autobiography, *First Down, Lifetime to Go*, fellow plebe Skip Orr recounted a memory from those early tryouts: "Larry Kocisko, who had gone to New Mexico Military Institute with Roger, was in my company. He asked me what position I played."

"Quarterback," Orr told him.

Kocisko laughed. "Forget it!"

In all twenty-two players tried out for the quarterback position, but only one would be destined to greatness at Navy.

As tryouts wore on, Staubach, along with Hill and speedster-halfback Kip Paskewich, were elevated to the second team. Gradually, their talents were being appreciated and recognized by the coaches, but the three were still convinced that they deserved to be practicing with the starters, and they were determined to prove it. An intra-squad game was scheduled for the end of the week, and Staubach shared his confidence with his two teammates. "On Saturday, there is a scrimmage," the young quarterback said. "On Monday, we'll be on the first team."

By the end of the tryouts, all three were selected for the squad and were prepared to see significant playing time. The plebe team was talented and deep. The team opened the season against Bainbridge Prep and posted a 43–6 victory. A headline in the *Capital* the following day read, "QB Staubach leads Plebes to easy win." Staubach had thrown for two touchdowns, and he ran 39 yards for another. Coach Duden called Staubach "a strong runner" and said he was "very pleased with the boy's showing."

Prior to the following week's game against the Virginia Tech freshmen squad, Duden was quoted in the paper saying that quarterbacks Staubach and Dan MacPhail were "coming along," a claim that was further validated by the plebes' 34–12 win against Virginia Tech. This was followed by a hard-fought 8–0 victory over Syracuse. A pleased Coach Duden commented, "It always feels good to get by a big and strong team like Syracuse." Of his quarterback, he added, "Roger turned in a fine all-around performance."

Navy went on to beat Penn State 26–0 and then George Washington 40–6. "Staubach sparks Plebes" read a headline. After the George Washington game, Coach Duden said his lanky quarterback "has been doing a fine job for us." In all, Navy won their first seven games before hosting an undefeated Maryland team at Annapolis.

Maryland and Navy are natural rivals, with campuses separated by a mere twenty-minute drive. Animosities between the schools have developed from both on-field and off-field events, including the very likely possibility that sharp-dressed midshipmen would travel to the University of Maryland campus to acquaint themselves with its co-eds. The upcoming battle between the two undefeated freshman football teams would only stoke the acrimonious fire between the two schools.

Hill scored two touchdowns that day, including a 98-yard kickoff return. Many of Hill's yards were gained via Staubach's favorite play, the Statue of Liberty. Despite Hill and Staubach's efforts, however,

Maryland earned a 29–27 victory thanks to a game-winning 23-yard field goal with fifteen seconds remaining.

In *First Down, Lifetime to Go*, Coach Duden spoke about the game against Maryland. "We lost that game because of me," Duden lamented. "They got possession of the ball and moved into position for that field goal because I sent in the wrong formation to Roger."

The Navy plebe football team won its last two games of the 1961 season to finish with a record of 8–1. Hill finished with seven touchdowns and five successful points after. Meanwhile, Staubach's list of admirers was continuing to grow. Coach Duden offered the following evaluation of his quarterback after his debut season: "Roger has size, ability, and a desire to excel. He did everything well—run, pass, and direct the team. He was our leader in every game. He had so many good games we came to expect them of him."

❈ ❈ ❈

Since 1959, the Midshipmen of the Naval Academy have played their home games at Navy–Marine Corps Memorial Stadium. Before then, they played at Thompson Stadium, which was built in 1914 on the Naval Academy campus and accommodated about 14,000 fans in wooden-plank seating that extended across the bleachers.

In 1957, led by Superintendent John Davidson, the academy put in motion a concerted effort to build a new, state-of-the-art football facility. Plans were drawn and the budget set at just over $3 million, all of which had to be raised through private donations. The academy hoped to have the stadium ready for the 1959 season, which allowed eighteen months to raise the funds and construct the stadium. Over this period, donations flowed into Annapolis from sources that were expected and some that weren't. That the Navy Athletic Alumni Association donated $1 million is not surprising, but the academy likely didn't expect four brigade members to donate their $500 winnings from an appearance on *Make Me Laugh*. The Dallas Naval Air Station chipped in $1,300 to memorialize thirteen men from the base who had lost their lives in active duty. The University of Notre Dame, which Navy had assisted with cash flow during World War II by making the campus a training area, donated $10,000.

In addition, a check for $1,107 was presented to the superintendent of the Naval Academy by the superintendent of the U.S. Military Academy, with funds donated by the cadets of West Point. A plaque was placed at the stadium and signed by the United States Corps of Cadets: "In tribute to their brothers in arms of the United States Naval Academy who have laid down their lives for their beloved country, the United States of America."

The funding goals were met, and the stadium was completed on schedule. On the white facades of the upper-level bleachers encircling the stadium, the list of battles that the Marines and Navy have courageously fought are branded in blue type as follows:

Blue Side (West): Southern France, Anzio, Belleau Wood, Chateau Thierry, Pearl Harbor, Java Sea, Wake, Coral Sea, Midway, Savo Island, Eastern Solomons, Santa Cruz Islands, Guadalcanal, New Georgia, Bougainville, Rabaul, Cape Gloucester, Hollandia, Market Time, Quang Nam, Quang Tin and Quang Ngai.

Gold Side (East): Marianas, Tarawa, Kwaj-alein, Sicily, Philippine Sea, North Africa, Peleliu, Leyte Gulf, Lingayen Gulf, Iwo Jima, Okinawa, Salerno, Normandy, Inchon, Chosin Reservoir, Battle of the Atlantic, Mekong Delta, Thua Thien, Quang Tri, Yankee Station, Desert Storm and Aleutian Campaign.

When William & Mary assistant coach Lou Holtz first walked onto the field and read the names of the battles ringing the stadium, he commented, "Boy, they play a tough schedule."

In the end, typical of the efficiency of the Naval Academy, Navy–Marine Corps Memorial Stadium was completed on time and under budget. On September 26, 1959, the stadium was dedicated on homecoming weekend. The ceremony featured speeches by five former superintendents, flyovers by an aerial stunt team, marching and drill exercises, and the dedication of a plaque, which read:

> This stadium is dedicated to those who have served and will serve—upholders of the tradition and renown of the Navy and the Marine Corps of the United States. May it be a perpetual reminder of the Navy and Marine Corps as organizations of men trained to work hard and play hard; in war, defenders of our freedom; in peace, molders of our youth.

❨ ❨ ❨

Wayne Hardin was born in rural Smackover, Arkansas, in 1927. His childhood started in the waning days of the "Roaring '20s" and wound through the dark days of the Depression. The Hardin parents moved the family to Stockton, California, where Wayne would attend a local high school, excelling in football, golf, and baseball. His golf game was so promising that some local businessmen offered to sponsor his potential pro golf career.

Following high school, Hardin attended classes at Stanford University but left to enlist in the Coast Guard while war waged in the Pacific and Europe. When he returned to California after discharge, he enrolled at the College of the Pacific, where the five-foot, eight-inch 175-pounder became a three-sport star, earning a record eleven letters (four football, four basketball, three golf) and ultimately being named to the College of the Pacific's hall of fame.

In golf, Hardin not only led the team as a scratch golfer but also was responsible for starting the team, volunteering his assistant football coach to provide adult supervision. His basketball coach, Chris Kjeldsen, described his forward as "fast, aggressive, and a fairly good shot." Following a game in which Hardin scored two baskets in the last ten seconds of overtime to earn Pacific a 54–53 victory, the *Reno Evening Gazette* called Hardin "a hard running forward." Even with his successes in the former two sports, football was where he established himself as a star. Under the tutelage of coach and football pioneer Alonzo Stagg, Hardin learned the finer points of the game on both the physical and the cerebral level. Stagg, who was then well into his eighties, still possessed boundless energy and enthusiasm. This spirit emanated from him and filled his players with the same vigor. Stagg demanded total commitment from his team and in return shared his knowledge, theories, and strategies in great depth. From his football coach—who didn't drink, smoke, or swear—Hardin learned the power of positive thought and the importance of organization.

Stagg took to Hardin, recognizing that he had superior athletic abilities, and selected him to play quarterback. Hardin, however, didn't want to play a position where your primary responsibility was to receive a snap from the center and then turn and hand the ball off to the halfback. He preferred to be the halfback, who could impact the game on a more direct level.

Coach agreed and defaulted to his second choice for quarterback, Eddie LeBaron. LeBaron would go on to realize all-American status and be voted onto four National Football League Pro Bowl rosters. Ironically, LeBaron would be the first great scrambling quarterback in college football. Two decades later, as coach, Hardin drew upon his experiences playing alongside LeBaron in the backfield and applied them to nurture the similar skills of his young, mobile quarterback, Roger Staubach.

After graduating in 1949, Hardin remained at Pacific and served as a volunteer assistant for Stagg. One year later he accepted a job at Ceres High School teaching English, teaching six physical education classes, and coaching football, basketball, and baseball for the total stipend of $2,950. In the football season prior to Hardin's arrival, the team had failed to win a game. During his two years as head coach, the team compiled a 16–1 record. In the 1951–1952 season, he coached the basketball team to a 25–2 record before accepting an offer to return to his alma mater as the defensive backs coach for the College of the Pacific.

The *Modesto Bee and News-Herald* reported that Hardin would join the College of the Pacific's staff, working for Head Coach Ernie Jorge and alongside fellow assistant Hugh McWilliams, who Coach Alonzo Stagg once called the best athlete he ever coached. (Years later, both Jorge and McWilliams joined Wayne Hardin on the Navy coaching staff, bringing with them great experience and first-rate resumes.) Jorge led Pacific to two Sun Bowl appearances.

Upon Hardin's departure from Ceres High School, principal Nick Koshell offered this assessment of the coach: "He is a hard worker and very serious minded. He doesn't stand for foolishness, and his standards are high as to physical conditioning. Hardin wants his players to demonstrate unity and not individuality. His athletes are out to win and win fairly—but out to win. Finally, Hardin is a fundamentalist who has the ability to sense the weakness of the player, his own and the opposition, and knows what he's about at all times."

After his stint at Pacific, Hardin's coaching career moved on to Porterville Junior College, then to the Chicago Cardinals before he accepted a position at the Naval Academy for the 1955 season. The twenty-eight-year-old Hardin was assigned the position of secondary coach under Head Coach Eddie Erdelatz. The head coach called his new assistant a "real hustler. The boys will learn a lot from him."

After four years as an assistant, Hardin was promoted to head coach of Navy football in April 1959, at the age of thirty-two. Erdelatz had resigned after Navy officials decided against participating in a bowl game following the 1958 season. After the announcement of Hardin's promotion, George Minot of the *Washington Post* wrote that Hardin "doesn't look like the popular conception of a head coach. He isn't gruff or paunchy. . . . He's a nice guy type, who reminds you of the kid next door. . . . He has a big grin that lights up his freckled face and fading red hair."

Navy officials were convinced that Hardin was their man not only because of his resume and abilities, but also because he was an individual who "knows the problems at the Naval Academy and sympathizes with them," a Navy spokesman commented. "He's our boy, and we hope and expect him to have a long and successful tenure."

In his book *Time Enough to Win*, Roger Staubach called Hardin "a tremendous competitor. He's a fiery redhead, very emotional at times and very demanding all the time. He expected everything from his players." Like most coaches, Hardin was an amalgamation of life experiences with great influence from a man he most admired, Coach Stagg, who demanded total commitment from his team. If Hardin perceived that he wasn't receiving 100 percent focus from a player, that player would be subjected to a reddened face, piercing eyes, and penetrating comments. Coach Hardin has been called moody, confident, undiplomatic, an offensive genius, and sarcastic.

In a 1963 *Sports Illustrated* article, Hardin professed that he would prefer that people not understand him. "I don't want anybody to know me. I don't want anybody to know what I think. The less they know about me, the less they know about my teams."

For many, Coach Hardin was an enigma, which was exactly how he wanted to be perceived. He preferred his opponents to be distracted by wonder and his players to be concerned only with the task at hand. Hardin was known to say, "A lot of people have tried to figure me out and not one has yet. Not even my mother."

As Beano Cook, former sports information director at the University of Pittsburgh, said, "I would hire him in a second to be my coach. I just wouldn't want to go away on vacation with him."

With his green fedora on his head, Coach Hardin paced the sideline, pushing his charges to be the best football players they could be. His players would respond, hoping to earn his approval. And though personal approval was restrained, Hardin recognized the team as a whole and saw their eagerness to succeed.

"They have a quiet, serene approach to the game, and they have the same approach off the field. They want to be good Midshipmen and Navy officers, as well as good football players." He expounded upon this theme in an Associated Press story, saying, "Any team rises or falls on its unity, and this team has it. It is probably the closest knit squad I have seen."

Navy squads comprised boys from different backgrounds and origins. Players were directed to the academy by Navy "bird dogs" and persuasive assistant coaches who only promised a good education, a chance to play Division I college football, and the pledge that someday a battleship would be named after them. This sole purpose galvanized the team, a purpose nurtured through the guidance of Coach Hardin, who was surrounded by a top-notch staff and administration, from school Superintendent Rear Admiral Charles C. Kirkpatrick down to young sports information director Budd Thalman. The solid staff of administrators provided great support to the football program, allowing the coaches to focus on the job of coaching football and putting the team in the best position to win.

Superintendent Rear Admiral Charles C. Kirkpatrick, a graduate of the Naval Academy of 1931, was lovingly known to the brigade as "Uncle Charlie." A war hero in the Pacific theater of operations during World War II, Admiral Kirkpatrick was awarded three Navy Crosses and a Distinguished Service Cross as a commander of the submarine *Triton*, from which he patrolled the Pacific Ocean with ferocity. On one mission, he sank a submarine and six merchant ships; on another, he downed two Japanese destroyers. As a naval officer, Kirkpatrick was present at Yalta when Stalin, Churchill, and Roosevelt met.

As superintendent of the academy, Admiral Kirkpatrick was an enthusiastic advocate of the brigade as a whole, but especially the football team. The 1964 edition of the yearbook, the *Lucky Bag*, said, "Pep rallies never seemed to click until 'Uncle Charlie' made his appearance . . . and then we went wild. If the Forty-One Hundred had a single living embodiment of its spirit, the Admiral was it. He was the team's most loyal supporter and his enthusiasm never slackened."

At rallies and meetings and walks through the yard, Uncle Charlie was forever motivating the midshipmen with pumped fist and his famous saying, "you can do anything you set your mind to do, and don't you forget it!" It wasn't simply a statement of casual intention. Superintendent Kirkpatrick embodied the sentiment and believed it with every fiber of his body. He wanted the best for the men of the brigade and believed they were capable of the best.

The saying was so associated with the man that when he took the podium at pep rallies, the 4,100 midshipmen would recite in unison before he could get the words out of his mouth, "you can do anything you set your mind to do, and don't you forget it!"

# CHAPTER 4

# Army vs. Navy

IN NOVEMBER 1890, ARMY CADET DENNIS MICHIE challenged the more established Navy football team to a match at the campus on West Point. Navy was victorious, 24–0. From that day forward, the two academies have met regularly on the gridiron to determine football superiority.

The Army–Navy competition—held annually, with a few exceptions, since 1890—is considered by many to be the greatest amateur rivalry in all of sports, one of the rare sporting events that transcend the arena in which it's played. The respective football teams merely act as a proxy for the men who serve or once did—the Navy squad playing for the brigade, the Army unit for the corps. From submerged submarines and the decks of aircraft carriers to tents and barracks around the world, the hopes and aspirations of millions of active and former military service men and women are embodied by the men on the football field. The game is a mark of pride. It's a game in which every tackle is harder, every block held longer, every victory relished longer, and every loss mourned deeper. For the participants, it is an experience that lasts a lifetime.

Army's Pete Dawkins, who won the Heisman Trophy in 1958 and later ascended to the rank of brigadier general, described the honor of playing in the Army–Navy game as a "responsibility to perform well and not to let the Corps down or the coaches or the team." Dawkins perceived his football season as two separate parts: the nine games prior to the service-academy game, and the rivalry game itself.

Great military leaders such as General Dwight Eisenhower, General George Patton, Admiral Bull Halsey, and Lieutenant General Bill Carpenter participated in their respective programs. A great wide receiver and future inductee in the College Football Hall of Fame, Carpenter was made famous by Newsreel Films that showed him as the "lonely end" who never joined the huddle but somehow knew the play. The Army–Navy game held a special place in Carpenter's heart and memory.

> It's not a state or regional rivalry but instead a national rivalry . . . . It's long-standing; it's fierce; it's symbolic of the best in amateur sports. In any game, you play for your teammates; a loss means you've somehow let them and your coaches down. Against Navy, you're letting down the Corps, the U.S. Army, and a big hunk of the nation in addition to yourself and your teammates. The rivalry was very special—the epitome of all that is great in college football.

For over a century, the Army–Navy game has held the fascination of the nation, and this interest was perhaps never more apparent than in 1926. In his book *Navy Football: Gridiron Legends and Fighting Heroes*, Jack Clary chronicles this legendary match-up in which a 7–1 Army team met a 9–0 Navy team at Solider Field in Chicago. More than 115,000 attended the game, including Knute Rockne, who skipped his own Notre Dame game versus Carnegie Tech to watch the much-anticipated service-academy contest. (While Rockne was watching Army and Navy tie 21–21, his Fighting Irish team was upset in South Bend. The loss cost Notre Dame an undefeated season and the national championship.)

At times, the intensity of the Army–Navy rivalry has extended beyond the boundaries of sportsmanship, occasionally to the point that authorities have been compelled to suspend play. Following a 6–4 victory for Navy in 1893, senior officers from the services attempted to resolve a dispute from the game by challenging each other to a duel.

Cooler heads prevailed, but the game was cancelled for the next few years, with the announcement, "The Army–Navy game constituted a distracting influence out of character with the orderly routine of the two schools."

A decade later, President Theodore Roosevelt attended the rivalry game only to leave the contest appalled by the level of violence. In that game, eleven different players were carted off the field as victims of the mass play called the Flying Wedge.

Mass plays such as the Flying Wedge pointed entire units at one player on the other team with the intent of breaking the blocking chain at its weakest link. Schemes like this led inevitably to an epidemic of deaths on the fields of college football. In 1905 alone, eighteen players died. Both Army and Navy had recently mourned the deaths of players.

It would take an executive order from President Teddy Roosevelt to encourage authorities to ensure that the game was conducted in a safe and appropriate manner. In a letter to Secretary of War William Alger, Roosevelt wrote, "I should like very much to revive the game between Annapolis and West Point. . . . If authorities of both institutions agreed to take measures to prevent any excesses."

Given the passions about the rivalry, the participants were often held in reverence at their schools and throughout the nation. When General George C. Marshall needed a recruit for a special assignment in World War II, he requested "an officer for a secret and dangerous mission. . . . I want a West Point football player." It's the type of game that creates living legends.

❨ ❨ ❨

Both the Army and Navy schedules in 1961 allowed for an off-week prior to the rivalry game in order to provide the teams and the students with ample preparation time. On the Friday prior to the 1961 contest, former Navy football star Joe Bellino was invited to the White House to reacquaint himself with President Kennedy. Ensign Bellino was joined by fellow Naval Academy graduate and football alumnus Sid Driscoll. During their visit, the two ensigns presented Kennedy with the Navy yearbook, called the *Lucky Bag* in the tradition at the academy.

The following day, on December 2, Kennedy was among the 102,000 spectators at the game, making him the first commander in chief since Harry Truman in 1950 to attend the rivalry game. Kennedy's immediate predecessor in the Oval Office, Dwight Eisenhower, was a former Army player and thus decided against attending the games as president, concerned that his allegiance to the Cadets would be misinterpreted by Navy personnel. Eisenhower and General Douglas MacArthur were such avid followers of the Army team that they were often given weekly updates on the team by Army coaches.

In the weeks leading up to the 1961 contest, Army coach Dale Hall, fighting to keep his job, was working twenty-one-hour days, reading and rereading the 1,500 pages of notes his four scouts had compiled on the Navy team. In a preview of the game in the *New York Times*, Hall pledged, "We will beat Navy." Army was favored by one point, and the Navy coaches were predicting a "nip and tuck game."

Navy, however, was led by the fiery coach Wayne Hardin, who was blessed with the ability to create, inspire, instigate, and manipulate. Not much older than the players he coached, Hardin was brash and unrelenting. Unafraid to annoy or provoke the media, opposing coaches, his players, or even the Navy administration, his mission was singular: put his team in position to win football games.

Both teams entered the game with 6–3 records, and there was talk before kickoff that the winner would be invited to play in the New Year's Day Rose Bowl against UCLA. The Army–Navy game was to be televised on ABC, and the black-and-white technology of the time made it difficult for viewers at home to identify the strange color of helmets Navy receivers were wearing when they took the field. Hardin, always in search of an extra edge, had instructed his equipment manager to paint the helmets of his pass receivers (halfbacks, ends, and wide receivers) fluorescent orange, while the linemen wore the traditional gold helmets. The word "Beat" was on the right shoulders of the Midshipmen, "Army" on the left.

UPI writer Oscar Fraley wrote, "The Middies, as so often is the story, exploded on the scene with ingenuity, inventiveness, and daring. The Cadets appeared with nothing new and listless." Hardin was never one to let the fear of criticism deter him from seeking every advantage and making bold statements.

❰ ❰ ❰

The venue for the 1961 match was Philadelphia's Municipal Stadium, as it had been in all but two years since 1936. Built in 1926, the giant cement edifice located in South Philly served as home to the National Football League's Philadelphia Eagles, and it also hosted concerts and championship boxing matches, including Gene Tunney's 1926 victory over Jack Dempsey and Rocky Marciano's win over Jersey Joe Walcott in 1952. "The great concrete igloo in the Philadelphia wastelands," as Arthur Daley of the *New York Times* called it, was a fitting stage for one of college football's greatest spectacles.

On a sunny, crisp Saturday in early December 1961, 102,000 spectators filled the stadium's concrete bleachers, poised for the contest. Among the spectators was Navy plebe Roger Staubach, who recalled in his book *First Down, Lifetime to Go*, "I remember sitting in the stands my freshman year and dreaming about playing in the game next year. I knew I had a chance."

Revenue from the 1961 game was divided between the two schools, and the amount generated from ticket sales, which averaged $7.50, and TV proceeds, which exceeded one million dollars, paid for each school's football program for a year.

On the field, the game was a hard-fought defensive battle. In the first half, President Kennedy sat in the front row on the Army side, his hat by his side, and braved the chilly December day in suit and tie, without an overcoat. He even refused the heater that past presidents had used. A week later, comedian Bob Hope roasted the president at the

College Football Hall of Fame dinner in New York about his wardrobe at the game. "What scared me was he was out there with no coat and hat. I mean, we know he doesn't need a hat, but the coat? Do you think we're spending too much for missiles?"

At halftime, Kennedy crossed the field to the Navy side, where he was greeted by Secretary of the Navy John Connally and his three sisters, Pat, Jean, and Eunice, who sat on the Navy side along with Vice President Lyndon Johnson and Lady Bird Johnson.

The president, who was seen to frown when Army scored, was full of life on the Navy side. His enthusiasm for his team was apparent. Smoking a cigar, he intently watched the game from his box of honor. With the score 7–3, Navy back Bill Ulrich ran for a 13-yard touchdown to give the Middies the lead for good and bringing the president to his feet. It was the foot of Navy's Greg Mather that would prove decisive in the game.

Prior to the 1961 season, the NCAA had voted to widen the goalposts, and Mather took advantage of the change to lead the nation in scoring, kicking nine field goals, with a long of 45 yards. In his pre-game analysis of the Army–Navy clash, Associated Press writer Bob Hoobing suggested that "field goals could prove a factor," adding, "Navy end Greg Mather or Army specialist Dick Heydt may have the answer to the sixty-second annual services football clash Saturday in the year of the Field Goal." Daley took it a step further in his pre-game column in the *New York Times*, giving Navy the edge in that regard. "At least it's nice to see that the foot has returned to football," Daley wrote. "By nightfall tomorrow, though, Army may regret that it has, because Mather of Navy could be the deciding factor."

Mather was such a concern of Army's that before the game, the Cadets put on a skit in which a cheerleader dressed up as the Navy kicker. A two-foot-high goalpost was placed in front of the impersonator, who drew great laughs when he continued to fail to kick the ball through the miniature uprights.

On game day, though, Mather laughed loudest. The nearsighted midshipman from California who possessed 20/300 vision kicked two field goals and an extra point, leading his team to a 13–7 victory.

After the game, Hardin stood on a bench in the locker room with the game ball that the team had presented him and yelled, "We won the greatest game we ever played. There is no feeling like the feeling of beating Army!"

In the post-game celebration, Navy director of athletics, Captain Asbury Coward, shouted to Hardin, "Wayne, you're the greatest football coach in the United States." Coach Hardin was now 3–0 against Army, wielding his aggressive and innovative style.

Navy receiver Jimmy Stewart observed that his team's orange head gear "shook up the Army and certainly helped our passing attack."

When Hardin and his team of forty-four returned to Annapolis, they were greeted by cheers of "Go-Go, four in a row!" Over five thousand well-wishers gathered in front of Bancroft Hall, singing "Anchors Aweigh."

> Stand Navy down the field, sails set to the sky.
> We'll never change our course, so Army you steer shy-y-y-y.
> Roll up the score, Navy, Anchors Aweigh.
> Sail Navy down the field and sink the Army, sink the Army Grey.

The midshipmen then counted along as Hardin and Superintendent Kirkpatrick rang the Japanese Bell, which was claimed in Okinawa and brought back to campus in 1851 by Commodore Matthew Perry. In all, the bell was rung thirteen times to signify the number of points scored against rival Army, followed by one ring by each Navy player.

A headline in the *Washington Post* the next day proclaimed, "Kennedy Talks Politics, Cheers Navy at Game." The president's allegiance to the Midshipmen football team was further articulated by Admiral George Anderson Jr., who sat with the president in the second half:

This was a close game. The President throughout the half in which he sat next to me was thoroughly interested, showed his complete awareness of all the technicalities of the game, and certainly manifested to me another facet of his extremely human qualities. Fortunately, the Army did not take care of all the opportunities that were given to them and the Navy won the game, and we had the pleasure of sharing Naval enthusiasm over this victory. In spite of the fact that the President was trying to be impartial, there was no question in my mind that he at the game did have a deep loyalty to the dark blue suit and the gold braid.

On the train ride back to Washington, D.C., President Kennedy sat with former Army coach Earl Blaik and expressed his concern about the Naval Academy's dominance over the Cadets. "When you have Army and Navy playing before the entire country, as it were, looking at it on TV," Kennedy said to Blaik, "and they judge the academies to a degree on how they played and how the game went—if one side dominates and the other gives a sad effort, it's not good." Soon thereafter, Kennedy wrote to former Army assistant coach and then current Green Bay Packer coach, Vince Lombardi, hoping to persuade him to return to West Point as head football coach. The president's request was respectfully declined.

When Kennedy arrived back at the White House, he wrote to the superintendent of the Naval Academy, Rear Admiral John F. Davidson, to tell him how he "thoroughly enjoyed" the game in Philadelphia. "Thank you very much for the hospitality shown to all of us," the president wrote, "and please extend my best wishes to the Brigade of the Midshipmen and their fine football team."

As for plebe Roger Staubach, he reflected on the impact of the game in his book *First Down, Lifetime to Go*: "Whenever that happens [Navy beating Army], plebes are allowed to 'carry on' from right after the game until Christmas leave. The entire plebe system is off. You can walk down the hall naturally instead of holding your chin in, almost at a brace. There were no come-arounds, no square meals [sitting on the

## U.S. Naval Academy (7–3)
## @ U.S. Military Academy (6–4)

Municipal Stadium . Philadelphia, Pennsylvania

December 2, 1961 . 1:15 p.m. kickoff . Attendance 102,000

|       | 1 | 2 | 3 | 4 | Final |
| ----- | - | - | - | - | ----- |
| Navy  | 0 | 3 | 7 | 3 | 13    |
| Army  | 0 | 0 | 7 | 0 | 7     |

|                |                                     |
| -------------- | ----------------------------------- |
| Navy           | FG, Mather, 32 yards                 |
| Army           | TD, Rushatz, 1-yard run (Heydt kick) |
| Navy           | TD, Ulrich, 12-yard run (Mather kick) |
| Navy           | FG, Mather, 36 yards                 |

|                  | Navy  | Army |
| ---------------- | ----- | ---- |
| First Downs      | 15    | 11   |
| Rushing Yards    | 113   | 97   |
| Passing Yards    | 116   | 88   |
| Pass Att.–Comp.  | 17-10 | 11-5 |
| Fumbles Lost     | 0     | 1    |
| Interceptions by | 1     | 2    |
| Penalty Yards    | 35    | 15   |

edge of your chair and bringing all food from your plate straight up and then at a 90-degree angle into your mouth], nothing."

Victory is sweet, indeed, especially for plebes.

According to Blaik, following the 1961 game, as the Midshipmen players marched off the field, they were heard to say, "Wait till they see Staubach."

In the *Washington Post*, George Minot added, "Waiting in the wings are the rookies from the best plebe team in years. The yearlings had about everything."

Navy supporters hoped that this third victory in a row over Army was only the beginning of a lengthy streak. They clearly were looking forward to the arrival of Staubach & Company on the scene.

On the other side of the rivalry, Coach Hall and his Army squad had again failed to beat Navy. His job already in jeopardy, Hall said after the game, "All I know is that I have another year to go on my contract. The administration hasn't said anything to me one way or another."

The 1961 Army–Navy game was Hall's last as coach of Army football.

# CHAPTER 5

# President Kennedy at Quonset Point, 1962

QUONSET POINT IS LOCATED ON A RHODE ISLAND PENINSULA in the town of North Kingstown, just northwest of the exclusive town of Newport. For years the area was used as a summer colony, where vacationers would occupy the row of cottages that were situated on the Atlantic Ocean waters of Narragansett Bay. In 1939, as part of the Lend-Lease program, the lands were acquired in anticipation of the spreading world conflict and converted to a naval air base and neighboring shipyard for aircraft carriers. The property had sufficient housing and facilities to host eleven squadrons. At its height, the base was the number one employer in the state.

The summer humidity of Annapolis, Maryland, can be stifling and thus not conducive for two-a-day football practices. Consequently, the 1962 Navy team was commissioned to travel north to the naval air base at Quonset Point, Rhode Island. It was the third straight year that Coach Wayne Hardin conducted preseason practices on the naval base and airport grounds. For ten days, one hundred players were put through grueling double sessions at the base, which in the early 1900s was used for a summer camp for children and was known as Camp Happyland. Camp Hardin was anything but a happy land. During these never-ending drills, Coach Hardin would learn if his current team liked to hit.

Roger Staubach was coming off his highly successful plebe season, in which he led the high-scoring Navy team to an 8–1 record, and he was brimming with confidence. Many at the camp felt that, despite his third-class (sophomore) status, he was the best quarterback on the team. That perception, though, wasn't shared by old-school Coach Hardin, who maintained the belief that young players hurt more than they help. He was known to say, "It costs you one touchdown for every sophomore that starts."

Staubach, though, remained sure of his abilities and those of his teammates from the previous season, including Fred Marlin, Jim Freeman, Pat Donnelly, and Kip Paskewich. All arrived at camp prepared to compete for playing time and contribute to the 1962 team. Missing from the heralded group was the electric halfback Darryl Hill, who had shown so much promise the previous fall but had decided to transfer to the University of Maryland at the urging of Maryland's freshman coach, Lee Corso. Despite Hill's absence, Navy's sophomore class was still one of the finest in the nation. Throughout camp, the players established themselves as potential contributors and were determined to be defined by their production, not their age.

Camp was winding down, and Hardin was pleased with the team's progress. In a *New York Times* article by Joseph Sheehan, the Navy coach assessed his squad. "This is a closely knit team now," Hardin said, "and the boys have fine spirit and really want to play. I think we're pretty good up front in the line, but I consider the passing game our biggest asset. We'll probably throw the ball a lot." Sheehan, in his team preview, shared Hardin's analysis, citing as the team's chief assets a "good passing game, stalwart first line, [and] experienced depth," while noting its only deficiencies as "lack of an established punter and place kicker."

When a group of second-year midshipmen assembled for a photograph with Hardin, Staubach leaned over to his irascible coach and declared, "Okay, coach, here's your starting lineup." Indeed, included in the *New York Times* college football season preview on August 31, 1962, was a note regarding Navy that said, "Staubach is scheduled to break in on the offensive unit."

On that same day, August 31, President Kennedy was busy at the White House finishing up the business at hand before departing for a long Labor Day weekend. That morning in the Oval Office, he signed into effect the Communications Satellite Act of 1962. The president said of the legislation, "Its purpose is to establish a commercial communications system utilizing space satellites which will serve our needs and those of other countries and contribute to world peace and understanding."

Business taken care of, the president prepared for his trip, scheduled to depart from Andrews Air Force Base at six o'clock in the evening. His destination: Quonset Point Naval Air Station to meet wife Jacqueline and four-year-old daughter Caroline, who would be arriving from their twenty-three-day trip to Italy and the Mediterranean.

On the practice field at Quonset Point, Navy players were completing their final drills of the camp under the watchful eye of their red-headed coach. Hardin's practices were always scripted, to the very last second. Players were responsible to know the agenda and, when a whistle blew, to report to the proper station. Practices were crisp and efficient. Conditioning was achieved not through running drills but instead by sprinting from station to station. There was no walking, there was no down time. Hardin never deviated from a day's plan.

Of course, there's an exception to every rule.

An officer approached Coach Hardin to inform him that the team's departure from the airfield would be delayed because President Kennedy would be landing that evening. Hardin was excited about the prospect of crossing paths with the president and consequently asked the Navy officer to call Air Force One to request the opportunity to meet Kennedy. The officer left and soon returned, informing Hardin, "The president will be happy to meet the team."

After ten long days of double sessions under an August sun, the team was looking forward to leaving Rhode Island and returning back to the Naval Academy. But instead, they were ordered to report to the tarmac of the Quonset naval base in their starchy white summer uniforms, complete with nametag and shined shoes. The exhausted team stood in line as the sun set. Hardin was in suit and tie, standing with Navy senior officers, including six admirals, while he held onto a team-signed football that was adorned with "19 N 62"—the year and "N" for Navy.

Just before seven o'clock, they heard the roar of Air Force One as it descended from the southern sky. When the plane touched down, the team was called to attention. President Kennedy appeared at the landing of the rollaway stairs, and a rousing cheer exploded from the 1,500 civilians present. Kennedy was dressed in a tailored blue suit with blue tie, holding hat in hand. As he walked down the walkway and made his way over to Coach Hardin and the Navy officials who were on hand, he was greeted by a rendition of "Hail to the Chief" and a twenty-one-gun salute.

At the conclusion of the formalities, President Kennedy engaged the coaching staff in conversation. Commenting on the coming year's game against Army, Coach Hardin responded that Navy would play a game "fit for a president." This answer brought a smile to former Navy man Kennedy's face.

Hardin then walked with the president down the line, right to left, introducing him to the players who stood at attention in three parallel lines. Kennedy stopped at each player and offered some words and shook hands. (When he came to halfback Pat Donnelly, he looked at his nametag and complimented, "Good Irish name.") He then told the players that he would be "following the team this fall. I wish you well." The president was so impressed with the team and coaches that he sent a staff member to retrieve brother Bobby from Air Force One to also meet the team.

Later, the coaches were invited onto Air Force One for a tour given by the president. The coaches were most impressed by the "red phone," a component of the much talked about phone system used in case of war or other catastrophe. Kennedy then turned to Assistant Coach Rick Forzano and invited him to take a souvenir, which he did in the form of Air Force One letterhead. Forzano then humbly requested if the president would be so kind as to send an autographed picture to his father. The president obliged.

A month later, Forzano's father received the very special signed photograph.

Rick Forzano was the defensive backs coach for Navy. As a teenager he suffered an eye injury that compelled him to become a coach so he could stay involved in sports. He also was responsible for recruiting and focused primarily on Ohio, where he had previously coached high school football in Akron. He knew that Ohio was a proud state that lived by the motto, "if you want to be somebody you have to go through Ohio." He also knew he was competing for athletes with the Big Ten schools and especially Woody Hayes of Ohio State.

But Forzano was an extremely persuasive person. When he got into a living room, he was able to apply his people skills while allowing the special qualities of the academy to speak for themselves. Forzano's recruiting achievements included Ohio high schoolers Tom Lynch, Pat Donnelly, and Roger Staubach. What made the Staubach commitment so special was that not only did Forzano have to convince him to go the Naval Academy but also to prep school in New Mexico so that he could improve enough academically to qualify.

In the summer of 1963, Forzano spent two days with defensive mastermind John Ray, who coached at John Carroll University and later at Notre Dame and Kentucky. Throughout their session, Ray instructed the Navy coach on the advantages of the defensive alignment called the Split Six. When Forzano returned to Annapolis and implemented the system of three down lineman and three linebackers who filled gaps, it gave the defense the flexibility to pressure the quarterback or drop back into coverage to blanket potential receivers. Forzano called the alignment "impossible to block if you haven't seen it before."

Players often heard Coach Forzano imploring them not to fumble or get beat deep for three reasons: Stacey, Ricky, and Kristie. Those were his three kids, who would suffer if he lost his job because his players didn't comply with his instructions. With a voice that would resound across a football field, Forzano could tease and prod until each of his players finally "hit harder than [his] daughter Kristie."

The meeting with Kennedy in the summer of 1962 was a tremendous experience for all involved. The coaches departed Air Force One as the Kennedys' private plane, the *Caroline*, was coming to a stop just feet from the nose of the president's plane. The president greeted his daughter, dressed in a pink dress with white dress gloves, and his wife, who was dressed in a long white coat, drawing the eyes of the Navy players from a distance.

The Navy team and the president parted ways, Kennedy to enjoy a weekend of swimming and sailing in Newport, and the team to commence school and prepare for the football season. One month later, Coach Hardin received a letter from the president's secretary that read:

> Dear Mr. Hardin,
> This note conveys the President's thanks to you and the USNA football team for the autographed football you wanted him to have. He appreciated receiving the memento and extends his very best wishes to each of the players for a most successful year.
> Sincerely yours,
> Evelyn Lincoln
> Personal Secretary to the President

☾ ☾ ☾

The ten days of brutal double sessions for the Navy football team had ended with a once-in-a-lifetime encounter. Players and coaches alike were thrilled with the chance to meet with the commander in chief, and he was thrilled to meet them. Just months earlier, he had outwardly cheered their victory over Army. Now he looked forward to the coming season with his new acquaintances.

Later that night, the team flew back to the academy filled with promise and hope. At Quonset Point the Navy football team came together as a unit beneath the strain of an August sun. Years later, two teammates and friends returned to the base, not for football but instead to serve their country.

Pat Philbin and Mike Burns first met on the football field of their high school, St. Francis of Xavier in New York. As teenagers they played the sport they loved for a hard-nosed coach known as Boiler Burns. Coach Burns was a New York City detective who also happened to be the father of Mike Burns.

Philbin and Burns were best friends and followed each other to the Naval Academy. Mike Burns was described as a big teddy bear whose killer instinct would only manifest itself on the football field. He was known as "Wimpy" to his teammates because of his legendary appetite for hamburger, reminiscent of the character from the Popeye cartoons.

Following graduation, Philbin and Burns reported to Quonset Point Naval Station, deployed in the antisubmarine warfare division. Mike would pilot a helicopter and Pat would fly an S2F airplane, which hunted submarines. As they had done for years on the gridiron, they supported each other as part of the same air group.

As part of their training, they often took part in training missions hunting submarines over the waters of the Atlantic. During one winter night's mission, the skies were ominous and northeast winds gusted, turning a winter's day brutally cold and blustery. The conditions created havoc with Burns' helicopter. Flying next to him, Pat Philbin could only watch as his comrade's aircraft began to drop from the sky into the Atlantic Ocean.

Below Philbin, Burns' helo rose and fell in the water's crests and troughs as the airman fought to free himself. Finally escaping, he swam to a life raft and climbed on board. Up above, his linemate breathed easy.

Burns, seemingly safe, prepared himself to be picked up by a rescue helicopter. During the effort, however, complications exposed the fallen pilot to the frigid ocean. In short time, the forty-degree waters enveloped the exposed body, and within minutes he was dead.

At Quonset Point in 1962, the Navy football team had made wonderful memories and strengthened their sense of camaraderie, hope, and youthful exuberance. Years later, the same location was a tragic stage of death. For over a decade, Pat Philbin and Mike Burns had stood shoulder to shoulder ready to support the other at all costs. Pat was asked one last time to support his friend. At the request of Burns' wife, Philbin was asked to escort the body of his teammate to Arlington Cemetery, where Burns would be laid to rest in honor of his service to his country.

# CHAPTER 6

# Of Mediocrity and Missiles: Kickoff, 1962

THE 1962 SEASON GOT OFF TO A DISAPPOINTING START. In the opening game against Penn State, the Nittany Lions dominated the Midshipmen, quashing them by a score of 41–7. The following week, the heavily favored Navy team had to hold on against William & Mary to eke out a 20–16 victory. One week later, the Midshipmen were manhandled by defensive end Carl Eller and the University of Minnesota. The Navy offense that had been so highly touted before the season was shut out by the Big Ten school, 21–0. Three weeks into the season and suddenly a Navy team of great promise was on the verge of disaster. Coach Wayne Hardin couldn't wait any longer—he began to re-evaluate the depth chart and his reliance on upperclassman.

In the first three games, senior quarterback Ron Klemick started, but the offense was stagnant and listless. Hoping to breathe new life into the team, Hardin decided to alter the offense by replacing the entire line and backfield for the Cornell game. Junior Tom Lynch moved to center and was flanked by Jim Freeman, Al Krekich, Erwin Storz, and Chuck Durepo. In the backfield, Hardin turned to the freelancing and creative—and sophomore—Roger Staubach, who had been impressive the previous season and at camp. To date, Staubach had seen limited action, throwing four incomplete passes and running for a negative 14 yards. He was joined in the backfield by halfbacks Bob Orlosky and Dick Earnest.

Prior to the October 11 Cornell game, it was written in the *Washington Post*, "The Ivy League seems to be more Navy's speed this year than the Big Ten." The record 23,358 fans in attendance at Marine Corps Stadium were treated to a star performance by sophomore quarterback Roger Staubach. He led the team on six touchdown drives, two of which he scored himself, en route to a 41–0 victory. In total, Staubach ran for 89 yards, including a 59-yard, zigzagging run that brought Navy fans to their feet. The six-foot-two sophomore also threw for 99 yards on efficient 9 of 11 passing.

In the following day's *Washington Post*, the story of the Navy quarterback's prowess was chronicled under a headline that read "Staubach Leads Rout of Cornell." Within the article, writer George Minot concluded, "Before the afternoon was over, he [Staubach] had won the #1 job away from Ron Klemick."

❨ ❨ ❨

Unbeknownst to Americans as they turned the pages of their Sunday morning papers, a U-2 spy plane was flying over Cuba, snapping pictures and recording intelligence of the Caribbean island. The previous August, intelligence reports had documented that thirty Russian ships had arrived at Cuban ports, containing two thousand Russian "technicians," MIG 21 planes, surface-to-air missiles, and patrol boats armed with missiles. These reports incited President Kennedy and his military staff to intensify their scrutiny of the neighboring country, which sits just ninety miles off the coast of Florida.

When the pictures from the spy plane were analyzed the following day, it became apparent that the construction and installation of missile launch sites was underway in the town of San Cristobal, 65 miles west of Havana. It was further detected that the weapons consisted of nuclear missiles with a range of one thousand miles, capable of reaching Cape

Cod, Massachusetts, and two thousand miles, which had strike capacity as far north as Canada.

In Russia the operation was known as "Anadyr" and called for the delivery and installation of missiles on Cuba. The spread of communism in the Western Hemisphere was of great concern to the president, as of course was nuclear destruction. With a great burden upon his shoulders, President Kennedy gathered his cabinet and military leaders and discussed strategies that ranged from a blockade to an all-out invasion of the island.

The president soon received additional intelligence further confirming Russia and Cuba's intention of armament build-up. In addition to the launch sites, a Russian Ilyushin 28 twin-engine bomber had also arrived in Cuba, having the ability to carry nuclear bombs and deliver such weapons as far north as Tampa, Florida.

By Saturday, October 20, concern had evolved into crisis. To this point, the White House had made "business as usual" a point of emphasis as it evaluated the situation in Cuba, but now Kennedy had no choice but to return to the White House from his normal presidential travels. Press Secretary Pierre Salinger announced that the president was suffering from a minor illness, thus it was prudent to return to Washington. The *New York Times* headline the next day read, "President Cuts His Tour Short, Flies to Capital, Has Mild Cold—Speculation Rises on Possible Urgent White House Business." Vice President Lyndon B. Johnson also acquired a cold, it was announced, and as a result would also be returning to Washington, D.C.

As both rushed back to Washington, at the Naval Academy Roger Staubach was awarded the start in the game against Boston College. When Navy took the field that day, Boston College coaches and officials were confused. Coach Hardin had decided to dress his team in its home blue uniforms marked by white shoulder stripes, topped off by the Midshipmen's traditional gold helmets. This outraged the Boston College coaches, because protocol called for visitors to wear white. Differentiating between the two teams was difficult for fans and players alike. The sun that day was low and blinding as autumn was moving toward winter. Potentially unnerved by the likeness in uniforms, the Eagle quarterbacks threw four interceptions, including a crucial third-quarter pick by Midshipman Al Krekich on the Boston College 10-yard line.

Staubach apparently had no such problems. He threw for 165 yards, completing 14 of 20 passes and 2 touchdowns. After the 26–6 victory, Hardin, who originally was reluctant to play the young quarterback, now fawned over him. "We knew he was good," the coach said. "He has come along the way we planned. All he needed was experience." He continued, "He's cool but not cocky."

As Saturday unfolded, the White House press corps was growing suspicious. The *New York Times* reported, "All over town high officials failed to show up to dinner parties or left suddenly murmuring apologies." When reporters asked about getting a comment from the president, they were told he wasn't in the White House—even though he could be seen through the Oval Office windows. Rumors of troop movements were starting to circulate. Marines from California reported to bases in Puerto Rico, while a squadron of Phantom jets arrived in Key West, Florida.

During high-level meetings, three options were being discussed in the White House: blockade of the country, air strike, or all-out invasion. The choice was blockade, with the official term being "quarantine," which called for an armada of American ships to block all ships destined for Cuba that were carrying cargo connected to offensive weapons.

On Sunday, October 21, forty-three letters were written and delivered to embassies around the world with instructions that they were to be delivered to heads of state. On Monday, fighter jets were sent across the country to pick up congressmen whose presence was requested back in the capital. Simultaneously, Pierre Salinger alerted television stations that President Kennedy needed thirty minutes of airtime to address the nation at seven o'clock. Later in the afternoon, Secretary of

State Dean Rusk summoned Russian ambassador Anatoly Dobrynin to the State Department. When Dobrynin arrived, he greeted the waiting media with casual indifference. When he emerged from the meeting he had a copy of the president's speech in his possession and was reported to be ashen.

During the football season, the Navy football team always gathered at the Boat House on Mondays to watch the game film, eat dinner, and listen to the scouting report of the following week's opponent. During the film session, the game from the previous Saturday would roll off the tape spooled on a 16mm projector. The captive audience would watch the game replayed in black and white on the screen—sometimes in slow motion, sometimes backward and forward—over and over again. Depending on the outcome of a certain play, characters in the audience would recoil or smile a satisfying grin.

Following the film, the players would be treated to a team dinner, which served as an escape from the regimen that existed back at Bancroft Hall. Players could eat without restrictions. When dinner was finished, the team would then file into the "classroom" of Assistant Coach Steve Belichick, where he would deliver the scouting report on the following weekend's opponent. Coach Belichick was known as the preeminent college scout in the country. It would be during this session that the players would learn about their opponent's tendencies, strengths, and weaknesses.

On this particular Monday, though, Coach Hardin decided that the team should delay the scouting report and interrupt the routine to sit as a team and watch the president address the country.

Preceding the president's speech, broadcast stations previewed the potential purpose of the address while detailing for viewers the best practices in an event of a missile attack. Unbeknownst to the American people as they sat anxiously in front of their televisions, the president ordered missiles to be launch ready, DEFCON to be lowered to stage two for the first and only time in American history. Twenty SAC bombers equipped with nuclear bombs were sent airborne.

At seven o'clock, a stoic but determined President Kennedy, dressed in a dark suit with a thin dark tie and white shirt, sat behind two microphones and began his speech.

> Good Evening my fellow citizens. Within the past week, unmistakable evidence has established the fact that a series of offensive missile sites is now in preparation on that imprisoned island. The purpose of these bases can be none other than to provide a nuclear strike capability against the Western Hemisphere.... This sudden, clandestine decision to station strategic weapons for the first time outside of Soviet soil is a deliberately provocative and unjustified change in the status quo which cannot be accepted by this country, if our courage and our commitments are ever to be trusted again by either friend or foe.... We will not prematurely or unnecessarily risk the costs of worldwide nuclear war in which even the fruits of victory would be ashes in our mouth; but neither will we shrink from that risk at any time it must be faced.... Our goal is not the victory of might, but the vindication of right; not peace at the expense of freedom, but both peace and freedom, here in this hemisphere, and, we hope, around the world. God willing, that goal will be achieved. Thank you and good night.

Ted Sorensen, in his book *The Counselor*, notes, "It was not the best speech of JFK's presidency, but it surely was his most important. It fully informed the American people and the world of what appeared to be the greatest danger to our country in history."

In Moscow, Russian officials called the speech, "A step along the road of unleashing thermonuclear war."

In Cuba, leader Fidel Castro ordered his country to "order of combat" while assuring all within the sound of his voice, "We are not alone," which spoke to the significant presence of the Russian military in Cuba. Reports estimated the number of Russian "technicians" at two thousand, but the real number was closer to forty-two thousand.

At the United Nations, U.S. ambassador Adlai Stevenson addressed the Security Council, expressing grave concern with Russia's provocative actions. He followed his address with an impromptu inquest of the present Russian ambassador Valerian Zorin, from whom he demanded an answer to the question of whether Russian missiles indeed existed in Cuba.

The world was now convinced of Russia's intentions and grappled with the possibility of a third world war.

Just ninety miles north of the island of Cuba, the hamlet of Key West, Florida, was placed under the virtual control of the American military. At the municipal airport, the army corps of engineers was busy constructing a radio tower while swarms of military jets and bombers landed at the airfield that was so congested that pilots were forced to back their missile-equipped jets onto the main highway. Just north of the airport, a radar and communications station was being assembled. At the town's baseball field, Wicker Stadium, tents and makeshift quarters were assembled, and hotel rooms were taken over by the more than one hundred thousand troops who arrived and prepared for an amphibious assault on Cuba.

Confrontation seemed inevitable, then a best-case scenario began to unfold: Twelve of the twenty-five Russian ships were turning around rather than testing the will of the American blockade. In the Oval Office, the president and staff breathed a partial sigh of relief. Secretary of State Dean Rusk commented, "We're eyeball to eyeball, and I think the other guy just blinked."

❆ ❆ ❆

Despite the ongoing crisis, college football games would be played on Saturday, October 27. The grave tone and subject matter of the president's speech earlier in the week impacted Navy players both as citizens and as future military officers. Following the speech, the players walked into the classroom with heads hanging down and distracted thoughts. It was one of those times as a midshipman that commitment to service transcends college life.

Coach Belichick was conscious of the enormity of what these kids had just heard and the possible consequences, and he wanted to bring their minds back to football, easing their concerns. The national crisis was out of his and the players' hands. Looking out at the team, he said of the leaders of the United States and the Soviet Union, "I don't think those guys realize that we are playing Pittsburgh this weekend."

Belichick's joke broke the tension and allowed the players to focus on the matter at hand. All the coaches were aware that it was different at the Naval Academy. Their players not only had to concern themselves with their studies and their playbook but also the security of the world order. In the following day's *Capital*, Coach Hardin articulated the special nature of his football players' concerns and how they related to the world outside of the sport. "We're not a football factory here at Navy," Hardin said. "We're training Naval Officers, but football might help if they have to fight. Cuba is on their minds, but we're confident the kids won't forget about the game."

The upcoming game against eastern power Pittsburgh would provide them the perfect distraction. In preparation for the game, Coach Hardin had decided to add a wrinkle to his arsenal of plays. The play, which relied on trickery and perfect execution, was called the "Sleeper Play."

The offensive ruse called for a lineman to roll out of bounds following a kickoff return, leaving only ten players on the field for the first-down play. While the team gathered to discuss the pending play in the huddle, wide receiver James Stewart, who stood only five-foot-eight and was known as the "world's smallest football player," would limp toward the sideline signaling for "replacement" Dick Earnest to rush onto the field. As Stewart made his way toward the bench, Navy would break the huddle, rush to the line of scrimmage, and snap the ball, at which time Stewart would sprint down the sideline to receive a pass from Staubach. The play could result in positive yards or even a touchdown, but even more it could demoralize the opponent via embarrassment. Hardin was determined to use the play on the first offensive down subsequent to Navy's first kickoff return.

The game was played at a neutral site in Norfolk, Virginia. Every year two eastern schools were selected to participate in the Oyster Bowl, with proceeds from the gate donated to the local Shriners Hospitals for Children. On the Friday before the game, the team traveled to Norfolk. During the trip, sports information director Budd Thalman shared the details of the play with the team's beat writers, laying evidence of the play's premeditated purpose.

Prior to taking the field on Saturday, the team was told the play was on. The Midshipmen received the kickoff and returned it to their 34-yard line. As the team huddled for its first play from scrimmage, Stewart broke and hobbled to the sideline. The team trainer started to walk onto the field to assist the "injured" player but was restrained. Halfback Earnest rushed onto the field past Stewart to join the huddle, waving his hand to officials (who had been warned of the play prior to the game), drawing the attention of the Pittsburgh defenders. Stewart arrived at the designated spot along the line of scrimmage, signaling for his teammates to sprint from the huddle and snap the ball. Stewart pulled out of his limp and raced down the field. The stunned Pittsburgh players could only stand frozen as Staubach lofted a perfect pass to what Assistant Coach Rick Forzano later called the "most open receiver in football history." The play went for a 66-yard touchdown. Navy used the slight of hand as a springboard to a 32–9 victory. On the day, Staubach was a perfect 8 for 8, passing for 192 yards.

The ruse fooled not only the Panthers players and coaches but other observers as well. Shirley Povich of the *Washington Post* noted that Stewart was "limping pitiably," while George Minot added that Stewart deserved an Oscar. Arthur Daley of the *New York Times* compared the play to the deception conjured up by Coach Pop Warner at Carlisle, when he had his quarterback slip the ball under his shirt. Coach Hardin denied any attempt to deceive, connive, or cheat. "If this happened," he remarked with not-completely-sincere remorse, "I apologize."

After the game, Pittsburgh's Coach John Michelosen was still smarting from the trickery. "Take a look at the code of ethics," he said, referring to the NCAA rule book, "and see if it doesn't say something about a tendency to deceive."

❨ ❨ ❨

By that Saturday afternoon, the crisis in Cuba reached its pinnacle when intelligence reports noted that the U-2 spy plane over the island had fallen out of contact and an American B-52 ventured into Russian air space off Alaska, forcing the Russians to scramble jets to escort the bomber out of its air space.

The president preached patience as he sought an end to the crisis. He and Ted Sorensen drafted a letter that was delivered to Moscow. The following morning, General Secretary Khrushchev agreed to the terms of the letter in principle, and the world, which had teetered on the abyss of nuclear devastation, now stood at the walkway of a new spirit of cooperation and understanding.

In the *Counselor*, Ted Sorensen ends the chapter on the Cuban Missile Crisis with the following:

> The discovery that the Soviet Union had secretly rushed nuclear missiles into Cuba tested JFK's wisdom, courage and leadership as no president since Lincoln and FDR had been tested. No other test so starkly put at stake, depending on the president's choices, the survival of our country. It was for that moment that he had been elected and it was for that moment that he will most be remembered.

As October 1962 wound down, the country was on the rebound thanks to the deft actions of its leader. In Annapolis, Navy football was on the same path. After starting the season 1–2 and with more questions than answers, its record now stood at 4–2, its resurgence in no small part due to the team's new on-field leader, quarterback Roger Staubach.

Sixteen-year-old John F. Kennedy (front row, second from right) poses with the junior football team at Choate School in Connecticut, 1933. The future president was a lifelong fan of the game of football. *AP Images*

Robert Kennedy receives a pass from older brother John at Robert's home in Hickory Hills, Virginia, 1957. The Kennedy family touch football games were a veritable American institution. *Paul Schutzer/Time & Life Pictures/Getty Images*

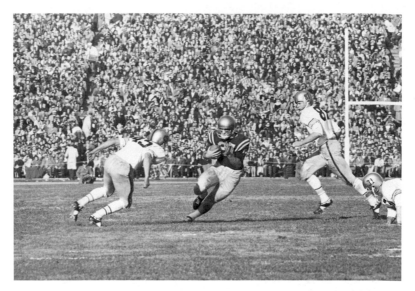

Joe Bellino heads for the end zone through an opening in the Army defense during the Army–Navy game on November 26, 1960. Navy won, 17–12, the second of what would be five straight wins for the Midshipmen. *AP Images*

President-elect John F. Kennedy (in sunglasses, center) cheers on the Navy Midshipmen at the Orange Bowl on New Year's Day 1961. The day proved disappointing for Kennedy and his team, who lost to Missouri, 21–14. *AP Images*

Joe Bellino (far left) hands a football signed by the entire Navy team to president-elect Kennedy at Kennedy's Georgetown home. With Bellino are four teammates who also come from Massachusetts. *Photo courtesy of Joe Bellino*

President John F. Kennedy is escorted across the field during halftime of the Army–Navy game on December 2, 1961. As per tradition in the rivalry game, the president sits on each team's side for one half so as not to show favoritism— although the preference of the former Navy hero was no secret. *AP Images*

Navy halfback Al Hughes rushed past the line of scrimmage during the fourth quarter of Navy's 13–7 win over Army in 1961. Hughes was also a star on the Navy basketball team. *AP Images*

President Kennedy, holding a football, meets with Coach Wayne Hardin and the rest of the Navy Midshipmen during a stop at Quonset Point Naval Aviation Center in August 1962. It was a profound moment for all the members of the team. *John F. Kennedy Presidential Library and Museum*

Flanked by flag bearers, President Kennedy tosses the coin before the annual Army–Navy game, on December 1, 1962. With Kennedy are Army team captain John Ellerson, to the left of Kennedy, and Navy team captain Steve Hoy, right. Navy won the toss—and the game. *AP Images*

A man, later identified as Vincent Pelzer, ran onto the field as Kennedy was changing sides during halftime of the 1962 Army–Navy game. Pelzer (second from right) was grabbed by Secret Service agents and arrested for breach of the peace, disorderly conduct, and drunkenness. *AP Images*

Kennedy enjoys the view of the Army–Navy game from an upholstered easy chair in his presidential box at Philadelphia's Municipal Stadium in 1962. To his right is deputy defense secretary Roswell Gilpatric. *AP Images*

Navy's star quarterback Roger Staubach led the way in the Midshipmen's easy victory over the Cadets in the 1962 contest. "Roger the Dodger" passed for 220 yards and ran for two touchdowns in the 34–14 win. *James Drake*/Sports Illustrated/*Getty Images*

Army coach Paul Dietzel (left) confers with his quarterback, Rollie Stichweh, on the sidelines. Stichweh, an all-around athlete and a star on defense before taking over the quarterback job as a junior, was unable to get the better of fellow star QB, Roger Staubach. *Photo from* The Howitzer, *U.S. Military Academy yearbook*

# CHAPTER 7

# Southern California vs. Navy, 1962

ON NOVEMBER 9, PIERRE SALINGER ANNOUNCED at a news briefing, "President Kennedy hopes to attend the Army–Navy football game in Philadelphia on December 1. But the attendance will depend on the status of the Cuba crisis."

Navy, though, had a November 17 meeting with the University of Southern California, the number-one team in the nation, to worry about before the team turned its attention to Army. The Midshipmen headed out west with a 4–4 record to face the number one team in the nation at the Los Angeles Memorial Coliseum.

USC was favored by 16 points, clearly a formidable opponent, and Coach Hardin needed to find an edge. After watching the films, Hardin and Assistant Coach Steve Belichick were confident that they could win. The Trojans would look at Navy's .500 record, underestimate the Midshipmen's ability, and most likely be looking ahead to the following week's game against archrival UCLA. Belichick anticipated the Navy team being taken lightly and actually predicted to Beano Cook before the game that they would upset the Trojans.

Hardin, never afraid to be unpopular if it meant putting his team in a better position to succeed, decided to wage a battle in the newspapers and try to set doubt in the minds of the USC offense and the officials who would be calling the game. During his weekly press conference he announced, "I've never seen a team with more illegal procedures and tactics against the football rules than this one [USC]. . . . They have illegal sets; illegal motions before the ball is snapped. I'm not crying, just pointing out facts."

In California, USC Coach John McKay was furious about the implication. Jerome Hall of the *Press Telegram* of Long Beach, California, wrote of Navy's coach, who they were calling Whimpering Wayne on the West Coast, "Hardin is the one that dredged up the sleeper play. . . . brought embarrassment upon the US Navy from Saigon to San Diego." Another California writer said, "Lock up your women and children, Navy is coming to town," while another wrote, "Hardin doesn't win games, he steals them."

❮ ❮ ❮

When the Navy players walked out onto the Coliseum field, 51,701 Trojan fans were ready for them. But Navy was ready for the Trojans and their fans, whose venom was targeted at Hardin and would serve as a distraction for the USC team throughout the game. At the end of the half, USC maintained a 7–6 lead, but in the locker room, McKay was disturbed. His players were not respecting the Navy team.

In the second half, USC scored to bring the count to 13–6. Navy had a chance to tie the score if not take the lead in the waning moments, but halfback Pat Donnelly fumbled on the goal line. McKay told reporters after the game that Navy deserved credit and that the Midshipmen would be competitive in USC's powerful Pac-10 conference. Hardin, who had put officials on notice prior to the game, noted that the game was well-officiated.

Roger Staubach used the visit to the West Coast to "introduce" himself to that part of the country. He ran for 126 yards and threw for 106. Alex Kahn of UPI wrote, "In defeat, Navy sophomore quarterback Roger Staubach put on a one-man show, which was as brilliant as any ever seen in Memorial Coliseum." For his efforts, Staubach was awarded the Pacific Coast Player of the Week, despite the fact that he played on an East Coast squad.

### U.S. Naval Academy (4–5)
### @ #1 University of Southern California (9–0)
Memorial Coliseum . Los Angeles, California
November 17, 1962 . 1:30 p.m. kickoff (PST) . Attendance 51,701

|      | 1 | 2 | 3 | 4 | Final |
| ---- | - | - | - | - | ----- |
| Navy | 6 | 0 | 0 | 0 | 6     |
| USC  | 0 | 7 | 6 | 0 | 13    |

|                 | Navy  | USC  |
| --------------- | ----- | ---- |
| First Downs     | 14    | 16   |
| Rushing Yards   | 196   | 254  |
| Passing Yards   | 106   | 94   |
| Pass Att.-Comp. | 17–11 | 19–6 |
| Fumbles Lost    | 4–3   | 5–4  |
| Interceptions by| 1     | 0    |
| Penalty Yards   | 35    | 16   |

Navy — TD, Staubach, 18-yard run (kick failed)

USC — TD, Bledsoe, 7-yard pass from Beathard (Lupo kick)

USC — TD, Brown, 56-yard run (kick failed)

The Trojans went on to win the national title that season, with John McKay named coach of the year. He received the award in Washington, D.C., and presented President Kennedy with a team-signed game ball.

❬ ❬ ❬

The West Coast visit was a bit of a homecoming for Hardin, who lived in Stockton for many years and later played football for the venerable Alonzo Stagg at College of the Pacific. Hardin and Navy threw a one hundredth birthday party for Stagg prior to the 1962 season. At the ceremony, President Kennedy sent a cable that read, "Good wishes, a persuasive and shining example of leadership." Coach Hardin said of his former mentor, "Amos Alonzo Stagg is the only man I have ever known with ideals next to God and all the ability to live up to them."

Wayne Hardin had been enrolled at Stanford University but was unable to continue there when he enlisted in the Coast Guard during World War II. When he returned home, he applied to and was accepted at College of the Pacific. Now, years later, the opportunity to be part of the Stanford family would be presented to him, as Stanford was interested in hiring a new coach. Hardin was at the top of the list.

Hardin met with Stanford officials, confident after the meeting that the job was his if he chose to accept it. When he returned to the hotel, he spent a restless night weighing his options. He would love to return to California. Of course, that would mean he would be leaving a Navy team that was improving every week and would be returning a bevy of talented lettermen, including an up-and-coming quarterback.

Talks between Hardin and Stanford University intensified, and the Navy coach became the front runner for head football coach. Leaks of the meetings soon made their way into the press. While playing at the Bing Crosby Golf Tournament at Pebble Beach Golf Course, Hardin was compelled to deny rumors that he was "on the verge of taking the Stanford position" and that the recently fired Cleveland Browns coach Paul Brown would be named head coach at Navy. Back in Annapolis, Athletic Director Bill Busik rebuked reporters who alluded to the rumors about Hardin and Brown. "Paul Brown? That's the first I've heard of that," Busik said. "We have a coach, and at the moment we're not even in the market."

In the end, Hardin remained as coach at Navy. "Turning down the Stanford offer is the toughest decision I have ever had to make in my life," he said. "Both Navy and Stanford are wonderful institutions." He later elaborated on the special nature of coaching at Navy: "They're the greatest kids I've ever met anywhere, and I couldn't leave them. Five years and a lot more money wasn't enough to compel me to leave."

After coming up short against the eventual national champions and wading through the distractions of the meetings with Stanford, Navy head coach Wayne Hardin now had to focus on preparing his team for the game against Army, coming up just two weeks after the USC game.

# CHAPTER 8

# Army vs. Navy, 1962

THE 1963 DREAM SEASON OF THE NAVAL ACADEMY started in December 1962, when Navy stepped onto the field to battle Army. Here, third classman Roger Staubach had his national coming out party in front of not only a national audience but also the president of the United States.

In a preview of the rivalry game, Harry Grayson wrote in the *High Point Enterprise* about the special quality of the contest, those who participated, and those who cheered. "If Nikita Khrushchev could peek in on the Army–Navy game in Philadelphia's Municipal Stadium December 1," Grayson surmised, "President Kennedy's troubles with the Cold War might be concluded. The power and spirit displayed by the officers in training would have to deeply impress even the table-pounding premier with American might."

In the days prior to the game, new Army coach Paul Dietzel appeared on the cover of *Sports Illustrated*: "Flashy Paul Dietzel Gets Army Ready for Navy." The tall blonde was brought to Army with two mandates: resurrect the once-glorious program and beat Navy and Coach Wayne Hardin, who had compiled a 3–0 record in the series. The third win had cost Army coach Dale Hall his job.

Dietzel had led Louisiana State University to the 1958 National Championship and was named national coach of the year. When the coaching position at West Point became available after the 1961 season,

Dietzel, who had twice been an Army assistant, kept an open mind despite the fact he still had four years remaining on his LSU contract.

When Army's Athletic Director Joe Cahill contacted Dietzel to gauge his interest, he was ecstatic to hear that the hottest coaching talent in the country was interested. After assessing the sincerity of his interest, Cahill asked Dietzel when he would be available to travel north to interview for the job. The question caused excitement to turn to coolness on the Louisiana end of the phone. Speaking directly, Dietzel informed the athletic director, "I don't have to be interviewed to prove I can win." Soon after, Paul Dietzel signed a five-year contract to coach the Cadets of West Point for an annual stipend of $18,000. Dietzel arrived in West Point in the spring of 1962.

With Coach Dietzel at the helm, interest in the program reached a fever pitch. On the first day of spring practice, Dietzel had to send his equipment manager to the sporting goods store to buy more uniforms because so many candidates reported to tryouts. Throughout the pre-season, General Douglas MacArthur, former President Dwight Eisenhower, and General Omar Bradley all could be seen at practices monitoring their favorite team's progress in its quest back to prominence.

When Coach Dietzel arrived on the Army campus, he not only brought excitement and meticulous organization with him but also his famous three-unit system. The three units were defined as follows: The most talented players who saw the most significant time on both offense and defense were called the Regulars. The second unit, which served as the backup offensive team, was called the Go Team. But it was the third unit that captured attention for Dietzel at Cincinnati, then LSU, and now West Point. This team was called the Chinese Bandits. The Chinese Bandits group was made up of not necessarily the most talented players on the team but, in Dietzel's words, "the eleven toughest football players." Their uniforms were identified by a patch of a bandit on the shirt and an image of a Chinese Bandit on the socks. The third unit was assigned the red bench on the sideline and was treated wildly by the cadets, who would all don Chinese

Coolie hats and ring a gong whenever they took the field. (Hardin was quoted that week as saying, about Army's third unit, "Don't think we're going to be scared just because we're playing some guys named Chinese Bandits.")

Army had compiled a 6–3 record before the Navy affair. In the week leading up to the rivalry game, the excitement at both academies was palpable. At West Point, Dietzel and his team were overtly conscious (and somewhat preoccupied) with the potential of Coach Hardin's gimmicks. During practices, Army assigned the junior varsity squad to play the role of the Navy team. The players wore "Beat Army" on their shirts, as the Navy team had done in the 1961 game.

At a luncheon at the Thayer Hotel on the Army campus, Dietzel met with the boosters of the team to discuss the past game and plans for the subsequent contest. During his speech he joked about Hardin and the infamous Sleeper Play against Pittsburgh, "Wonder how poor Jimmy Stewart is? At least we know what we're up against."

Later, the Army coach spoke of Coach Hardin's tactics and coaching style. "I will be very surprised if Wayne does not come up with some gimmick in Philadelphia," Dietzel said. "Maybe it will be a platoon of WAVES [Women Accepted for Volunteer Emergency Service] parachuting onto the field to disconcert my boys. The only way to handle a psychologizer like Hardin is to expect anything and stay loose."

For Hardin's part, he filed a formal concern with the governing body of East Coast officials stating that the forward handoffs by Army on kickoff returns were illegal and should be watched carefully in Saturday's game. Both sides were waging psychological warfare.

The night before the final practice at West Point, a cadet drove a sixty-ton M48 tank to Dietzel's front door. Behind the tank marched 2,500 cadets, who arrived at the house to serenade their coach. At the following day's practice, Dietzel hung an effigy of Navy's Roger Staubach on the practice field and allowed his thirteen seniors to take their best shots while the entire corps looked on along with Superintendent General William Westmoreland.

Following practice, the student body stood at attention for Taps and then was allowed to fall out to enjoy a barbecue in which the main course was goat meat, in honor of the Navy mascot. At the end of dinner, the team boarded buses and was escorted to the front gate of the academy by tanks and cadets carrying torches.

In Annapolis, the dining hall of Bancroft Hall was the scene of a spontaneous rally. One by one, midshipmen approached the football players, who sat with their respective companies, and hoisted them on their chairs, parading them around the hall to the cheers of their class-mates. Following dinner they walked out to Tecumseh Court, where a blazing bonfire greeted the crowd. One by one, speakers induced the crowd into a lather of excitement. At the end of each speech, the cry of "Beat Army" punctuated the presenters' thoughts. By the time Coach Hardin made his way to the microphone, the crowd was roused to a fever pitch. The moment induced a great spirit of community. Hardin, just hours from kickoff in Philadelphia, was overcome by the unavoid-able rush of adrenaline. As he looked out over the brigade he said, "We're not only going to beat Army. We're going to kick the shit out of them!" And with that the fuse was lit. The brigade was ignited and raring for Saturday. Hardin further stirred up Army disdain when he told a Phila-delphia newspaper that his team would not only win but run up the score and beat Army by the largest margin in the rivalry's history.

In preparing for the game, Coach Hardin was determined to top last year's orange phosphorous helmets and "Beat Army" logo on the shoulders of the players. Looking to neutralize the buzz created by Army's Chinese Bandits, Hardin had the idea to stencil "Beat Army" in Chinese on the gold helmets of the Navy team. To accomplish this, the art department employed the services of midshipman Ted Sadamoto. The only problem was that Sadamoto was Japanese, not Chinese. Nev-ertheless, he spent the week on the phone with his mother attempting to trace the Japanese characters of "Beat Army." When he succeeded in depicting the basic characters, the Japanese translation of Beat Army was then sketched onto the helmets. Also placed on the helmets, directly in front above the face mask, was a menacing skull-and-bones design known as the Jolly Roger. The Jolly Roger was known throughout nautical history as a rampaging symbol of those who owned the seas without loss.

This continued the taunting that led up to the big game. Earlier in the week, the Navy brigade took out a $3,500 ad in the *New York Times* that read, "Reward offered for the capture of Chinese Bandits on the premise of the [stadium]." There was a picture of a goat eating a coolie hat and a depiction of a frowning Chinese Bandit.

The chairman of the brigade activities committee, W. D. Davidson, spoke to the *New York Times* about the purpose of the ad. "It will shake the morale of the enemy forces and reduce their spirit to rubble." He continued offering his editorial opinion, "And the goat chewing up the inadequate Chinese bandit, wow! It's the greatest thing since the advent of the wheel."

☾ ☾ ☾

More fun and games took place just prior to kickoff. A makeshift Chinese junk was rolled across the field, only to be chased by a Navy battleship, which proceeded to fire on the junk and "sink" it while the Navy team stretched and loosened up before the game. On the Army side, cadets spelled out "Today Is Ours" on the tops of their hats.

While the previous year's affair took place on a cool autumn day, this day was perfect, with a high sun and mid-sixty-degree temperatures. Odds-makers had the game as a "pick 'em," calling the teams even despite the fact that Army entered the game with a 6–3 record compared to Navy's 4–5 mark.

Army had decided not to warm up on the field before the game. When the team finally did take the field, members sported white cleats, along with an unoriginal "Beat Navy" patch sewn on their jerseys.

Moments before kickoff, the public address announcer said, "Ladies and gentlemen, the President of the United States." President Kennedy walked to midfield while the honor guard presented arms and the bands played "Hail to the Chief." Following the national anthem, the president shook hands with Army Captain John Ellerson and Navy Captain Steve Hoy before flipping a silver dollar with his right thumb and catching it in his right hand. Still concealing the coin, he turned it over onto the back of his left hand and asked the Army captain his preference. When the president unveiled the coin, Navy had won the toss, and the coin was awarded to the Navy captain.

The president was then escorted to the Navy side of the field for the first half. His presidential box sat halfway up the bleachers at Philadelphia Municipal Stadium. In the prior year, the president's front-row seat had hindered his efforts to watch plays develop and enjoy the game as a true fan. Consequently, his box for the 1962 game not only was moved higher but also was equipped by concessionaire Jack Nilon (boxer Sonny Liston's manager) with a rocking chair and fine china for tea.

On the field, the Cadets, still stiff from foregoing pre-game warm-ups, proceeded to hand the first points to Navy after a snap from center went over the punter's head for a safety. By the end of the first half, it was apparent which was the better team. Navy held a 15–6 lead, highlighted by a brilliant 20-yard cut-back run by Roger Staubach for 6 points and another touchdown pass to Neil Henderson. The dominance over the dreaded Chinese Bandits brought great satisfaction to the Navy faithful. All through the game whenever the over-hyped unit took the field, the midshipmen in the stands would wave American flags in defiance of the much-talked-about defenders.

The president and Navy football loyalist also revealed, if subtly, his preference in the game. According to Arthur Daley of the *New York Times*, "The Commander-in-Chief of all the armed forces spent the first half with Navy and was observed applauding vociferously. Then he switched to the Army side [in the second half] where his cheering didn't seem quite so enthusiastic. Officially, he was neutral. But since he was the skipper of a Navy PT boat during the war, it was easy to guess which team he was neutral for."

Toward the end of the first half, President Kennedy sat with his brother, Attorney General Robert F. Kennedy, and Admiral George Anderson, who was a member of the ExComm during the Cuban Missile Crisis. As Navy continued to move the ball up and down the field, both the president and his brother voiced their concern for the Army team. Some years later, Admiral Anderson recounted how Navy's big advantage by the end of the half, and the superb performance by Staubach, led Bobby Kennedy to exhibit great sympathy for the Army team. "Bobby made the remark that he didn't think it was good to have Navy licking Army for so many years in a row," Anderson recalled. Following the game, Anderson had written a joking letter to the president, in which he commented that he would "bitterly resent any possible suggestion that the Attorney General might make Roger Staubach be transferred to the Army."

At the end of the half, as per tradition, the president was escorted across the field to the Army sideline. Rumors that he would remain on the Navy side throughout the game proved unfounded. As he was walking with his escorts, a man in a green sport shirt broke through layers of security and Secret Service men and made it to within feet of the president before being apprehended. The man was whisked off the field as he yelled, "I just wanted to shake his hand." The man, Vincent Pelzer of Wyckoff, New Jersey, was profoundly inebriated and attempted the presidential meeting on a dare from his friends.

The encounter was taken lightly by neither the press nor the public, as a letter received by the Secret Service dated December 5, 1962, attests:

> Like a million other Americans I sat in horror as I watched on TV a man approach the President of the United States without anyone attempting to stop him. He was only a drunk, but he might have been someone with less well intended ideas. The President of the United States is entitled to and should receive better protection than he was afforded last Saturday at Philadelphia.

Included along with the letter was an article by Bill Lee of the *Hartford Courant*, which said:

> Paul Dietzel and the segment of the Secret Service responsible for the safety of the President of the United States must reexamine their preparation for last Saturday's Army–Navy game. . . . The need for even more painstaking security was evident to one hundred thousand spectators live and a few million more television viewers. . . . Where the President is concerned, these things are not funny. The drunk could have been a mad man with evil intentions. Nobody gave the character a tumble until he was almost on top of the President.

Pelzer was charged with breach of the peace, disorderly conduct, and drunkenness. He was fined $12.50 and released.

Navy's dominance continued in the second half of the game, with the key play coming on a 65-yard touchdown toss to Nick Markoff—the longest play in the history of the rivalry game. Staubach had rolled left and thrown against the grain, to the right, while Army defenders bore down. The pass found a wide-open Markoff, who rolled down the right sideline for the score. Staubach later added a 2-yard touchdown run, and the romp was on. The Chinese Bandits were embarrassed.

As the score differential widened, President Kennedy and his brother were further concerned with the apparent lack of competition between the two academies. Army General Earl G. Wheeler, then chairman of the joint chiefs of staff, sat with the two in the second half and recalled the mood:

> We were getting the hell kicked out of us by a very fine Navy team. When [President Kennedy] got to over to our side . . . I think he was a little shocked by the fact that Army was getting beaten so badly. . . . When I saw him not too long after that in his office, he asked me what I was going to do about getting some football

players. He said, "you know you've got to go out and recruit them. You've got to go out and get these people. They just don't come to you."

Navy had now beaten Army a record four straight games. The Midshipmen defense pressured the Cadets throughout the game, forcing a safety, three fumbles, and two interceptions. The offense had unmasked the folklore of the Chinese Bandits. The *Hartford Courant* noted that "the white cleats really looked silly in the end." The most points Army had allowed in a game all season was 14. On this day, Navy scored 34 despite resting the starters as the game progressed.

The star of the game was clearly Staubach. He threw for 220 yards, completing 12 of 15 attempts while running for two touchdowns and throwing for two others. His creative, unorthodox scampering and running led President Kennedy to comment to his aide, "There ought to be twenty out there like him."

In the *New York World Telegram*, Joe Williams called Staubach's passing and running "superb" and added that "the dazzling Dutchman performed feats of sorcery that left the Cadets gasping in disbelief. They could have him completely surrounded, only to find when they closed in that he had magically evaporated into the shimmering Philadelphia sun."

Joe Bingham of *Sports Illustrated* contributed to the praise for Staubach, writing, "Never in the long history of Army–Navy has a quarterback so dominated a game."

With the victory, Coach Hardin was carried around the field on the shoulders of the Midshipmen. When he spotted Staubach also hoisted on the shoulders of his classmates, the two leaders were let down so that they could acknowledge each other. Hardin, the man who wouldn't let anyone understand him or unveil himself to players, press, or even his own mother, walked over to his star player and put his arm around Staubach's shoulder. They had beat Army for a fourth consecutive time. Nothing could be better.

## U.S. Military Academy (6–4)
## @ U.S. Naval Academy (5–5)

Municipal Stadium . Philadelphia, Pennsylvania

December 1, 1962 . 1:00 p.m. kickoff . Attendance 98,543

|      | 1 | 2 | 3 | 4 | Final |
| ---- | - | - | - | - | ----- |
| Army | 0 | 6 | 0 | 8 | 14 |
| Navy | 8 | 7 | 7 | 12 | 34 |

|                 | Army | Navy |
| --------------- | ---- | ---- |
| First Downs     | 13   | 17   |
| Rushing Yards   | 120  | 102  |
| Passing Yards   | 138  | 220  |
| Pass Att.–Comp. | 13-8 | 15-12 |
| Fumbles Lost    | 3    | 1    |
| Interceptions by | 0   | 2    |
| Yards Penalized | 35   | 55   |

| Navy | Safety |
| Navy | TD, Henderson, 12-yard pass from Staubach (pass failed) |
| Navy | TD, Staubach, 21-yard run (Von Sydow kick) |
| Army | TD, Parcells, 1-yard run (pass failed) |
| Navy | TD, Markoff, 65-yard pass from Staubach (Von Sydow kick) |
| Navy | TD, Staubach, 3-yard run (run failed) |
| Army | TD, Seymour, 2-yard pass from Lewis (Ellerson pass from Lewis) |
| Navy | TD, Campbell, 5-yard pass from Klemick (pass failed) |

Following the celebration, the teams made their way to the school bands. As was tradition, the teams and coaches from the two academies stood at attention for the playing of both alma maters. The losing team's song was played first, followed by the winner's. At the conclusion of the Navy song, the teams made their way off the field and underneath the stands to the locker room.

As Hardin walked with a smile on his face, he came upon a black limousine that was working its way from the underbelly of the stadium. As he got closer, the window rolled down, and President Kennedy's face appeared with a big smile. The two made eye contact, and Kennedy stuck his hand outside of the car and gave Hardin a thumbs-up of approval.

In the post-game press conference, Hardin was asked what the turning point of the contest was. He replied, "When we walked on the field."

Later that night, the Midshipmen players arrived back on campus and were engulfed by a riotous brigade, which had started the rally without them. The team rang the Japanese Bell thirty-four times in recognition of the number of points they scored against Army. Navy trainer Red Romo jokingly put tape across Hardin's mouth and told him not to say a word. His words weren't necessary. All that needed to be said was already uttered by Staubach, who announced to his mates, "Those people up on the Hudson think it's their turn to beat Navy. But I have news for them: We don't take turns in this game."

At the end of the rally, as calls went out from the crowd proclaiming "Staubach for President," Superintendent Rear Admiral Charles C. Kirkpatrick quieted the gathering and replied, "President Kennedy is happy where he is, and I want Staubach with me, and he's happy here." The crowd roared their approval. Motioning for quiet again, the super then proposed, "Let's make it drive for five. That's our new slogan."

The slogan was adopted, ready for the next chapter in the Army–Navy rivalry. The story of the 1962 game was of a young, lanky quarterback, a brash and unrelenting coach, and a president who found great joy in the success of Navy football.

In honor of the victory, the Naval Academy brigade was allowed to "carry on" for the rest of the semester.

# CHAPTER 9

# We Have a Happy Ship: Kickoff, 1963

IN MARCH 1963, WAYNE HARDIN WAS BACK IN ANNAPOLIS running errands, including a trip to his local butcher shop. After exchanging greetings, the butcher shared with the coach a bold prediction for the coming season. "Coach this is going to be your year," he said. "Navy is a team of destiny."

Soon thereafter, Hardin gathered his players for a team meeting at the Boat House, where the coach had a captive and anxious audience. The momentum from the team's strong finish the previous year, which featured a competitive game against national-champion USC at the Coliseum and a dominating win over Army, set the program on a path for great things.

Hardin spoke about the importance of the spring practices in the coming months and the expectations for the 1963 season. He told his players and fellow coaches that the team had the chance to be truly great. At the conclusion of the speech, he shared with them his butcher's assessment that this fall Navy football would be a team of destiny. "I believe it," Hardin concluded, "so you should believe it." On his desk he placed a sign that read, "Team of Destiny."

When the players returned to the Naval Academy after a summer tour on the high seas, to a man they were excited about the prospects of the coming season. The team had worked hard in the offseason and returned a great nucleus, especially at the skill positions, including

Roger Staubach, Pat Donnelly, Johnny Sai, and tight ends Jim Campbell and Dave Sjuggerud. In all, twenty-four lettermen returned from the previous season.

Although in prior years Navy had held its summer football practices at the Quonset Point Naval Air Station in Rhode Island, in 1963, the coaches and administration elected to remain on campus. The players reported on August 22 and were immediately greeted by Maryland's stifling summer heat and humidity. Double sessions were planned, with one two-hour practice in the morning and another in the late afternoon. When lineman Larry Kocisko suffered heat stroke, however, the practices were scaled back to seventy-five-minute sessions.

Hardin remained positive about his team's progress. "Things are fine down here," he told a reporter from the *Washington Post*. "We have a happy ship. Everything is as smooth as can be."

Earlier in the summer of 1963, before the team gathered for camp in Annapolis, Hardin had traveled through Europe with other college coaches giving football clinics. During that time, he worked on an option-roll-out offense that would maximize Staubach's talents as both a passer and runner. "He's the only player I've ever had who made me change my offense," Hardin said. "I prefer to use a drop-back pass, but Roger is a roll-out scrambling type of quarterback, so we've adjusted to him."

In the book *The Heisman* by Bill Pennington, two-way stalwart Tom Lynch talks about the blocking scheme utilized in such an offense. "Everyone learned pretty quick that blocking your man wasn't going to be good enough," Lynch said. "Roger would be back there running around for several seconds, and frequently something good happened. Everyone knew that you better block your first guy and then look for two or three more."

Assistant Coach Steve Belichick said Lynch was the most charismatic leader he had ever coached in his decades in football. Lynch came to the Naval Academy from Lima, Ohio, where he was captain of the football team, a basketball forward, and shot-putter for Lima Central Catholic High School. At the conclusion of his high school career, he was awarded the Thunderbird Trophy for his "leadership, adherence to discipline, and team spirit." The *Lima News* wrote that Lynch "has good speed, and loves to tackle and block and he has good leadership skills. On top of that he is an excellent student." The inborn leadership skills that bloomed at Lima Central Catholic were further strengthened at the Naval Academy. Lynch eventually served as superintendent of the Naval Academy and reached the rank of admiral.

Lynch was recruited by nine colleges, including perennial power-houses Ohio State, Purdue, Northwestern, and Tennessee, but he chose Navy in part because he was influenced by a *Life* magazine article he read about Heisman Trophy winner Pete Dawkins of Army and by the persuasive recruiting efforts of Assistant Coach Rick Forzano.

The 1963 Navy football team was connected by a bond of which Tom Lynch was the custodian. Lynch pushed his teammates from day one to be the best they could be. The six-foot-one, 210-pound captain—who also was a two-time heavyweight boxing champion at the academy—was able to command the attention of his teammates without needing to ask for it. Players were inspired by his words and his actions. The captain was so loved and revered that his fellow players never wanted to disappoint him. Years later, teammates estimated that Lynch's leadership was worth two or three extra wins in 1963. He was a galvanizing force who drew people together and united them under a common goal.

Lynch's first start at center corresponded with Roger Staubach's first start as quarterback. From that day forward, the two had a wonderful chemistry on and off the field. *Washington Post* writer George Minot once wrote, "If Tom Lynch doesn't do anything more than hand the ball to Staubach, he has earned his place in Naval history."

From the first day of school in the fall of 1963, the team was ready to transform its focus from summer camp into the more structured schedule of coursework and football practice. The academy allotted two hours for practice each day, but because Coach Hardin was so organized, practice was often completed in ninety minutes. Drills and practice methods were geared to put his players in the best position to succeed, with no wasted energy or time. There was always a purpose and intensity to Coach Hardin's practices, which were conducted in a brisk fashion, with players and coaches sprinting to their next assignment, eliminating the need for special conditioning practice.

Players were expected to read and understand the schedule, which was taped in the locker-room next to the current depth chart.

- Monday: Sweats for running, light practice, report to Boat House to watch films, eat dinner, and chalk-talk with Steve Belichick.
- Tuesday: Helmets and pads, going hard.
- Wednesday: Helmets and pads, going hard.
- Thursday: Sweats.
- Friday: Travel. (Navy had just three home games in 1963.)
- Saturday: Game day.

Following practice on the first day of classes, Coach Hardin assessed the session and the team's goals for the year, and then he released the players for the day. Tired and sore from a long three weeks of summer camp, many of the players started to drag themselves toward the locker room for a hot shower, followed by a stop at Bancroft Hall for dinner and studies. Before they got off the field, however, they saw Tom Lynch with football in hand.

Without warning or discussion, Lynch called for the first unit to line up and run plays the length of the field. There was no word of dissension or question. The exhausted first unit lined up and began to run traps, screens, square-outs, and option plays until they reached the far end zone. When they completed the task, Captain Lynch offered applause and encouragement. He knew this type of additional effort would be valuable to draw upon throughout the season when times got tough. For the remainder of the season, the team incorporated this post-practice drill into every session.

"I don't see how any Navy team ever could have had a finer captain," surmised Coach Hardin.

At a White House gathering in the summer of 1963, Superintendent Charles Kirkpatrick had the opportunity to visit with President Kennedy and reminisce with him about the most recent Army–Navy game. It was apparent to Kirkpatrick that Kennedy was still excited about the game and its outcome. During the conversation, the president leaned back and simulated throwing a football. "Do you still have that man [Staubach]?" he asked. The superintendent assured him that the Naval Academy's quarterback was returning for his junior year.

Kirkpatrick then invited the president to return to the academy to mark his twentieth anniversary as skipper of the PT 109. Kennedy accepted, as his Navy experience, and that moment in the South Pacific in particular, had deeply affected his life.

In early August 1963, President Kennedy appeared on the steps of Bancroft Hall to address the members of the new plebe class upon completion of their orientation.

As the president stood at the rostrum, he looked out over the plebe class and encouraged the midshipmen to be resilient. "I want to express our strong hope that all of you who have come to the academy as plebes will stay with the Navy," he said. "I can imagine no more rewarding career. . . . Any man who may be asked in this century what he did to make his life worthwhile, I think can respond with a good deal of pride and satisfaction: I served in the United States Navy."

A few weeks later, Admiral Kirkpatrick sent Kennedy a copy of the football schedule and a note extending an open invitation to the president and first lady to attend any of the games, including the Army game.

# CHAPTER 10

# West Virginia vs. Navy, 1963

EDWARD "SKIP" ORR, A REDHEADED, FRECKLE-FACED KID, came to the Naval Academy in 1961 as an all-star quarterback from Chaminade High School in the village of Mineola on Long Island. It was his hope to continue playing quarterback at the collegiate level, and in his first game as a plebe, Orr came in as a backup quarterback and completed a 52-yard touchdown pass to Kip Paskewich against Bainbridge Prep. But with fellow plebe and future Hall of Famer Roger Staubach vying for the same position, it quickly became clear that if Skip wanted to play football for Navy, it would have to be at a different position. In 1962, he switched to flanker and played for the junior varsity team. The following summer, he was listed as the fourth receiver on the Midshipmen depth chart. His goal was simply to make the team. According to Hymen Cohen of the *Capital*, "Many of the writers in the Middies press conference never heard of him."

In the final days of camp in 1963, senior Dick Earnest sprained his knee. Suddenly, Orr was in the huddle staring up at starters. Despite doubts about whether he truly belonged among such a talented group, the six-foot-one, 183-pound flanker could barely contain himself. He had finally reached the highest tier of the Navy football caste system.

When Orr returned to Bancroft Hall, he phoned his father and told him, "Dad, I think I'm going to start." His father, a Brooklyn policeman, called three of his buddies, grabbed his police badge to allow for an expeditious ride, and began the seven-hour journey to Morgantown, West Virginia, where his son was about to play in his first varsity college football game.

In Mountaineer country, the state and university were in the midst of celebrating their centennial anniversary. Earlier in the summer, President Kennedy had appeared to commemorate the honored date. West Virginia had been good to the president in the election three years earlier, and he, in turn, was good to the state.

In honor of the centennial, West Virginia University petitioned the NCAA to allow its kicker, Chuck Kinder, to wear the uniform number 100 for the season opener.

At a preseason gathering for West Virginia boosters, Coach Gene Corum had told the crowd that the opening game with Navy would be a high-scoring, competitive affair. "I think the West Virginia team is ready for Navy," Corum said, "and if you've got your tickets for that one, you're sure going to get your money's worth."

In all, a sellout crowd of 35,000 was expected at the Saturday afternoon game at newly refurbished Mountaineer Stadium. As part of the renovations, the school built a new $143,000 press box, which housed press and politician alike. To accommodate more fans, officials placed 2,200 temporary seats behind the end zones. The forecast called for comfortable sixty-degree temperatures.

In preseason polls, West Virginia was projected to be the top team in the Southern Conference, and the Mountaineers were ranked as high as fifteenth in some national polls. They returned several key lettermen from the 1962 squad, which had gone 8–2. As the team prepared for the coming season, players spoke of aspirations that included winning the Lambert Trophy, awarded to the dominant football team in the East. The team boasted a big line on each side of the ball, outweighing the Navy players by more than seventeen pounds on average. The roster included a top-notch fullback, Dick Leftridge, who as one of two African Americans on the squad was making history as the first African-American player to appear in a West Virginia varsity football game. Also leading the Mountaineers team was quarterback Jerry "the Most" Yost, a third-team all-American the previous year. "There is some doubt as to whether [Staubach is] as good as they say he is," wrote A. L. Hardman of the *Charleston Gazette*. "Personally, we are Jerry Yost fans."

Since the preseason meeting in which Hardin told his players they were a team of destiny, the Midshipmen had been determined to fulfill that prophecy. Now it was time to put the new mobile offense and Split-Six defense to the ultimate test on the gridiron. Determined to realize its full potential, the team was further inspired when local newspapers printed pictures of sinking ships from Pearl Harbor to represent Navy's forthcoming demise in Morgantown. The Academy had suffered significant losses on December 7, 1941, and the tasteless and inappropriate depiction only fueled the Midshipmen's fire as they took the field.

Two Navy players in particular were inspired to realize success in Morgantown: Bob Orlosky and backup quarterback Bruce Bickel. Bickel was born and resided in Fairmount, West Virginia. His mother wrote for a local newspaper and had written in an article that Navy had a strong team and prospects were high for the coming season. Not soon thereafter, Mrs. Bickel became the source of West Virginians' wrath, who shouted disparaging comments at her and even dumped trash on her front lawn.

Orlosky had grown up in the town of Nemacolin, Pennsylvania, just miles from the West Virginia campus. For years, he had competed against current West Virginia players, including quarterback Jerry Yost, whom he had faced on the baseball field. Orlosky actually was offered a baseball scholarship to attend school in Morgantown, but instead, he accepted the invitation from Assistant Coach Steve Belichick to attend the Naval Academy, where he could play both baseball and football. After a disappointing plebe year, Orlosky contemplated focusing only on baseball, until Belichick suggested that he shouldn't sell himself short when it came to football. Three years later, Orlosky impressed teammates and coaches in summer practices, and Coach Hardin noted that Orlosky would see significant playing time during the upcoming season.

In the week leading up to the West Virginia game, Orlosky was quoted in a newspaper saying, "We just have to beat the Mountaineers. If we don't, I can't go home." Sadly, the night before the game, Orlosky's biggest fan, his grandmother Catherine, passed away. As she would have wished, Bob decided to play the game, and the team elected to dedicate the game to her memory.

As with every team that faced Navy in 1963, West Virginia's attention would be focused on quarterback Roger Staubach. Even though former West Virginia star Gerry Urda was quoted in local newspapers saying that Staubach was overrated, the Mountaineer locker room was blanketed with pictures of the Midshipmen quarterback, ensuring that all players knew who their main target would be.

❰ ❰ ❰

On September 21, 1963, more than two thousand Naval Academy followers—including Superintendent Rear Admiral Charles C. Kirkpatrick, Skip Orr's father and friends, Bruce Bickel's mother, the town of Nemacolin, the 105-person marching band, and six hundred members of the brigade, dressed in blue coats and white hats—were in Morgantown for the Navy–West Virginia game.

Prior to kickoff, the Midshipmen in the bleachers were active both in supporting their mascot and in baiting the home fans. While some in the white uniform of Annapolis thwarted Mountaineer students trying to kidnap Navy's mascot—the goat known as Billy XV—other Midshipmen built a makeshift hut on the sideline, which they called a "portable hillbilly comfort station." On top of the door, they wrote "W. VA Dressing Room." Then, just before the teams took the field, two men dressed in ragged clothes and long beards sprinted from the shack, only to be "shot" by those representing the Academy. In the crowd, classmates went wild tipping their white caps.

Enthusiasm elevated when the teams took the field, Navy in its road whites and gold pants; West Virginia in its home blue. After an exchange of possessions, Navy kicker Fred Marlin began the scoring with a 25-yard field goal, opening the floodgates of the onslaught. In the second quarter, leading 3–0, Navy had the ball on the West Virginia 26-yard line. Staubach took a snap from center Lynch and faked a handoff before rolling to his right, where he faked a pass to the sideline, drawing the safety and allowing Orr to break loose on a post pattern down the middle. Spotting Orr, Staubach threw off his back foot and launched a perfect spiral that Orr caught on the goal line for his first college touchdown. Flipping the ball to the referee, he made two subtle fists and with the restraint of a Midshipman simply punched the air in celebration. In the stands, his father swelled with pride.

West Virginia struggled to move the ball throughout the first half. In all, Navy ran fifty-nine plays to West Virginia's twenty-one. The home team's biggest gain occurred on a 15-yard personal foul, after Mountaineer defensive player Alan Hoover rode Staubach out of bounds. This perceived offense caused Coach Hardin, in his sport coat and green hat, to jump on the back of Hoover in defense of his star player. Within seconds, the Navy team surrounded the player. To offend one Navy player meant that player would have to deal with forty-three other shipmates and one fired-up coach. When Hoover was asked about Hardin hitting him, he answered, "Somebody was pouring it on."

Navy ended the first half with a commanding 24–0 lead after halfback Kip Paskewich added two more touchdowns on short runs, with the second set up by an interception by Nemacolin's own Bob Orlosky, thrilling those who traveled from his town and honoring his grandmother's memory.

The moods in the two locker rooms at halftime reflected the score. Amid the cheers and back slapping, Lynch sat in front of his locker and re-energized with orange slices, continuing to lead and urge his teammates to keep it up. At the end of the intermission, Lieutenant Commander Sam Jones slid over to Lynch's locker and shared with him a premonition. "Tom," Jones said, "I see the team scoring 27 points in the second half to make it 51." Smiling, he explained why,

"You're number 51; I graduated in 1951; there were 51 individuals on the plane up to Morgantown [44 players, 7 coaches] on a flight that took 51 minutes."

Lynch nodded respectfully, only concerned with winning, and then joined his team as they took the field for the second half. Navy was interested in keeping the foot on the gas pedal while West Virginia was compelled to open up the offense and put the ball in the air. "I believe in putting on pressure when you're ahead," Coach Hardin once said. "I don't believe in slackening."

In the preseason, Coach Hardin had commented that Orr was a solid player on both offense and defense. At the start of the second half against the Mountaineers, Orr flashed his sure hands on defense and intercepted a wayward Yost pass, which he returned 52 yards for his second touchdown of the game. Orr's father accepted handshakes from friends, knowing that the seven-hour ride back to Long Island would be a pleasant one.

As the game in Morgantown wore on, West Virginia players were seen with hands on hips as they struggled to catch their breath, proving the axiom that both Vince Lombardi and General Patton believed in: "Fatigue makes cowards of us all."

Halfback and track star Johnny Sai added another touchdown on a spectacular 47-yard run, breaking off left end and cutting back to the right, breaking tackles, and then outrunning opponents before leaping over a blocking teammate into the end zone. Dave Sjuggerud fell on a fumble in the end zone caused by a strip of the quarterback by Ed Merino. Navy finished the scoring on a touchdown pass by Bruce Abel to Neil Henderson.

In the crowd, midshipmen reveled in their classmates' success by chanting across the field to the now-silent home fans, "We can't hear you Mountaineers. We can't hear you Mountaineers. We can't hear you Mountaineers."

Final score: Navy 51, West Virginia 7. Lieutenant Commander Jones was proved to be a visionary.

### #9 U.S. Naval Academy (1–0)
### @ #15 West Virginia University (0–1)
Mountaineer Stadium . Morgantown, West Virginia
September 21, 1963 . 1:30 p.m. kickoff . Attendance 35,000

|  | 1 | 2 | 3 | 4 | Final |
| --- | --- | --- | --- | --- | --- |
| Navy | 3 | 21 | 14 | 13 | 51 |
| West Virginia | 0 | 0 | 0 | 7 | 7 |

|  | Navy | West Virginia |
| --- | --- | --- |
| First Downs | 21 | 9 |
| Rushing Yards | 194 | 13 |
| Passing Yards | 223 | 104 |
| Pass Att.–Comp. | 27–21 | 21–12 |
| Fumbles Lost | 1 | 2 |
| Interceptions by | 3 | 1 |
| Penalty Yards | 85 | 51 |

| Navy | FG, Marlin, 25 yards |
| --- | --- |
| Navy | TD, Orr 26-yard pass from Staubach (Marlin kick) |
| Navy | TD, Paskewich 2-yard run (Marlin kick) |
| Navy | TD, Paskewich 1-yard run (Marlin kick) |
| Navy | TD, Orr 52-yard interception return (Marlin kick) |
| Navy | TD, Sai 47-yard run (Marlin kick) |
| Navy | TD, Sjuggerud 12-yard fumble return (kick failed) |
| Navy | TD, Henderson 17-yard pass from Abel (Marlin kick) |
| WV | TD, Hauff 7-yard pass from Yost (Kinder kick) |

It was the Mountaineers' worst loss in twelve years. In the West Virginia locker room, the pictures of Staubach were taken off the wall. Taped on Navy's locker room wall, the itinerary for the day read: "Depart 6:00 p.m. after beating West Virginia."

Staubach finished 17 for 22 with 171 yards, despite playing only two and a half quarters and leaving the game with Navy ahead 38–0. Among the many praises bestowed in the post-game analysis, the *Charleston Gazette*'s Hardman re-evaluated his earlier assessment and called Staubach's passing performance the "most dazzling . . . old Mountaineer Field has ever seen." West Virginia head coach Corum called him "as good as most pro quarterbacks right now."

And the raves about the Midshipmen's talents were not limited to their star quarterback. In the *Washington Post*, George Minot wrote, "For anyone who saw him last year, Staubach's success was expected, but the game played by Edward A. Orr was a surprise." Orr finished with 2 touchdowns, 7 receptions for 89 yards, and 1 interception.

The offensive and defensive line for Navy was immense. Al Krekich, Jim Freeman, Tom Lynch, Fred Marlin, Tom Holden, Dick Merritt, Dave Sjuuggerud, Jim Campbell, Dave Gillespie, Larry Kocisko, Charles Durepo, Pat Philbin, John Connolly, and Ed Merino had not only protected their golden quarterback but also shut down the West Virginia running game, which only gained 13 yards on 27 carries.

Prior to the 1963 season, the number one concern of the Navy coaches had been the offensive line, which was decimated by graduation. After the first game, however, it was apparent that the unit had great depth, and suddenly a perceived potential weakness was an asset that would allow Staubach to fully utilize his skill set.

Navy had out-run, out-hustled, and out-conditioned the bigger West Virginia team. It was a trend that Navy hoped would play out through the season—the smaller Navy team running its bigger opponents to exhaustion as they chased Staubach from sideline to sideline, only to find an offensive lineman waiting for them.

By dominating highly regarded West Virginia, the Navy team put the nation on notice that it was a legitimate threat to capture the national championship.

Back home in Annapolis, an elated student body treated the team to a much-earned hero's welcome.

# CHAPTER 11

# William & Mary vs. Navy, 1963

COACH WAYNE HARDIN WALKED INTO THE LOCKER ROOM on the Monday following the West Virginia game, took off his green fedora, and held it in his hand. On Mondays, Hardin liked to set the tone for the coming game, but before talking about the Tribe of William & Mary, he turned his hat upside down and showed the team the inside of his lid. Inscribed on the elastic band that circled the hat was "WV," in honor of the first victory of the 1963 season.

Hardin was pleased with his squad but would never share that information with his players. The dominating performance against West Virginia had surprised him. Clearly, though, the team was molding together before his very eyes. Nevertheless, one week of lost focus could spell the end of a perfect destiny. As a result, Hardin closed practices to the media, drawing the ire of the men with the pen.

Hardin was confident that Lynch could steer the ship in the right direction, maintaining a course of progress rather than contentment. In the days leading up to the William & Mary game, Coach Hardin said that his team was focused and determined, and he was relatively unconcerned about overconfidence. Nevertheless, Hardin emphasized all week the importance of taking the season one game at a time; no doubt the fact that last year's Navy team barely escaped with a victory against William & Mary was still on his mind.

The date was Saturday, September 28, 1963. As was tradition, the first home game of the season served as homecoming for the Naval Academy. Four years after dedicating Navy–Marine Corps Memorial Stadium, thousands of former midshipmen and their families were expected to attend the festivities, as well as the Saturday football game versus William & Mary.

Navy had yet to lose at the new home stadium.

During the week leading up to the game, William & Mary coach Milt Drewer watched game films of Navy playing against West Virginia and told reporters that the film was like watching a "horror movie. . . . I didn't think they could be that good."

A pep rally, hosted by Superintendent Rear Admiral Charles C. Kirkpatrick, was held on Friday night to kick off the weekend. At the rally, he reminded the brigade that its members could conquer anything if they were determined.

The weekend activities included a meet and greet between families and staff, reunions for twenty-seven different Naval Academy classes, and tours of ships tied up alongside the Severn River, including the submarine the USS *Sealion* and the amphibious assault ship the USS *Thetis Bay*. The weekend was capped off with the football game.

Navy tore apart William & Mary. Staubach was a nightmare for the Tribe, throwing for 206 yards while running for 91, breaking the previous total yards output by a Navy player, Jim Maxfield, while leading the team to a 28–0 shutout victory. In the *New York Times* a headline declared, "Staubach is Star as Navy Wins 28–0." *Times* sportswriter Allison Danzig wrote about the Navy quarterback, "It was his resourcefulness, improvisations, and evasive action in getting away when trapped on an attempted pass that put the stamp of greatness on him. . . . Staubach sidestepped, circled, reversed his field, coolly waited to pick up his blockers, and then got away."

## #5 U.S. Naval Academy (2–0)
## vs. College of William and Mary (1–1)

Navy–Marine Corps Memorial Stadium . Annapolis, Maryland

September 28, 1963 . 2:00 p.m. kickoff . Attendance 19,230

|  | 1 | 2 | 3 | 4 | Final |
|---|---|---|---|---|---|
| William & Mary | 0 | 0 | 0 | 0 | 0 |
| Navy | | 14 | 0 | 14 | 0 | 28 |

|  | William & Mary | Navy |
|---|---|---|
| First Downs | 14 | 20 |
| Rushing Yards | 62 | 204 |
| Passing Yards | 174 | 263 |
| Pass Att.–Comp. | 25–17 | 23–14 |
| Fumbles Lost | 4 | 1 |
| Interceptions by | 1 | 0 |
| Penalty Yards | 40 | 95 |

Navy  TD, Staubach, 3-yard run (Marlin kick)

Navy  TD, Donnelly, 1-yard run (Marlin kick)

Navy  TD, Sai, 6-yard run (Marlin kick)

Navy  TD, Paskewich, 4-yard run (Marlin kick)

Following the game, Coach Hardin met with the team in the locker room and voiced his displeasure with the team's performance. He thought the players had lost focus and was struggling to understand how they could be so dominating against a strong West Virginia team and then one week later submit an uneven effort against an opponent of lesser talent. "You men can't just throw your jocks out onto the field and expect to win. You're not that good. You need to play hard every week."

The message was delivered. If the team of destiny was to achieve greatness, the margin of error was narrow. It was Hardin's job to not allow his team to misstep.

# CHAPTER 12

# Michigan vs. Navy, 1963

ANY GOOD COACH IS ABLE TO READ THE MOOD and state of his team and react accordingly to ensure that the team is on the proper path to success. In the week leading to the critical game against Big Ten powerhouse the University of Michigan, Coach Hardin sensed that his players were tight and anxious. Concerned, he decided to deviate from the usual structure of practice week to provide some relief. Calling the team together with the assistant coaches by his side, he first showed the boys the inside of his hat, where he had branded on the band the initials "W&M" in honor of their victory over the Indians. He then announced to the team that instead of the standard practice format, the coaches had decided to challenge the team in a game of Kennedy Touch Football.

Hardin knew that any connection with the president worked to strengthen the bond between the team and the commander in chief, which would further enhance the psyche of the team that, naturally, felt special to have the president of the Untied States as a fan. Second, the game allowed players to realize that the coaches weren't a separate entity but instead aligned with them in their efforts to achieve their goals. Lastly, the game gave the old coaches, who understood the intricacies of Kennedy Touch Football, the opportunity to have some good, pure fun as they dominated the much younger, more athletic Midshipmen. The coaches would have their way with the team on the touch football field that day. It was good fun that had now placed the team in a positive frame of mind for the big game coming up against Michigan.

The members of the Navy team played the game of football with chips on their shoulders. Individually and collectively, the players were motivated to prove to other schools and coaches that they made a mistake by ignoring them as potential elite college football players. The University of Michigan represented the type of program that the Navy players aspired to play for, but which too often passed them over. The storied program had laid claim to a piece of twelve national titles. They played in Ann Arbor's "Big House," where 100,000 fans would cheer every Saturday. To defeat Michigan would represent a greatly satisfying victory, through which the players could validate their abilities to compete at the highest level of college football.

❨ ❨ ❨

A massive crowd would attend Navy's game against Michigan, as the Wolverines tried to protect the honor of both their school and the Big Ten Conference. The game was on national television, which would allow the Navy program and its star quarterback, Roger Staubach, to showcase their skills. In the press box was an influential contingency of national media along with the most competitive and feisty Kennedy Touch Football player of them all, Attorney General Robert Kennedy, who was joined by family members and Under Secretary of the Navy Paul Red Fay, an old shipmate of President Kennedy's. Their passion for the team matched the commander in chief's.

Prior to the game, Associated Press writer William Grimsley wrote, "Navy 22–7—Wolverines have no antidote for Roger Staubach."

When the team buses pulled up to the stadium, the players stepped from their transport just outside of the stadium and were surprised at how small the famous Michigan Stadium, a.k.a. the Big House, appeared. Of course, the players were unaware that the stadium was actually built into a sunken bowl. After dressing and taking the field, the players were awestruck by how massive and intimidating the stadium actually was, with the throng of fans that looms over the field like an immense wall hoping to suffocate the opponent's spirit and energy. The bleachers seemed to rise out of the playing surface, surging upward and giving the impression to one player that the stadium and fans were more like the cliffs of Dover.

Coming into the game, Michigan's lineup had multiple professional football prospects, including eventual two-time all-American Bill Yearby. Yearby not only played on both lines but also on the kickoff team, as return man Johnny Sai discovered on the opening kickoff. Sai was running the kick back and was clotheslined by Yearby, almost separating the return man's head from his body. It took Sai some time to regain his faculties and account for all parts.

The first half was a hard-fought, physical affair. The defenses on both sides dominated play. While Michigan had the advantage of a mean and large force, the Navy defense had its own advantage in the form of advanced scout and assistant coach Steve Belichick.

Steve Belichick was a 1941 graduate of Case Western University, where he led his team to the Sun Bowl and was later voted into the school's hall of fame. After serving in the navy during World War II, he appeared in six games for the Detroit Lions of the NFL. After a stint as coach at the University of North Carolina, Belichick took a coaching job at Navy, and in the process increased his pay from $1,000 to $7,000. He was considered by many across the nation to be the best advanced scout in college football. The players looked forward to his Monday night sessions at the Boat House, when he would analyze and dissect the coming week's opponent, whom he had watched on the previous Saturday. Each week he was able to provide the Navy players a behind-the-scenes edge. To Coach Belichick, the team's next opponent was always the best team in the country, capable of mythic feats. To him, every team was capable of its best on that day—he wanted the players to prepare accordingly.

Coach Belichick was also responsible for recruiting in primarily the Pennsylvania region, where he was born and lived prior to his family moving to Ohio. Navy had a significant Pennsylvania and specifically

Pittsburgh contingent on its roster. When Belichick showed up at the house of candidate Nick Markoff of West Mifflin, Pennsylvania, Markoff's father was ecstatic to find out that the Navy coach was Croatian like him. The two men then proceeded to sit down at the kitchen table, where they never talked football. By the time they had emptied a bottle of plum brandy known as Slibowitz, Markoff was committed to the Naval Academy.

At the Boat House film session prior to the Michigan game in 1963, Belichick was able to identify a key for the defense that would indicate the direction of Michigan running plays. The previous week, Belichick had attended the Michigan game against Southern Methodist University and noted a subtle change in the lead fullback's alignment, which unintentionally tipped the direction of his team's running plays. Later, while reviewing the game films, he confirmed the conspicuous variation and subsequently shared it with the team. If the play was to be run to the right side, the fullback would unintentionally open his body to the right side by setting his right foot a few inches behind his left. Navy defenders were able to apply this information to slant in the detected direction, or to flood one side, stifling the bigger and stronger Michigan running game.

The first quarter ended scoreless, but it was apparent that Navy was starting to wear down Michigan's heralded line. Between plays, the Wolverine defenders would start to rest hands on hips as they sucked air.

Early in the second quarter, Navy had the ball on the Michigan 5-yard line when Staubach rolled left with the option to pass to Skip Orr in the back of the end zone or to tuck the ball and run. On the end, left tackle Larry Merritt had sealed his man by enveloping his defender, allowing Johnny Sai and Pat Donnelly to get to the second level and throw lead blocks, which opened up the end zone for Staubach. Navy 7, Michigan 0.

Playing with a lead on the road, Navy decided to run out the clock in the closing seconds rather than throw the ball downfield. In the press box, a *Time* magazine reporter who was assigned to pen a story on Roger Staubach remarked to other writers that the quarterback seemed to do everything well except throw the deep ball. On the play just before the scribe made his comment, Staubach had been content to sneak forward into the line while the clock continued to wind down. Unbeknownst to the reporter, as he was preoccupied with critiquing the Navy quarterback, running back Sai had returned to the huddle with the suggestion that he could beat his defender if Staubach wanted to chance a late throw from the team's 44-yard line.

Sai, who was a self-admitted possessor of hands of stone, was determined that he could get loose and was confident that his quarterback could get him the ball. Staubach agreed and called for the play Transcontinental 97, in which the back would circle out of the backfield and travel vertically down the field. Upon the snap, Staubach surprised many of his own players by dropping back to throw. From the right end, a massive Michigan lineman with the number 94 on his chest had not been fooled and bore down on Staubach. On the opposite side of the backfield, Pat Donnelly exploded from his quarterback's right side to throw his body recklessly into the oncoming defender, giving Staubach sufficient time to loft the ball down the left sideline.

With the ball in the air, Sai was running free with two defenders trailing. Looking over his shoulder, he saw the ball descending from its pinnacle. As it approached, Sai extended the softest of hands and grasped the ball in stride, proceeding into the end zone—where the Michigan band was standing. Like the *Time* writer, the band had assumed the half was coming to a quiet end, but instead Navy had exerted a devastating body blow to the Big Blue.

As Navy went into the locker room, the team took with it momentum and a 13–0 lead. For Michigan, the outcome was inevitable. Not only did the Wolverines trail the high-powered, over-achieving Navy team, but since the moment that Yearby clotheslined Sai to start the game, Navy proceeded to devastate the Michigan team. One Michigan player after another was dragged off the field, with many forced to go to the hospital. This included Yearby, of whom *Time* once wrote, "a vicious tackler, always on target, always gets his man." This time, Navy offensive lineman Al Krekich got his man, flattening the massive Yearby with an awesome pancake block, leaving the Wolverine motionless on the field.

Krekich was part of the rebuilt offensive line that took great pleasure in knocking down defenders and then knocking them down again as the agile Navy quarterback serpentined back and forth behind the line. During Staubach's improvisations, a Navy lineman could block two or three men as the quarterback scrambled in one direction, only to reverse his field and allow his linemen to peel back and blow up unsuspecting defenders pursuing Staubach in vain. The motto of the entire line was to never stop blocking and knocking people down, because eventually Staubach would be coming back around.

Krekich symbolized the heart of the Navy team. Inspired to attend the Naval Academy after watching the television show *Men of Annapolis*, Krekich, like his teammates, was motivated to achieve. Once during a practice in which he failed to execute a play on consecutive repetitions, Assistant Coach Rick Forzano applied some negative reinforcement and ordered him to sprint to the fence. Furious with himself, Krekich sprinted to the fence, filled with anger for not accomplishing the task. When he arrived at the fence he decided not to stop and proceeded straight through, bringing down the entire structure. Hearing the crash, Coach Hardin spun and shot a look at Forzano, who shrugged his shoulders and simply said, "I didn't tell him to go through the fence."

Now in Michigan, the Navy offensive lineman went through the wall of Yearby, who outweighed Krekich by forty pounds and stretched five inches taller. When the play was over and the dust cleared, Yearby lay prone and still. He would not play again during this game, nor would six other starters and thirteen teammates total, including two quarterbacks. The relentless Midshipmen ripped the heart out of the Michigan team, just as they had with the West Virginia Mountaineers two weeks earlier. Touchdowns by Neil Henderson and Pat Donnelly would cap off a dominating 26–13 victory, and Navy improved to 3–0.

It might have been the Navy quarterback's greatest game yet, as he connected on 14 of 16 passes for 237 yards, while running for 70. His highlight play of the game only resulted in a one-yard pass play, but it occurred after a 30-yard scramble backwards. It was plays like this that reminded Coach Hardin not to restrict Staubach by coaching but to let him play and allow his God-given gifts to manifest themselves.

Others agreed, with the accolades for Staubach mounting. "Staubach is a great football player," said Michigan Coach Bump Elliot. "Don't know when I've seen a better one." Assistant Coach Jocko Nelson added, "The only way to beat Staubach is to let the air out of the football." And Michigan three-time all-American and radio announcer Bernie Oosterbaan called Staubach the "best all-around player I've ever seen."

A week after the Michigan game, Staubach appeared on the cover of *Time* magazine after impressing the writer in the press box with his arsenal of skills, which included throwing deep.

When the team headed back to the Naval Academy following the game, with the buses proceeding down Maryland Street toward the campus, it was said that the players "gasped" as they saw the entire brigade waiting for them at the gates of the school. Hanging off the gates and walls and one another, midshipmen waved their hats while others held the flags of their respective companies with great pride. As the team got closer, many sprinted down the street and greeted the buses, which they escorted directly to Tecumseh Court for an impromptu pep rally.

A certain spirit was starting to manifest itself not only among the midshipmen but across the nation. The Navy football team had now showcased itself in front of a national audience. Little by little, the crest on which this Navy ship sailed was rising.

Throughout the game against Michigan, Navy physically dominated the bigger, faster, and more highly acclaimed Wolverine players. It was the type of disposition that Coach Hardin fostered in his team. He wanted his players to be physical and impose their will upon their opponents. He would say that his team "could hit with anyone [in the country]."

**#6 U.S. Naval Academy (3–0)**
**@ University of Michigan (1–1)**

Michigan Stadium . Ann Arbor, Michigan
October 5, 1963 . 2:30 p.m. kickoff . Attendance 55,877

|  | 1 | 2 | 3 | 4 | Final |
|---|---|---|---|---|---|
| Navy | 0 | 13 | 13 | 0 | 26 |
| Michigan | 0 | 0 | 7 | 6 | 13 |

|  | Navy | Michigan |
|---|---|---|
| First Downs | 18 | 16 |
| Rushing Yards | 154 | 84 |
| Passing Yards | 237 | 144 |
| Pass Att.-Comp. | 16–14 | 14–10 |
| Fumbles Lost | 3 | 1 |
| Interceptions by | 1 | 1 |
| Penalty Yards | 54 | 10 |

Navy TD, Staubach, 5-yard run (Marlin kick)

Navy TD, Sai, 54-yard pass from Staubach (kick failed)

Navy TD, Donnelly, 1-yard run (Marlin kick)

Mich TD, J. Henderson, 39-yard pass from Chandler (Timberlake kick)

Navy TD, N. Henderson, 8-yard pass from Staubach (kick failed)

Mich TD, J. Henderson, 20-yard pass from Chandler (pass failed)

☾ ☾ ☾

One Navy player in particular who loved to deliver hard hits on the football field was a New Jersey wisecracker named Tom Holden. To his teammates, the hard-hitting linebacker was known as "The Rat" because his smile revealed a three-tooth gap whenever he removed a tooth plate prior to a game or a fight. Holden was a natural leader who would light up a room with a grin and charm girls with his dimples. Whether on the field or at a party, Tom always had his teammates' or friends' backs. He was the man his teammates always said they wanted to "go through the door with."

Holden later brought this spirit with him to Southeast Asia as a first lieutenant in the United States Marine Corps. There, his charismatic ability to lead inspired men to follow and believe. During a combat mission on August 23, 1965—which happened to be his twenty-fifth birthday—Holden was wounded in battle. He later received a Silver Star and Purple Heart when, "fearlessly exposing himself to enemy fire, he led his men in a furious attack, routing the enemy and rescuing the beleaguered patrol." Fourteen months later he again put himself in harm's way when, during a torrential rainstorm, one of the other platoons in his company was besieged in a firefight. Lieutenant Holden heard the gunfire, grabbed his helmet and flak jacket, and took off to help with what fellow Marine Gene Carrington described as "a look in his eye that said no one could stop him from trying to help his men."

In a rice paddy ten thousand miles away from the Annapolis field where he had strapped on the Navy helmet to play the game he loved, Tom Holden died a hero trying to save his brothers. The citation that accompanied his Gold Star medal read, in part:

> First Lieutenant Holden moved aggressively to aid the Platoon. Upon learning that both the Platoon Commander and the Platoon Sergeant had been wounded, he took command of the platoon and directed the base of fire in an attempt to gain superiority over the enemy while simultaneously directing the extraction of that portion of the platoon which was pinned down. Although constantly exposed to the heavy volume of accurate enemy fire, he resolutely continued in the attack until he fell, mortally wounded. By his outstanding leadership, indomitable fighting spirit and unwavering devotion to duty, First Lieutenant Holden upheld the highest traditions of the Marine Corps and the United States Naval Service. He gallantly gave his life for his country.

Years later, Navy teammate and brother-in-arms Mike Chumer wrote, "Tommy was not a 'choir boy'—none of us were. However, we all had a sense of ethics joined at the hip with our sense of duty coupled with the courage to act accordingly, so important a lesson for each Midshipman."

# CHAPTER 13

# Southern Methodist vs. Navy, 1963

IN THE PRESEASON PREVIEW OF THE NAVY FOOTBALL SCHEDULE, the Annapolis newspaper, *The Capital*, described Southern Methodist University as a team in a rebuilding mode. Navy coaches, however, didn't see SMU in the same light. The Mustangs were coming off a 10–0 upset win over the tenth-ranked Air Force Academy. The team was led by linebacker John Hughes, whose 20-tackle effort against the Falcons so exhausted him that he lost consciousness in the SMU locker room after the game—but only after he had received the game ball as a memento of his performance. For his effort he was named the national linebacker of the week.

Heading into the game against SMU, Coach Wayne Hardin wouldn't underestimate the Mustangs. "From a coaching viewpoint, we're not overlooking SMU, and I don't think the kids are either," Hardin said in the *Capital*. "They have excellent speed. This is the type of team that gives us trouble."

Speed that matched Navy's would neutralize one of the Midshipmen's advantages. In Michigan, they had run the giant Wolverines off the field and to the hospital. SMU's offense would present a number of different looks to the Navy defense, up to fourteen different formations out of the team's "T" formation. Navy assistant coach Steve Belichick noted that the team from Texas had both speed and effort, which made them like Mexican jumping beans; the SMU fans would call them field mice.

Leading up to the game, the Navy team prepped per usual and received its advanced scouting report from Coach Belichick. In addition, the team had inside information on players and style. Navy guard Jim Freeman, who was considered the best of the offensive line's starters, had transferred from SMU in just the last year. In his critique of his old team and teammates, he warned his fellow Midshipmen of SMU's aggressive style of defense and dirty play, especially after the whistle. Freeman, who was from Denison, Texas, also had a brother who played on the freshman team of SMU.

((  ((  ((

The SMU–Navy game was in Dallas, part of a football festival weekend to be held at Cotton Bowl Stadium. The Midshipmen game was on Friday night, and on Saturday afternoon, first-ranked Oklahoma would play second-ranked Texas in the annual chapter of their heated contest known as the Red River Rivalry.

Temperatures Friday night were in the eighties, which, when combined with Texas humidity, served as a significant advantage for the home team, who in theory was more acclimated to such conditions. Prior to the game, Navy took the field first for warm-ups. When SMU ran onto the field, many of the SMU players felt that the Midshipmen were mocking them as they ran past. They interpreted the clapping and whistling of the men in white shirts and gold pants as an insult. Gary Cartwright of the *Dallas Morning News* wrote of the incident, "Navy football team stood sarcastically at attention and clapped. Then the sailors snickered."

"When they clapped for us," SMU halfback Billy Gannon said, "that's all we needed." Running back John Roderick was more direct: "If I had my way, I would have fought them [the Navy players] right there. When we went back in the locker room before the game, we said to a man, 'Win, lose, or draw—let's send them to the hospital.' We were set on whipping ass and taking names."

Clearly, SMU wasn't intimidated or afraid of the challenge. The team looked at the chance to play the number four team in the country as an opportunity, as opposed to a burden. SMU had a high-flying defense led by John Hughes, a high-energy coach in Hayden Fry—who had majored in psychology and would need every mind trick to help his team—and speedster Johnny Roderick.

Roderick came to SMU by way of Highland Park High School in Dallas. Highland Park has a rich football history, with graduates of the school including football greats Bobby Layne and Doak Walker. Roderick arrived on the SMU campus not as a football star but as a sprinter with Olympic aspirations. As a freshman he had validated his high aspirations by running a 9.4 in the 100-yard dash.

Roderick, a free spirit who hadn't played football since his junior year in high school, suddenly got the urge to play the sport in the summer of 1963. With the Olympic qualifiers for Tokyo within months, Roderick approached his track coach, who had granted him the athletic scholarship, to ask permission to play football. Unhappy, his coach allowed him to try out for the team, fearing he would lose his star athlete, who was slotted to lead the spring 400-meter relay team to a world record in the following year.

He made the football team.

Prior to the 1963 football season, Roderick was called SMU's secret weapon. It was his blazing speed that more than compensated for the fact that he hadn't touched a football in three years. In the game against Air Force, the rogue halfback scored the contest's lone touchdown. When he ran out onto the Cotton Bowl field to battle Navy, he was ready to exact damage upon the team that came into the game with the number one offense (423 yards a game), scoring average (35.0), and passing game (241 yards).

Early in the game, with each team scoreless, Navy quarterback Roger Staubach gathered his team in the huddle and called for a running play. On the other side of the line, reserve SMU lineman Johnny Maag paced back and forth, determined to follow through on the sadistic mission posed in the SMU locker room to send Navy players to the hospital. At the snap of the ball, Maag moved to Staubach's blind side as the quarterback handed off to one of his running backs. As the crowd and quarterback watched the ball carrier, Maag raced toward the defenseless Staubach and rammed his head into the back of the unsuspecting Midshipman, flipping him upside down and causing him to land on his left shoulder.

Instantly, Staubach knew that he was injured and exactly what it was. As a plebe playing baseball two years previous, Staubach had landed awkwardly while chasing a fly ball and dislocated his shoulder. During his time as a Navy athlete he would separate his humerus from his arm socket seventeen times, but this was by far the most severe instance. Watching the play just feet from the premeditated hit, the referee pulled his yellow flag from his pocket, held it, and then slid the yellow marker back into the pouch.

Inexplicably, the head official had allowed the play to go unsanctioned, setting a trend that would continue throughout the game. Staubach came to the sideline with his left arm dangling by his side, while Coach Hardin, in his fedora and short-sleeved white dress shirt, fumed. Staubach was helped to the locker room, where his injury was diagnosed as game-ending and potentially season-ending. Staubach, though, was determined to return to the game and insisted that the shoulder be popped back into the socket. As instructed, the trainers did so and then placed his shoulder in a harness that would restrict the non-throwing arm from rising.

On the field, backup quarterback Bruce Abel, a senior from Pittsburgh, Pennsylvania, moved the Navy team down the field. Abel, who his coaches and teammates knew could have started on most college teams, was relegated to the bench at Navy, stuck behind the top quarterback in the country. But on this day, Abel acquitted himself nicely in Staubach's absence. When Staubach miraculously but not surprisingly returned, the team scored the first points of the game on a Fred Marlin field goal to take a 3–0 lead. Later in the first quarter, Staubach added to the lead, running for a 1-yard touchdown before being piled upon by the determined SMU defense. Staubach, now on the bottom of the pile, was then subjected to attack by the SMU players, who scratched his face and ripped his helmet from his head. When he made it to the sideline, he was incensed. In Staubach's *First Down, Lifetime to Go*, Hardin stated that it was the only time he ever saw Staubach lose his temper.

With SMU now trailing 10–0, SMU quarterback Mac White led his team down the field. White, a sophomore, had never carried a ball in a college game. Earlier in the season, he had hurt his knee and was listed as questionable. Prior to the Air Force game, SMU coach Fry prodded his talented back by asking, "Are you going to play this year or should I just red-shirt you?" White wanted to play and answered accordingly. Before the Navy game, White was informed by the trainer that he would be starting against the high-ranked Midshipmen.

On the 22-yard line of Navy, White carried the ball for the first time in his college career. When he was tackled he rolled over to find that he was lying on the goal line and the ball was in the end zone. On his first run, White had scored a touchdown and drew his team within three points of the highly favored opponent.

Navy got the points back in the second quarter on a patented Johnny Sai dive over the line for a 2-yard touchdown, but by now the game had turned into a street brawl. Every play had late hits and other vicious infractions. Helmets were used to spear while arms were brandished as weapons. Every time Staubach touched the ball he was hit hard, late, and often. Even the sanctuary of out of bounds failed to offer protection, as Mustangs continued to put a helmet on him at every opportunity. It was apparent that the SMU game plan was to hit the Navy quarterback whenever possible.

By halftime, the electric Cotton Bowl scoreboard showed Navy ahead 18–13. When the teams returned for the second half, the play was just as mean, just as violent. Back and forth the teams moved the ball up and down the field. In the third quarter, Staubach would avoid pressure long enough to hit Ed Merino for a 17-yard pass, but his shoulder was again dislocated on a late hit, forcing him again to the locker room to have the shoulder subluxation put back in the socket. While in the locker room, a virtual unknown took over the game.

Johnny Roderick, who had begged for permission to play football and then was infuriated by a perceived lack of respect by Navy players before the game, was now shredding the Navy defense. Never before had the Midshipmen played against someone with such speed and quickness. With each pitch and outside option, Navy players assessed angles by using the historical data of past plays and players. But the denominator of Johnny Roderick's speed was impossible to configure. Roderick possessed speeds beyond any ball carrier they had seen previously, and thus when estimating arrival time, their calculations proved to be faulty. They were late at every turn.

Such elusiveness started to frustrate the Navy defenders, including Nick Markoff, who was determined to get a shot at the six-foot-one, 168-pound sprinter. He was so desperate that Markoff finally used the sideline to his advantage, hemming the Mustang flanker out of bounds on a punt return. When Markoff was getting Roderick out, a cheerleader named Conrad Archer swung his blow horn at the Navy tackler and shouted an unpleasantry at him. Then, according to writer Gary Cartwright, Markoff kicked the cheerleader. Markoff got back into the huddle, oblivious to the booing crowd.

Up in the press box, Navy's Assistant Athletic Director Rip Miller was starting to suffer from the stress brought on by the back-and-forth nature of the game.

Edgar "Rip" Miller arrived at Navy with a great football pedigree. He had played for Knute Rockne at Notre Dame and had blocked for the Four Horsemen. He and the other men who composed that storied team's front line were known as the Seven Mules. In 1924, his Fighting Irish team went undefeated and won the national title. A few years after graduating, Miller joined the Navy coaching staff as a line coach before taking over as head coach in 1931. Two years later, he led Navy to its first-ever win against his alma mater, securing a 7–0 win over Notre Dame. The following season, Miller reassumed his role of line coach, where he remained until being named assistant director of athletics in 1948, a position he held until his retirement in 1974, after nearly half a century of service at the Naval Academy. He was voted into the College Football Hall of Fame in 1966.

Despite his decades of experience, the stress of the SMU game was too much for Miller, and he left the press box and made his way out to the Cotton Bowl parking lot, where he drank a beer and listened to the game on the radio. Meanwhile, inside the stadium, Roderick was now virtually running downhill. Every time the ball was handed off or pitched to him, the Navy bench would yell in unison, "Get him, get him!"

In the third quarter, SMU had the ball on the Navy 45-yard line, trailing 25–13. The call from the Mustang sideline was to run the option using the speedy flanker as the trail man. Mac White accepted the snap from his center and rolled left, and with the fullback leading the way, he ran the option with Roderick shadowing him. As White broke the line of scrimmage he was confronted by Navy end Jim Campbell. Just before contact, White pushed a two-handed chest pass to Roderick, who took the ball in stride and moved downfield. Recognizing defenders in front he cut from left to right, avoiding and teasing Navy defenders who reached and dove as he crossed the field. When he got to the sideline, the man who had never been caught before from behind on a football field or a track sped into the end zone with an electric touchdown.

Every time the sprinter touched the ball, the 37,000 spectators in the Cotton Bowl bleachers rose to their feet. In the fourth quarter,

SMU delivered again, with Roderick scoring on a 2-yard touchdown. The Mustangs had their first lead of the game, 26–25.

SMU would get the ball back late in the fourth quarter, desperate to keep the ball from the one-armed Staubach, who despite the injury and shoulder harness continued to move the ball. With the ball on the Navy 42-yard line, SMU faced a fourth and 12, and a tough decision on whether to go for a first down or punt. Doug Gabriel, the SMU coach responsible for calling plays, decided to go for the first down and turned to a play that had worked the entire game: the option to Johnny Roderick.

As SMU made its way into the formation, head coach Hayden Fry was furious. With his rolled-up sleeves and sideline pass tied to his belt loop, flipping around, he asked who called the play. When Coach Gabriel admitted it was he, Fry fired him on the spot. Seconds later the ball was snapped and Roderick took the pitch and ran for 18 yards and a first down. Coach Gabriel was rehired.

Eventually, Navy got the ball back and drove down the field, settling for a clutch 20-yard field goal by Marlin to give Navy the lead, 28–26. But in this game, no player nor score was safe. With just 2:52 showing on the clock, Navy squib-kicked the ball to an upback who took the ball to SMU's 29-yard line—71 yards from the end zone. On the first play, SMU completed a long pass play, which was followed by another sweeping Roderick run of 29 yards, bringing the Mustangs to the Navy 22-yard line. On the ensuing play, SMU threw to the goal line, but the pass was tall and wide, giving the receiver no chance to complete the play—then emerged from the fog of the Texas humidity a referee's flag, floating through the air. Despite the fact that the ball was uncatchable, the officials called pass interference on Navy, and the ball was moved to the 1-yard line. SMU scored to take the lead, just seconds left in the game.

With one arm dragging by his side, Staubach never gave up hope. Time after time during this game he took his place beneath center and found a way to move the ball downfield while being subjected to hit after hit after hit. Almost miraculously, Navy had advanced the ball into Mustang territory, and Staubach dropped back to pass again as the rush came from all sides. Releasing the ball prior to being hit, he connected with Dave Sjuggerud at the SMU 15-yard line. Navy was now in position to win the game. But again, an official's flag was thrown. Navy was called for offensive interference. Frustrated but not discouraged, Skip Orr caught a pass, moving the ball to the 28-yard line.

With just seconds left, the crowd was wild as the game moved toward a crescendo, and Staubach again stepped to the center. Across the line, SMU defenders, drenched in sweat and anticipation, were set to chase the Navy quarterback again. Upon the snap, Staubach dropped back and then decided to run. He crossed over the 20, refusing to be brought down, lowering his head and decimated shoulder, resorting to running defenders over. When the warrior was finally tackled, he lay at the 8-yard line, his shoulder again displaced. In agony, he looked up at the scoreboard, where the clock continued to tick. Less than 10 seconds left, Navy without a timeout, Staubach hustled the team to the line and received the snap. Looking over the middle he released the ball, but the pass was deflected to the ground with two seconds left. The crowd exhaled, on its feet to watch the last play of the game.

In the huddle, a number of plays came to the quarterback's mind, but he decided to turn to his friend and number-one receiver, Orr, and ask him if he could get open. The nine other players turned their heads to Orr and strained to listen as the noise of the crowd filled the Texas night. All game, Orr had found success by running vertical routes and then cutting out toward the sideline. He suggested to his quarterback that, this time, he instead curl in. Staubach agreed. The team clapped as they left the huddle.

Across the way, SMU defensive back Tom Caughran (who months later would be Jack Ruby's jail guard) was assigned the task of patrolling the middle of the end zone. The noise from the crowd made productive thought impossible; players were just acting on instinct. It had been a vicious, hot, and exciting game, and it came down to one last play. The players on the sidelines moved onto the field to peer down at the right end zone. It was a play of sudden death. Each team with so much to lose, each with so much pain and effort invested.

Upon the snap, Caughran played a hunch and set his attention on Orr. Earlier in the year, Orr had been listed on the depth chart beneath three others, but now the team was turning to him to help save their dream of a national championship. When he broke from the line, Caughran put a hand on the wide-out to disrupt his route but then was supposed to release him inside. Reacting on his gut, the SMU defender decided to stay with the Navy go-to receiver. Out of the corner of his eye, the Mustang defensive back could see Staubach cock his arm. Suddenly, the ball released from Staubach's hand and spiraled in the direction of the Navy receiver. When the ball arrived, Caughran desperately extended his hand, deflecting the ball to the chest of Orr. The ball then ricocheted into the air, suspended in time. Orr spun desperately for the wayward ball, trying earnestly to corral it. Instead, it just drifted away—his dive was too late. Game over. Navy had lost on a hot, humid, and passionate night in Dallas. Staubach and team played like warriors, but on this night the sprinter from Highland Park, Texas, and the painful sight of lofted yellow flags were the Midshipmen's undoing.

Matty Bell, SMU athletic director, said that Staubach was the best quarterback he had seen. *Dallas Morning News* reporter Sam Blair offered, "Jolly Roger Staubach didn't look jolly as he trudged up the ramp to the Navy dressing room." Blair continued to write that the Navy quarterback had pointed to the clock beating the Midshipmen and not SMU. But it was more than the clock. Navy had outgained SMU 462 to 290 yards. Staubach had run for 107 yards while throwing for 128 yards, all with only one shoulder and tremendous pain. Navy back Pat Donnelly added 109 yards rushing, and Nick

## #4 U.S. Naval Academy (3–1)
## @ Southern Methodist University (2–1)

Cotton Bowl Stadium . Dallas, Texas

October 11, 1963 . 8:00 p.m. kickoff (CST) . Attendance 37,000

| | 1 | 2 | 3 | 4 | Final |
|------|----|---|---|----|-------|
| Navy | 10 | 8 | 7 | 3  | 28    |
| SMU  | 7  | 6 | 6 | 13 | 32    |

| | Navy | SMU |
|----------------|------|-----|
| First Downs | 24 | 11 |
| Rushing Yards | 319 | 201 |
| Passing Yards | 143 | 89 |
| Pass Att.–Comp. | 26–13 | 17–9 |
| Fumbles Lost | 2 | 1 |
| Interceptions by | 1 | 1 |
| Penalty Yards | 107 | 52 |

Navy    FG, Marlin, 27 yards

Navy    TD, Staubach, 1-yard run (Marlin kick)

SMU    TD, White, 22-yard run (Richey kick)

Navy    TD, Sai, 1-yard run (Staubach run)

SMU    TD, Hillary, 3-yard pass from Thomas (run failed)

Navy    TD, Merino, 17-yard pass from Staubach (Marlin kick)

SMU    TD, Roderick, 45-yard run (pass failed)

SMU    TD, Roderick, 12-yard run (Richey kick)

Navy    FG, Marlin, 20 yards

SMU    TD, Gannon, 1-yard (kick failed)

Markoff ran for 83 yards plus, reportedly, one kick of a cheerleader. SMU's Roderick, who the Navy players said ran like a deer in fear, was the player of the game, running for 148 yards on 11 carries, including 2 touchdowns, one of them for the ages. But the most telling statistic of the game was penalty yards: Navy was penalized for a total of 107 yards, SMU 52.

After the game, some observers questioned the integrity of the officiating. Multiple calls appeared to go beyond standard "home cooking." The violent roughing of the Navy quarterback was ignored by the on-scene official. The pass interference call late in the game, which placed the ball on the Navy 1-yard line, directly impacted the outcome, leading to the game-winning touchdown. And several times during the contest, plays of significance in favor of Navy had been called back by the unusual call of mutual offsides. Over time, rumors of impropriety began to circulate: stories of NCAA censure, FBI investigation, and an unusual swing in the Vegas point spread, from Navy being favored by 12 points in the morning to the game being called a pick-'em by kickoff.

Months before, when the game was scheduled, it was decided that the Navy team would spend the night in Dallas so it could attend the next day's contest between Texas and Oklahoma. After the loss, the team would have preferred to leave the city, but instead the players were trapped in Dallas for another day, where dressed in their white naval uniforms they would be the targets of barbs and taunts from locals. After returning to Annapolis, lineman Al Krekich penned a letter to his parents, noting how badly the team had been treated in Dallas and what a terrible experience the city had been.

*Dallas Morning News* reporter Roy Edwards voiced disgust with the behavior of the Navy players, noting their "flagrant display of extracurricular violence" during the game. Edwards continued, "You're astounded to see it from a team representing a United States military academy, for these are our future military leaders."

Days later, Nick Markoff was back in class when he was summoned to Superintendent Rear Admiral Charles C. Kirkpatrick's office. (Articles in Texas papers noted the Nick Markoff/cheerleader confrontation. The story would be later picked up by *Sports Illustrated* and noted in the national publication.) Nervous about the meeting's purpose, Markoff arrived at the superintendent's office and noted a pile of Western Union telegrams on the desk. Worried, he tried to read the face of the superintendent. The superintendent invited Markoff to take a seat and then said, "I'm getting lots of letters about your incident in Dallas. Why don't you tell me what happened?"

Markoff denied what was written and said that it was actually the cheerleader who instigated the contact. The superintendent mulled the proper response and then advised Markoff as only he could: "I hope you learned a valuable lesson."

Markoff wasn't sure where this was heading, so he sat and waited for a rebuke. Kirkpatrick finished, "If you're going to be accused of something, you better make sure that you get your money's worth. Now get out of here and go win a football game this weekend."

Decades later, the heart-stopping 1963 SMU–Navy game is still considered a classic, and it earned a spot on the Cotton Bowl list of greatest games. Later that year, the Mustangs were invited to the Sun Bowl despite their 4–6 record. Roderick would again be the hero, catching two touchdown passes. Soon thereafter, though, the music stopped for the SMU football team and its star, when the program was placed on two years' probation and Roderick flunked out of school. He also failed to qualify for the Olympics.

# CHAPTER 14

# Virginia Military Institute vs. Navy, 1963

NAVY COACH WAYNE HARDIN SHOWED UP AT PRACTICE MONDAY after the long and difficult weekend in Texas. He stood before his team and took off his green fedora to show the latest inscription on his hat: "SBT." It stood for "Screwed, Blued, and Tattooed."

The hangover from the SMU loss enveloped the Navy football team, days later still weighing heavily on the players who had aspirations of greatness. Nick Markoff was still receiving hate mail, and Roger Staubach was still suffering the discomfort of a dislocated shoulder. After arriving back in Annapolis, the quarterback was given a full examination by an orthopedist who determined that the injury was so significant he recommended season-ending surgery. Staubach opted for tightening the shoulder harness and rest. In addition to Staubach, Johnny Sai, Dick Merritt, Dave Sjuggerud, Doug McCarty, and Jim McGinn were all nursing ailments of varying degrees of severity.

Next on the schedule for Navy was the Virginia Military Institute. The game was to be played at the neutral site of Foreman Field in Norfolk, Virginia, in the traditional charity event known as the Oyster Bowl. The game, which was first played in 1946, is traditionally played between eastern teams, with proceeds from the event donated to the Shriners Hospitals for Children.

Hardin assured reporters his boys were over the loss and his quarterback was fine. In reality, he was greatly concerned. The team was not practicing well and was apparently still suffering the emotional and physical effects of the devastating loss in Dallas, to the point that the players took the field for Monday practice wearing sweats and cloaked in self-pity. Coach Hardin immediately noticed the lack of energy and that the team was distracted. Weighing the best course of action, he elected to allow the players latitude while they slowly purged the Dallas visit from their systems.

On Tuesday, the Midshipmen continued to struggle with execution and focus. The team only had limited time to practice and prepare, and that opportunity was starting to slide away. By Wednesday, Coach Hardin's patience had morphed to a red face and firm words. "If you guys want to wait to the game on Saturday to prepare," he said, "then you're going to learn a very difficult lesson."

During the midweek phone conference between coaches and media, all parties were careful to salute and not provide motivation. VMI coach John McKenna told the media, "We've run and rerun the movies of the Navy games, and we've come to one conclusion: There is no way to stop Staubach." On the other end of the phone, Navy assistant coach Steve Belichick compared the VMI defense to SMU's, calling them fast and relentless.

❮ ❮ ❮

On Saturday, the team bused down to Norfolk. When they arrived, sports information director Budd Thalman was informed that organizers had forgotten to procure a public address announcer and that he was selected to fill the void. Part of his duties were to narrate the pregame ceremony that commemorated the anniversary of the 1781 Battle of Yorktown. The ceremony included re-enactments of George Washington's big upset over General Cornwallis. It was just such an upset that Coach Hardin feared the Keydets of VMI were capable of doling out. He knew that the Midshipmen were distracted. VMI was a good, tough team. In the prior year, it had won the Southern Conference and was undeniably a formidable opponent. Before the game, VMI coach McKenna urged his team to play with unrestrained abandon. Navy was a three-touchdown favorite, and VMI decided to throw caution to the wind. That made the team dangerous.

In the first half, the Keydets blitzed and harassed the injured Staubach, chasing him around and across the field, pushing him back for a negative 21 yards rushing. In the closing seconds before intermission, with the game scoreless, Navy had the ball on the VMI 21-yard line. Staubach dropped back hoping to find an open receiver for the end zone, but the pressure was too much. Yet again, Staubach was thrown for a loss. On fourth down, Hardin called on his kicker, Fred Marlin, to attempt a 31-yard field goal.

Marlin, at age twenty-three, was the oldest player on the team. His odyssey to the Navy was chronicled in an article in *Sports Illustrated* as follows: "In 1958, Marlin played for Western Maryland. In 1959, he was in the Navy. In 1960, he played for the Naval Academy Prep School. In 1961, he played on the Navy Plebe team. In 1962 he was a sophomore. He has another season of eligibility."

The freckled lineman with the number 64 on his back and high-top black cleats was not only the kicker but also the leading tackler on the team. Marlin grew up in Woodbury, New Jersey, before joining the Navy prior to his arrival in Annapolis. Marlin was intense but also known to be one of the team's pranksters, along with fellow lineman Tom "the Rat" Holden and Jim Freeman, while Nick Markoff and Bruce Abel were blessed with quick wits. Marlin and his cohorts had ways to make practice, long bus rides, or a dead locker rooms fun.

Before the season opener in West Virginia, Dave Sjuggerud had been listed first on the depth chart at kicker, but during warm-ups in Morgantown, Marlin's kicks were solid and true. When Hardin asked him why he was kicking so well, Marlin joked, "Coach I always kick better with new shoes." At five-foot-ten and 196 pounds, Marlin was subsequently given the kicking duties and became a significant offensive force for the team, leading the nation in scoring in 1963. Prior to the season, Coach Hardin critiqued the kicker and expressed his limited expectations. "Marlin isn't great," the coach said, "but he's the best we have. He has power, but accuracy is the problem."

Now the team again called on Marlin to attempt a field goal and give Navy a 3–0 lead, as well as some degree of momentum leading to the intermission. On the VMI sideline, Coach McKenna wanted to keep the pressure on the Midshipmen. In case of a short kick, McKenna sent out third-string quarterback Mark Mulrooney to stand in the end zone as a safety, in case of a return opportunity.

Upon the snap and hold, Marlin, a straight-on kicker, swung his right leg back and then forward, launching the ball toward the end zone. As soon as the ball left his foot, Marlin knew that he had failed to kick it squarely. The ball spiraled through the air but appeared to be falling short of the goalposts. In the end zone, Mulrooney could see the ball was going to be shy of the posts, but he jumped up and swatted it away just in case. The kick was no good, and both teams started to make their way to the sidelines, except for Marlin, who remained on the field in disappointment.

As players from both sides ran to their respective sidelines, Marlin stood on the field and looked toward the end zone, where his kick had fallen short and was knocked down by Mulrooney. Then Marlin noticed that the official in the end zone was standing over the ball, but not picking it up. Suddenly, it struck Marlin like a bolt of lightening: The ball was live!

Instantly, the kicker began to run like hell, as his teammates would later describe his frantic charge to the end zone. When Marlin arrived at the ball, he reached down and picked it up. The referee walked up to him, looked at the ball in his hands, and threw both arms up in the air to signal a touchdown. Marlin's quick thinking gave Navy a most unusual touchdown. Marlin then converted the extra point, and the Midshipmen went to the locker room with a gifted 7–0 lead.

## #10 U.S. Naval Academy (4–1)
## vs. Virginia Military Institute (1–3–1)

Foreman Field . Norfolk, Virginia (Oyster Bowl)

October 19, 1963 . 1:00 p.m. kickoff . Attendance 31,500

|      | 1 | 2 | 3  | 4  | Final |
| ---- | - | - | -- | -- | ----- |
| VMI  | 0 | 0 | 0  | 12 | 12    |
| Navy | 0 | 7 | 14 | 0  | 21    |

|                | VMI  | Navy |
| -------------- | ---- | ---- |
| First Downs    | 9    | 17   |
| Rushing Yards  | 171  | 134  |
| Passing Yards  | 64   | 148  |
| Pass Att.–Comp. | 11-3 | 13-9 |
| Fumbles Lost   | 1    | 0    |
| Interceptions by | 0  | 1    |
| Penalty Yards  | 29   | 25   |

Navy  TD, Marlin recovered live ball in end zone (Marlin kick)

Navy  TD, Sai, 2-yard run (Marlin kick)

Navy  TD, Staubach, 1-yard run (Marlin kick)

VMI  TD, Deale, 21-yard run (pass failed)

VMI  TD, Talley, 16-yard pass from Nunally (pass failed)

When the Navy players arrived in the locker room to eat their oranges and drink water, they found an enraged Coach Hardin. His face was red, his words direct and firm. All week he had feared a lackluster performance like this, and these fears had come true. An undersized VMI team had out-worked and out-hustled the Navy squad, and were it not for a fluke play, the teams would be tied at halftime. He told his Midshipmen that they weren't big enough or talented enough to just show up and win a football game. They'd better make some adjustments—and fast!

Navy did make adjustments in the second half, resulting in two scores. One was set up by a Pat Donnelly 40-yard run on an option play, which led to a Johnny Sai 2-yard touchdown. The second score was set up by a Larry Kocisko fumble recovery, which Navy converted into a 1-yard Staubach sneak. VMI scored two late touchdowns, making the final score 21–12.

Despite the lackluster Navy performance, VMI coach McKenna heaped praise on one member of the Navy squad in the locker room after the game: "I still think [Staubach] is the finest quarterback I've ever seen."

Coach Hardin, for his part, was somewhat philosophical about his team's struggles in victory. "You can't get a team up every week," he said.

All the while Navy was battling VMI, up in Massachusetts, President Kennedy was feeling nostalgic. In Boston for a fundraiser, he had Secret Service agents drive him to Cambridge to watch his alma mater, Harvard, play Columbia. When he arrived, no one knew he was in the stadium until the Harvard band started to play "Hail to the Chief."

Navy had been outplayed and was lucky to escape the Oyster Bowl with its fourth victory. The sub-par performance endangered the team's entire season. Staubach ended the game with 1 yard rushing and 148 yards passing, completing 9 of 13 attempts.

Navy was fortunate to have survived with a victory. Next up was Navy's biggest game of the year to date, at home against third-ranked Pittsburgh.

# CHAPTER 15

# Pittsburgh vs. Navy, 1963

PRIOR TO THE 1955 GAME BETWEEN THE UNIVERSITY OF PITTSBURGH Panthers and Navy, students from Pitt snuck into Thompson Stadium at the Naval Academy and made their way to the pen of the Navy's goat mascot, Billy IV. They stole the goat, prompting this police bulletin: "Stolen from the United States Naval Academy at 1600 hours, one mascot goat by two young men wearing black sweaters. Goat placed in trunk of Model-T Ford convertible. Last seen heading west from Annapolis. Believed to be en route to Pittsburgh, Navy's next opponent."

The 1962 Oyster Bowl featured Navy versus Pittsburgh, and Navy quarterback Roger Staubach was eight for eight throwing the ball. One of those eight plays was after the team had run the old-school "Sleeper" play for an uncontested 62-yard touchdown, a play that created much disdain from the Pittsburgh camp.

Following the 1962 game and in preview of the coming week's 1963 contest, there was significant attention given to the play, which was called by UPI the most unusual play of 1962. During the week, Roger Staubach predicted that Pitt would be out for revenge because of last year's events, which was confirmed in Red Blaik's weekly college football column. "Pittsburgh is still irritated at the sideline sleeper play Navy used in victory a year ago and will be in a violent mood," Blaik wrote. Newspaper accounts compared the play to Pearl Harbor, which infuriated the Navy team and administration. One newspaper carried the headline,

"Navy Pearl Harbors Pitt," while another paper ran a picture of the USS *Arizona* sinking with the headline, "Pitt Remembers Pearl Harbor."

The fact that many of the Navy players were from Pennsylvania and were ignored by Pitt recruiters further fueled the fire. William Ulrich, Steve Shrawder, James Ounsworth, Nick Markoff, Gary Kellner, Richard Earnest, James Campbell, and Bruce Abel all were passed over because their measurements or times didn't adhere to the standards that Pitt Panthers evaluators deemed adequate to perform at their level. This chip that sat on the shoulders of these players emerged either when they faced a Panthers team on the football field or walked into a Pittsburgh tavern and found themselves scoffed at by Pitt fans.

This year's Pitt–Navy contest would determine eastern dominance and most likely the winner of the Lambert Trophy. On Monday, the two teams started preparation. In Pittsburgh, Coach John Micheloson stressed the number one priority to his team: contain Roger Staubach. "This fellow [Staubach] is supposed to be the best," Micheloson quipped to the media. "If anybody can defend against him, I'd like to know."

Pittsburgh's intention was to take Staubach out of the game by committing as many players as necessary to restrict his ability to maneuver and manipulate in the pocket. "The offensive line is tough, sometimes throwing two or three blocks for him because he becomes a mad dog so quickly [in the backfield]."

In Annapolis, Coach Hardin opened practice to the media for the first time all season. It was the second half of the schedule, and the requests for answers to questions about his team (and quarterback) were mounting. The team dressed in its home blue uniforms and stood for pictures and answered questions. Staubach was said to be polite and courteous, even telling reporters that he did have an interest in playing professional football but only after serving his military obligation.

Coach Hardin answered questions and provided little fodder for the Pittsburgh locker room. "Pitt has size, speed, experience, flexibility on the offense and toughness on defense," he said. "There is no question they are a great team."

As he did every Saturday, Assistant Coach Steve Belichick traveled to scout the coming week's opponent. While charting the Pittsburgh–West Virginia game, the perceptive coach noted that Pittsburgh's defensive strength was a combination of talent and design. Their 5–3 defense gave the Panthers options in defending multiple styles of offense. When he returned to Annapolis, Belichick sat down with Hardin and the other members of the staff to try to expose the holes in that particular alignment.

Over and over again they drew up plays on the chalkboard, drawing and erasing and drawing again until they all finally agreed they had solved the puzzle. On Thursday at practice, they introduced the new formation and design to the team. The play that they had designed to work against the Pittsburgh defense called for the two tight ends to line up on the same side. One of the tight ends would then move behind the offensive line to the other side prior to the ball being put into play. Upon the snap of the ball, the two halfbacks would spread out, one to each flat, drawing linebackers with them. The ends then would run down the field 10 to 15 yards and curl in, forcing the remaining lone linebacker to choose which end to cover.

Navy was blessed with two gifted tight ends, Dave Sjuggerud and Jim Campbell. Their teammates called them the perfect pillars around which to build the team, bookends of a great offense. Of Sjuggerud's defensive prowess, Army coach Paul Dietzel said, "He is one of the most underrated players in the country. The way he runs down ball-carriers from behind is amazing."

Of Sjuggerud and his tricky name, the *Washington Post* wrote, "The Middie with the name only a mother can pronounce . . . 'Sugar? rude' it is, and that about sums up the player. He's 'sugar' and spice and everything nice off the field, but he's rude indeed, to enemy ball carriers." His teammates called the six-foot-four, 205-pound senior "Shug." As a high school star at Menomonie High School in Wisconsin, he starred in football and track, and he averaged over 20 points per game in basketball. His senior season he was offered scholarships to Wisconsin and Minnesota, but he decided to attend school in Annapolis because his family had limited financial resources. Not only would the Naval Academy be free for Shug, but the midshipman also got paid a stipend.

As a freshman he was sometimes described as awkward, but Sjuggerud improved dramatically each year. His first real contribution of significance occurred against Notre Dame his sophomore season. With the Fighting Irish driving inside the Navy 10-yard line in the closing minutes to win the game, he made a game-saving tackle and fumble recovery to secure victory.

His tight-end partner was Jim "Soupy" Campbell, whose hometown was Homestead, Pennsylvania, just southeast of Pittsburgh. The six-foot-two end weighed in at 208 pounds and was considered by Belichick to be the greatest athlete he had ever coached. His teammates would say that if they did a movie about him, only Gary Cooper could play him. He was known to be the most intense player on the team, one who always went 100 percent, whether in a game or at practice. Along with football, Campbell played on the basketball team and was so gifted that he took up lacrosse in college and was a contributor on Navy's national champion lacrosse team.

"We may have had an end who was better individually," Coach Hardin was quoted in the *Capital*, "but we never had a pair who were so strong in every department—blocking, tackling, and pass receiving."

On Thursday, the team showed up for practice in their sweats to walk through plays and continue to piece together the game plan. During the session, the probing play with the two ends was introduced to the team. On the chalkboard and walking through the play with no defense, the play was unstoppable. But in reality, there was still a level of uncertainty. Prior to the game, former Navy great George Welsh was in town scouting for his employer, Penn State. In the locker room after exchanging greetings, Coach Hardin rolled the chalkboard over and drew the "two-end" play on the board. He then asked Welsh if he should run the play over and over again, forcing the Pitt team to adhere to Navy's rules, or save it for just the right moment.

It was Welsh's recommendation that Hardin hold the play for the right moment, but the Navy coach disagreed. He always liked to run successful plays over and over again to force the other team to adjust to his team. In the 1962 game against Boston College, Navy had a sequence of plays in which Roger Staubach rolled out and threw across the field for a first down, only to have the play called back for a penalty. On the ensuing play, with Navy needing 20 yards, Hardin called the same exact play, which was completed for a first down, only to have that called back for a penalty. Now third and 30 yards, Hardin called the same play for the third straight time, which was completed successfully for a first down. It was the type of football experience that convinces a coach to go with something until it doesn't work.

❨ ❨ ❨

In the local papers that weekend, pictures of Roger Staubach throwing good luck pennies at the replica of Native American Tecumseh and of Pittsburgh all-American Paul Martha sitting on the statue of the Pitt Panther appeared on the front pages of their respective sports sections. The game was the most anticipated football event in Annapolis history. Portable bleachers were brought into the stadium to accommodate what would be a record crowd at Navy–Marine Corps Memorial Stadium. Navy still hadn't lost at its new home stadium, compiling a 9–0 record since its completion in 1959.

Prior to the game, Senator Joseph Clark of Pennsylvania had requested that the Pittsburgh team be invited to meet with President Kennedy on its way to Annapolis. The president, during his tenure, had met with high school teams; Punt, Pass, and Kick contestants; and Heisman winners. Pitt was told the president couldn't find the time to meet with the squad.

The president had been desperate to attend the game but was instead scheduled to speak at the dedication of the Robert Frost Library at Amherst College. Frost had been asked by the president to read a poem at his inauguration in January 1961. For months the poet had worked on the poem, titled "Dedication." When he stood at the podium outside of the capitol building, the glare of the sun off the snow blinded him, forcing him to forgo his work and recite from memory his poem "The Gift Outright."

Representing the president at the game was his brother Robert Kennedy and the president's friend and undersecretary of the navy, Red Fay. Also at the game was 1960 Heisman Trophy winner Joe Bellino.

It was the biggest game of the year in college football, with bowl game and national championship implications. At 12:30 p.m., the brigade of midshipmen conducted their march below a perfect autumn sky with temperatures in the low seventies. On the grass hill behind the north end zone in the open bowl, the words "Plaster Pitt" were laid in lime.

The game featured two high-flying offenses. The conductor for the Navy team was its great quarterback, while the man pulling the strings for the Pittsburgh team was its school's chancellor, Ed Litchfield. In an offseason meeting with Coach Michelosen, the chancellor made it clear he wanted the football team to be exciting in the form of a wide-open offense. The head of the college even stated his preference for high-scoring over winning football.

In the Navy game, the ultimatum from the chancellor manifested itself early on, when a free-throwing Pittsburgh team put the game in the hands of its highly touted quarterback, Fred Mazurek, who Steve Belichick called "a stud." The good news for Navy was that this approach somewhat kept the ball out of the hands of Pitt's all-American halfback, Paul "Rambling Rose" Martha, who to that point in the season was averaging 6.5 yards per carry.

Alas, the wide-open offense ordered by the academic leader of the school would have immediate consequences for Pitt.

Early in the first quarter, Pittsburgh had the ball on its own 25-yard line. Mazurek dropped back to pass. In his read, he failed to see that Navy middle linebacker and captain Tom Lynch had dropped back into coverage. Lynch intercepted the pass, giving Navy the ball deep in Pittsburgh territory. The play wasn't just a turnover; it established the momentum of the game. The interception effectively put doubt in the heads of the Pittsburgh quarterback and his teammates, and it ultimately gave Navy an early lead, as the turnover led to a Fred Marlin 36-yard field goal.

In the second quarter, the wide-open offense mandate of Pittsburgh would again prove its undoing. With the team driving deep into Navy territory, Pat Donnelly made a shoestring interception of a Mazurek pass, giving Navy the ball on its own 20-yard line.

Coach Hardin decided that this was the moment in the game to expose the 5–3 defense of Pittsburgh. Breaking the huddle, Campbell and Sjuggerud started their dance—one in motion, both breaking off the line, curling in some 10 to 15 yards downfield. The design of the play jumped off the chalkboard and came to life on the football field. As projected, the Pitt linebackers had fanned out to cover halfbacks in the flat, leaving open ends for Staubach to choose from. Like an electric current the ball spiraled to Campbell, who caught it and moved up the field for an 18-yard gain. On the sideline the coach with the green fedora yelled, "Run it again!" And again, one end went in motion to balance the line. Upon the snap, both broke downfield, turning-in in synchronicity. Staubach again drilled the ball to Campbell, who bobbled and then secured the ball for 14 more yards. The Navy team went wild on the sideline. The players knew the game was theirs to win. They had the best coaches, the best plan, the greater will. It was revenge. Revenge for the laughter and taunting in the Pittsburgh taverns, revenge for the absent Pitt recruiters.

A fired-up Hardin prowled the sideline yelling with enthusiasm, "Run it until I tell you to stop!" And again, the ends made their way downfield, and again the combination of Staubach to Campbell connected, for 18 more yards; and a fourth time for 9 more yards. Navy had marched 80 yards, all the way into the end zone, against the third-ranked team in the country. The Navy football team was forcing its will upon its opponent, unleashing the power of its unit—coaches and players working together for one common goal, representing the entire brigade and all for which it stands.

The Pittsburgh team and coaches were bewildered. It was too late for a switch in the defensive scheme. Navy had forced Pitt out of its element. The Midshipmen went into the locker room at halftime with a 10–0 lead.

In the second half, the game was never in jeopardy for Navy, though the battle on the field became a war. Earlier in the week, the Panthers had disclosed that they would commit as many men as necessary to quash Staubach. In the second half alone, players threw the Navy quarterback with the aching shoulder for 93 yards in losses, but the Midshipmen always came up with an antidote for any pressure Pitt thrust upon them. Twice, Hardin called for Staubach to hand off to halfback Pat Donnelly and go out on pass patterns himself, which resulted in two 19-yard receptions on balls thrown by Donnelly to Staubach. At every turn, Navy exposed the Pittsburgh team, its coaches, and its chancellor. The wide-open offense would result in two more interceptions, one by Bob Orlosky that led to a score. The interception by Jim Campbell encapsulated the Navy defense: Pressure was exerted by Pat Philbin up the middle, forcing an early release of the pass, which was tipped by James Breland. The ball deflected to Campbell, who lateralled to Donnelly, who ran the ball to the 5-yard line, setting up another touchdown for the offense. In addition to the four interceptions, the Navy defense forced and recovered two fumbles and sacked the Pittsburgh quarterbacks four times, with one each by Campbell, Sjuggerud, Lynch, and Breland.

Though Pittsburgh scored two late, meaningless touchdowns, it was Navy's day. In front of the brigade, Robert Kennedy, and the country, Navy had established itself not only as the eastern college football power but as a candidate for the national championship. The boldness of Coach Hardin, the insight of Assistant Coach Belichick, the creativity of Staubach, the dance of Campbell and Sjuggerud, the brilliance of a defensive unit led by its captain, Lynch, all came together in the victory.

## #10 U.S. Naval Academy (5–1)
## vs. #3 University of Pittsburgh (4–1)

Navy–Marine Corps Memorial Stadium . Annapolis, Maryland
October 26, 1963 . 1:30 p.m. kickoff . Attendance 30,231

| | 1 | 2 | 3 | 4 | Final |
|---|---|---|---|---|---|
| Pittsburgh | 0 | 0 | 0 | 12 | 12 |
| Navy | 3 | 7 | 0 | 14 | 24 |

| | Pittsburgh | Navy |
|---|---|---|
| First Downs | 12 | 13 |
| Rushing Yards | 76 | 11 |
| Passing Yards | 173 | 187 |
| Pass Att.–Comp. | 26–11 | 21–16 |
| Fumbles Lost | 2 | 0 |
| Interceptions by | 0 | 4 |
| Penalty Yards | 30 | 83 |

| | |
|---|---|
| Navy | FG, Marlin, 36 yards |
| Navy | TD, Sai, 1-yard run (Marlin kick) |
| Navy | TD, Staubach, 1-yard run (Marlin kick) |
| Pitt | TD, Crabtree, 39-yard pass from Lucas (pass failed) |
| Navy | TD, Donnelly, 1-yard run (Marlin kick) |
| Pitt | TD, Martha, 74-yard pass from Lucas (pass failed) |

Perhaps Steve O'Neill of the *Baltimore News-Post* said it best when he wrote, "Proving once again that he is the premier quarterback in all the land—and on the high seas and airways as well—Staubach guided the Tars safely past one of the rocky shoals on their course, and with astonishing ease too."

The 1963 match-up with Pitt epitomized Navy football's strengths as a cohesive unit working toward a common goal. On its home field, in blue shirts and gold helmets and green fedora, Navy football shined bright under the beautiful October sun.

# CHAPTER 16

# Notre Dame vs. Navy, 1963

AS A PROMISING HIGH SCHOOL QUARTERBACK, Roger Staubach, whose heroes were Y. A. Title and Johnny Unitas, had his heart set on attending and playing at just one college: the University of Notre Dame. It seemed like a natural progression for him, a Midwestern school in which he could not only develop as an athlete but also as a student and as a Catholic. Overtures made by the Staubachs and family representatives to the Irish coaches were rebuked. Word from South Bend was that their quota for quarterbacks had been met, thus the program had no interest.

Staubach received scholarship offers from at least forty other schools. Woody Hayes of Ohio State once called the Cincinnati-born quarterback on seven straight nights of a week. And though this attention provided him many options, none of the forty seemed to be his destiny. Eventually, he committed to Purdue University in Indiana even though he felt the campus was too big for him. Because it didn't feel right, he continued to search, hoping to find the college that would be the perfect fit. During this time, Staubach was introduced to Navy assistant coach and recruiter Rick Forzano, who was recruiting in the Ohio area. Forzano was a very convincing man who was passionate about selling the Naval Academy to worthy candidates. Staubach, who had visited the campus at Annapolis and was taken by it, was convinced not only to commit to the Naval Academy but also to a year of junior college at New Mexico Military Institute to improve his grades to a level worthy of a midshipman.

The summer after high school graduation, Staubach participated in the Ohio all-star game, a game in which he truly established himself as a player of significance and great potential. After the game, Staubach received considerable attention from college scouts, including from Notre Dame. Young Staubach, though, was a man of principle. He felt that Notre Dame had its chance and missed it.

In Staubach's book, *First Down, Lifetime to Go*, Forzano talks about that particular Ohio high school all-star game. "Roger was tremendous in that game," Forzano recalls. "He had all those unassisted tackles . . . made two great catches. As a quarterback he was two for two passing and got loose on a long run which excited everyone. In the locker room after the game all those college scouts, including Notre Dame's, were mobbing him. I said, 'Uh, oh.'"

Staubach was true to his commitment and attended a prep year at New Mexico Military Institute, where he led his team to a 9–1 record and was named a junior college all-American. It was after his fine ju-co season that Forzano predicted the quarterback would win the Heisman Trophy.

When the six-foot-two, 193-pound Staubach arrived on Navy campus, he didn't ask where the football field was, but rather his first question was, "What time is the daily Catholic mass?" In high school he considered joining the priesthood. As a midshipman he would regularly attend the 5:30 a.m. mass and serve as an altar boy. Along with schoolwork and sustaining his religious beliefs, he also was a great baseball player, hitting .421 as a sophomore, and he played basketball on the varsity team. At the conclusion of his second year at the Naval Academy, he was presented the Thompson Trophy, which recognizes the student who has most impacted athletics at the Academy. Never before had a second-year man won the award.

Ironically, his worst day as a Navy football player occurred against Notre Dame during his sophomore season, when on a stormy

Philadelphia day, Staubach was held to 57 yards passing and 8 yards rushing in a freezing, icy, windy 20–12 loss.

Prior to the 1963 Notre Dame game, a headline in the *Washington Post* read, "Staubach Has Old Score to Settle." Staubach wanted to show Notre Dame personnel that his destiny had all along been to play in Annapolis and not under the shadow of the Golden Dome.

The annual Navy–Notre Dame game dates back to 1927, making it the longest uninterrupted intersectional rivalry in college football. Notre Dame had dominated the series up to that point, winning 27 of the 37 contests, 11 of which were shutouts, and settling for one tie.

The Navy team arrived in South Bend, Indiana, the Friday before the game. It was the Catholic holy day All Saints Day, so the Notre Dame campus was quiet with students observing the day and preparing for homecoming weekend festivities. By Saturday morning, gray skies had blown into town, bringing rain with them. On the field, the tarpaulin was laid from end zone to end zone while in the catacomb-like locker rooms, players got taped and focused on the game plan, as well as how special it was to participate in this storied rivalry.

For nearly all the Navy players, this game had great significance. It was widely believed that if you couldn't play *for* Notre Dame then you wanted to play *against* Notre Dame. For years the players had read about the exploits of Notre Dame football and Knute Rockne, and all the mystique that surrounded this national program of prominence. It was on newsreels at the local theaters that they would watch the men of South Bend win each week, sparking aspirations to someday play football at such a level.

❮ ❮ ❮

While waiting to take the field, Navy player John Connolly looked around the locker room and marveled at the setting and situation. Coach Hardin, who had donned a winter coat and a Navy baseball cap for the game, was conscious that some of the players were in awe of the Notre Dame aura. In the *South Bend Tribune*, Coach Hardin noted the unique experience and difficulty of playing in South Bend. "When you walk on the campus and see that Golden Dome," Hardin said, "you almost feel the hush. It's not like any campus anywhere. You look for their legends. You can almost feel them, it bothers you."

Recognizing that Connolly's face was filled with a mixture of wonder and trepidation, the coach walked over, put his hand on his shoulder, and said, "Don't worry son, the boys in the other locker room have the same feelings that you are feeling right now."

The players finished putting on their shoulder pads (Staubach, his left shoulder harness) and shirts and sat through the final anxious, pent-up moments prior to taking the field. Finally, as a team they rose to their feet and filed out of the locker room. As the players marched onto the field beneath the goalposts, the experience was almost surreal, as if they were watching the scene unfold on the television or movie screen. When they arrived at their sideline, they realized that they were the first team on the field. It was tradition at South Bend that Notre Dame allow the other team to take the field first so that when the Notre Dame players sprinted down the runway and onto the field, their opponents would be intimidated by their gold helmets and great size.

Even though the team was a long way from home, the Midshipmen always had great support wherever they traveled. As Notre Dame was a national team, Navy was an international team, with interest on every continent and every sea. For this game, the Navy team was accompanied by eighty midshipmen who joined the Notre Dame band as they marched on the field. Also present was an impressive list of Navy brass, including loyal followers Superintendent Rear Admiral Charles C. Kirkpatrick and Under Secretary of the Navy Paul Red Fay.

Back home in Annapolis, the rest of the brigade, along with Assistant Coach Steve Belichick's son, Bill, gathered at the Halsey Field House to watch the game on a big-screen television via closed circuit. Behind the Navy bench, the team set up loudspeakers that were connected by telephone cable to the gym so the cheers from Annapolis could be communicated to the team.

Tom Lynch went out for the opening coin toss, looking down—he couldn't believe the size of the Notre Dame players, their feet, calves, thighs. He stopped there. Notre Dame won the coin toss and elected to receive the ball.

Throughout the first quarter, the defenses dominated play, with punters and tacklers most prevalent. On Notre Dame's first punt of the day, the Navy players peeled off to set up a return and lure the Irish's punt team into a false second of security. On the next two punts Navy would put nine men on the line of scrimmage and both times pressure Notre Dame punter Dan McGinn, forcing him to try to run and pass, both times unsuccessfully. The second turnover set up the first score of the day, Navy 7–0, a Staubach pass to Gary Kellner followed by the Marlin point after.

Notre Dame took the ensuing kickoff and marched down the field to tie the game going into halftime. Coach Hardin was furious. The victory over Pittsburgh would all be for naught if the team didn't win this game. Realizing he needed to light a fire under his players, he found it necessary to diminish the aura of Notre Dame, which appeared to be greatly affecting Navy's play. He would get on the team the moment they walked into the locker room.

As they sat eating oranges, the players could tell by the red face that glowed behind the freckles of their coach that the team was in for a lashing. Hardin knew that Notre Dame had faded in the second half in their losses to Wisconsin (13–9), Purdue (8–7), and Stanford (24–14). Thus his Navy team needed to get a lead and knock the opponent out. The coach, pacing back and forth, took off his Navy baseball cap and started, "The Four Horsemen are dead. They're not playing against us." Pausing for effect, he continued, "And another thing: God isn't on their side. We have more Catholics than them. You boys are doing a disservice to yourself and the brigade! You need to start busting your butts out there and play like you're the number-four team in the country." Hardin then held up the speech to allow Captain Tom Lynch to escort Roger Staubach out of the locker room under false pretenses so that the coach could complete his speech.

Once Lynch and Staubach were out on the field, Hardin continued: "Now you boys know that Roger has a chance to win the Heisman. But if we don't win this game it's over for him. Just give him some time out there. He'll do the rest. Doesn't he deserve that from you?"

The other players loved Roger Staubach, as he loved them. There was no false pretense in him. He was humble and considerate. The team wanted good things for him not because of the player he was but because of the person he was. So when the team took the field to rejoin its quarterback and Lynch, it was filled with a fury to succeed. Assistant Coach Carl Schuettee told Hardin later that it was his greatest speech. Coincidentally, the speech occurred just feet from where the legendary coach Knute Rockne used to inspire his Notre Dame players.

Navy received the opening kick of the second half. Taking the ball on the 30-yard line, the Midshipmen proceeded to march down the field. First on a middle screen to Donnelly, followed by a jump pass to Kip Paskewich, and finishing in the end zone on a roll-left pass to Donnelly from the 8-yard line to the front of the end zone. In three minutes, the Navy men had paraded down the field and propelled themselves into the end zone.

On Navy's effort, George Minot wrote in the *Washington Post*, "It was a different Navy team that came out of the dressing room to answer the second half whistle."

It was on the chalkboard, during film sessions, and in advanced scouting that Navy was able to expose its opponents' weaknesses. Prior to the Pittsburgh game, the staff solved the riddle of the 5–3 defense by using their two ends. On the Thursday prior to the Notre Dame game, Coach Hardin introduced the option play to his team. Twice in the second half, Navy used the play successfully. Donnelly would be the recipient of two wonderful, two-handed chest passes by Staubach. One led to a long gain down the right sideline, while the other was nothing more than the Xs and Os moving exactly as drawn by the coaches. From the Notre Dame 41-yard line, Staubach took the snap and moved left. Surrounded by four Irishmen, he stopped and pushed the ball with two hands just over the outstretched arms of Jack Snow of Notre Dame to a streaking Donnelly, who moved on his left. On his knees, Pat Philbin blocked two defenders while Jim Campbell cracked back and flattened one player while taking out a second. Johnny Sai, who had led Donnelly out of the backfield, wiped out his man, and the run was finished off when Dave Sjuggerud put his assignment on the ground.

Navy would score four times in the second half, which included two more touchdowns in a span of 44 seconds—one on a patented Sai dive into the end zone, followed up by Gary Kellner's second touchdown of the game on an 8-yard interception return, which was forced by a marauding Neil Henderson, who was draped all over the Notre Dame quarterback.

Prior to the game, Assistant Coach Steve Belichick noted that Notre Dame was struggling with its passing game. This, like most Belichick observations, was spot-on. In the second half, the Irish would throw the ball 13 times and complete zero passes while throwing three interceptions, two to Steve Moore and one to Kellner.

The final score of the game was 35–14, the most points Navy had ever scored in the series. The second half was played for Staubach, but the star of the game was the quarterback's traveling roommate, Donnelly. In Minot's *Washington Post* column, he said of the halfback, "A fine broth of an Irish lad, Pat Donnelly ran wild." Minot added, "Navy laid the old shillelagh to Notre Dame today."

Donnelly, an A student, president of his class, and an all-American lacrosse player on the Navy team that would win three straight national titles, was considered by many to be one of the top backs in the country. On the defensive side, he tackled and intercepted, while as a quick kicker he averaged over 50 yards. His coach would say of the five-foot-eleven, 193-pound back, "He is strong and runs like a fullback, and he can go, too, like a halfback." A quiet, unassuming kid from Maumee,

**#4 U.S. Naval Academy (6–1)**
**@ University of Notre Dame (2–4)**

Notre Dame Stadium . South Bend, Indiana

November 2, 1963 . 1:00 p.m. kickoff (CST) . Attendance 59,362

| | 1 | 2 | 3 | 4 | Final | | Navy | Notre Dame |
|---|---|---|---|---|---|---|---|---|
| Navy | 0 | 7 | 21 | 7 | 35 | First Downs | 16 | 11 |
| Notre Dame | 0 | 7 | 0 | 7 | 14 | Rushing Yards | 191 | 109 |
| | | | | | | Passing Yards | 91 | 28 |
| | | | | | | Pass Att.–Comp. | 15–9 | 18–2 |
| | | | | | | Fumbles Lost | 3 | 0 |
| | | | | | | Interceptions by | 3 | 0 |
| | | | | | | Penalty Yards | 46 | 73 |

Navy — TD, Kellner, 2-yard pass from Staubach (Marlin kick)

ND — TD, Budka, 2-yard run (Ivan kick)

Navy — TD, Donnelly, 8-yard pass from Staubach (Marlin kick)

Navy — TD, Sai, 1-yard run (Marlin kick)

Navy — TD, Kellner, 8 yard interception return (Marlin kick)

Navy — TD, Donnelly, 41-yard run (Marlin kick)

ND — TD, Kantor, 10-yard run (Ivan kick)

Ohio, he was recruited by both Michigan and Ohio State. It was in the biggest arena of them all where he shined most, running for 127 yards on 14 carries and 41 receiving yards with 2 touchdowns.

Donnelly and his other teammates had been determined to win for their quarterback. The defense suffocated Notre Dame in the second half, with Lynch leading the way with 13 tackles. The offensive and defensive lines of Navy were singled out by Notre Dame coach Hugh Devore after the game. "Pursuit was the best word to describe Navy's forward wall," Devore said. "With their aggressive charge, interior linemen like Pat Philbin, Captain Tom Lynch, Fred Marlin, John Connolly, and Al Krekich applied pressure throughout the game." Joe Doyle from the *South Bend Tribune* described the Navy lines as "fast and aggressive" on both sides of the ball. "They pursue the opposition continually and don't hesitate to pile on."

Of his team's effort, the executive vice president of Notre Dame, Father Edmund Joyce, who was previously affiliated with the Naval Academy, appeared in the locker room to tell the Navy team, "That showing was unacceptable. We'll make sure it doesn't happen again." Notre Dame would go on to win its next forty-three match-ups with Navy, winning every meeting of the rivals from 1964 to 2007.

So it was, on the field of Notre Dame Stadium—within the shadow of the golden dome where Staubach had once dreamed of playing his college ball—that Staubach's teammates showed their love and respect for him by sustaining the dream of a Heisman Trophy to recognize him for his special talent.

As Navy battled Notre Dame, the two other service academies, Air Force and Army, were waging battle at Soldier Field in Chicago, just west of South Bend. President Kennedy, always an advocate for the service academies, believed that athletics should serve as a showcase for the country's brightest and strongest. The president was scheduled to attend the contest and conduct the pre-game coin toss with the team captains.

President Kennedy penned the following message to be printed in the game program.

> To the Falcons and the Black Knights, my best wishes and good luck. Both teams can be counted on for a spirited, determined game.
>
> At any athletic event in which two of our service academies participate we see the spirit; the physical readiness and the mental alertness which carries forward into later professional careers of service to our nation. It is an inspiration to me, as Commander-in-Chief, and to all Americans to see these fine young leaders compete in Chicago today.
>
> We wish them well,
>
> John F. Kennedy

Unfortunately, President Kennedy was unable to attend the game, much to the disappointment of Chicagoans who were expecting a glimpse of the leader of the free world. Though the reason given for his absence was a disturbance in Vietnam, subsequent reports cited security precautions as the reason. Secret Service agent Abraham Bolden, in his book *The Echo from Daley Plaza*, explains that an assassination team of Cuban nationals was detected by a hotel worker who saw rifles with telescopic sights, as well as a map documenting the president's parade route. Another potential assassination team included Thomas Valle, an expert marksman who was apprehended by Chicago police carrying an M1 rifle, a handgun, and three thousand rounds of ammunition.

Days later, the president sat down and dictated a letter of explanation to the mayor of Chicago, Richard Daley.

11/8/1963

Dear Mr. Mayor,

I was extremely disappointed that I was unable to come to Chicago on November 2 for the Air Force–Army football game at Solider Field. I am well aware that the last minute change in my plans created numerous problems for you and this I regret sincerely. My decision to remain in Washington was taken with all concern and reluctance as I am sure you know you were most gracious to receive my guests and the members of my staff and to accord them the many courtesies of which they have informed me. I am especially grateful for your consideration in meeting them at the O'Hare International Airport and escorting them to the hotel and to the stadium.

All of the arrangements made by you and the members of your staff reflect the continuing hospitality and cordiality of the city of Chicago. I am most appreciative of this effort you expended and I extend my sincere thanks.

Sincerely,

John F. Kennedy

# CHAPTER 17

# Maryland vs. Navy, 1963

BENEATH THE SHINE OF THE FLOODLIGHTS, Lieutenant Commander Sam Jones stood at the microphone in front of Bancroft Hall and looked out over the twenty-four companies of midshipmen and roared, "Gentlemen of the brigade, I give you the number one team in the country!" On cue, the Navy band struck up "When the Saints Go Marching In," and the Navy football team marched forward. In the sea of midshipmen, white hats moved back and forth in concert with the notes of the music. It was the perfect forum in which to anticipate Saturday's upcoming game.

At the Friday night pep rallies, students would get the opportunity to personally send off their shipmates as they left to represent the Naval Academy. It was also an opportunity for Superintendent Rear Admiral Charles C. Kirkpatrick to tell his men, "Whatever you set your mind to do, nothing can stop you," and for Coach Wayne Hardin to make a pledge, "Tomorrow will be no different! We have a major opponent, but we have the brigade behind us and we will win."

From the first day a midshipman puts a Navy helmet on, he is indoctrinated with one goal: "Beat Army." Second to that sentiment is one that plebes head coach Dick Duden always preached: beat intrastate rival, the University of Maryland. "Gotta hate the hell out of these guys," Duden was known to say.

Separated by only thirty miles, the Naval Academy and the University of Maryland are natural rivals. Over time, the schools have morphed from competitors into outright antagonists. Animosities born through both athletics and proximity increased over time—the schools would compete not only for lacrosse championships (since 1936 Navy has won eight national championships to Maryland's seven) but also for co-eds. Midshipmen in sparkling white uniforms and shiny shoes were seen to have a competitive advantage with Maryland co-eds at dances and local taverns.

The rivalry began in 1888, when the Maryland Agricultural School football team beat the Navy team in the first sporting event between the schools. From that point forward, each ensuing sporting contest served to stoke the intense fire of competition that existed between the two institutions, as numerous examples attest.

- In 1910, the two schools were tied in baseball 1–1 after nine innings. As the game went to extra innings, the sun began to fall. By nightfall neither team would agree to surrender, so lanterns were brought in to light the field. Eventually, the game was called after fifteen innings and the teams still locked in a 1–1 tie.
- In 1917, the Navy football team beat the Old Liners of Maryland 62–0, and months later the Midshipmen basketball team beat Maryland 58–1. No mercy.
- In 1930, Maryland lacrosse beat an undefeated Navy team at Annapolis during graduation weekend, thwarting the Midshipmen's national title aspirations. At the end of the game, the Maryland band stormed the field and played "Maryland, My Maryland."
- In 1934, Maryland accused Navy footballers of using ineligible players in their 16–13 victory.
- In 1939, the Navy–Maryland lacrosse match had national championship implications. The *Washington Post* described the scene: "In a driving rain with players swearing and swinging

at each other, . . . the rivalry began to get serious, and on a time out two minutes later, Meade had a large cut over his eye. Munson's shoulder was cracked sufficiently to remove him from the game and [coaches] 'Rhythm' Moore and Bill Cole were squaring off."

- In 1950, the football game was played for the first time since the 1934 illegal player dispute. Navy administration warned the brigade "to behave like gentlemen and go straight home after the game."
- Before the 1951 football game, an "N" was painted on a Maryland campus building and on the football field.
- In 1952, seven players were ejected from the football game, which Maryland won 38–7.
- In 1959, Maryland supporters vandalized the statue of Tecumseh with spray paint.
- In 1961, the battle between the two undefeated freshman football teams was a hard-fought game that further spread seeds of acrimony that would blossom in the coming years.

The intensity of Navy–Maryland fire was further stoked in 1963 by the appearance of Darryl Hill in a Maryland uniform. Hill had been a member of the highly successful Naval Academy plebe team in 1961, whose only defeat was a devastating and highly emotional 28–26 loss to Maryland. Just months after Maryland coach Lee Corso witnessed Hill's first-rate performance against his Terrapin freshman team—in which the back scored two touchdowns, including a 98-yard kickoff return—Corso encouraged Hill to transfer to Maryland.

Hill was the first African American to play football for Navy. As his first year as a midshipman progressed, his doubt that he was in the right place grew stronger. The idea of being an officer did not appeal to him, nor did the restrictions that were placed upon him at the Naval Academy. He felt restrained and incapable of fully expressing himself as a student, player, and teenager. Ultimately, he convinced his parents that Annapolis wasn't the place for him. The following fall,

Hill was on the campus of the University of Maryland. Upon taking the field for the Terps, Hill broke the color barrier in the Atlantic Coast Conference.

The week before the game offered displays of gamesmanship on a couple of fronts. In anticipation of continued rivalry high jinks, for the 1963 Crab Bowl Navy administrators took unprecedented steps to protect the statue of Tecumseh and the team's mascot, Billy XV. The goat was kept at an undisclosed off-campus location and would be transported to the game by armed escorts.

In his comments leading up to the game, Maryland coach Tom Nugent expressed the sentiment that Navy was far and away the better football team, adding that his team would have to score at least 35 points if it had any chance to compete with the Midshipmen. His opinion was that his defense was incapable of holding the Navy team. Maryland's athletic director, William Cobey, spoke at a press conference of the Terps' lack of confidence: "We see that the small craft warnings are up around here, and we're afraid they're going to still be up on Saturday, and we're just hoping to sail in and sail out in full sail."

The newspapers also featured bulletin board material from Hill, who stated, "I'm pointing to this game." There were sixteen players on the 1963 Navy roster who had played with Hill on the 1961 plebe team. Some of them had a negative opinion of their former teammate and felt he had been a bad teammate and was afraid to get hit or work hard. They looked forward to the opportunity to administer some Navy hospitality whenever he touched the ball.

The Maryland game was the third Navy game that was featured by the media as a contest between all-American quarterback candidates. In the season opener, the press anticipated that West Virginia's Jerry "the Most" Yost would match Staubach pass for pass. In the end, the Mountaineers scored only seven points. Similarly, Pittsburgh's stud quarterback, Fred Mazurek, ultimately wilted against the Midshipmen and ended up watching the game from the bench. Maryland boasted a first-rate quarterback, Dick Shiner, and thus the headlines in the papers proclaimed, in one form or another, that the game would be a duel between Shiner and Staubach.

❨ ❨ ❨

From the moment Hill appeared on the Navy–Marine Corps Memorial Stadium field, he was booed. Right or wrong, the brigade viewed Hill as a quitter who turned his back on the Academy. As far as the midshipmen in the crowd were concerned, this was the perfect forum in which to express their displeasure with Hill.

The Navy players effectively expressed themselves too. They swarmed the Old Liners on both sides of the ball. Fred Marlin intercepted a Shiner pass at midfield, leading eventually to a Staubach 2-yard touchdown. They followed that with a Sai touchdown run and a vintage Staubach play to convert the two-point conversion, where he scrambled 15 yards back only to find Navy's number one tennis player and halfback Bob Teall for two magnificent points.

The final Navy touchdown was scored by Jim Ounsworth, who scampered 8 yards around end and into the end zone. Ounsworth was known to his teammates as "Snorter" because of the way he grunted while he ran. Coach Hardin admired the six-foot, 185-pound fullback's ability to get the most out of his skills and always get the job done.

In the fourth quarter, Darryl Hill caught his only ball of the game, for a 23-yard touchdown, his seventh of the season. That was the play of the day for Hill, who, being the source of the entire brigade's attention, lashed out to defend himself. As described in the following day's *New York Times*, Hill and Dick Melcher were "tossed out of the game for throwing punches in the closing minutes, and these were about the best offensive gestures Maryland made all day."

When all was said and done, Navy had put 35 straight points on the scoreboard and 42 overall. The play of the game was when Kip Paskewich made a one-handed interception on the Navy 24-yard line

## #4 U.S. Naval Academy (7–1)
## vs. University of Maryland (2–6)

Navy–Marine Corps Memorial Stadium . Annapolis, Maryland

November 9, 1963 . 1:30 p.m. kickoff . Attendance 30,035

|          | 1 | 2  | 3 | 4 | Final |
| -------- | - | -- | - | - | ----- |
| Maryland | 0 | 0  | 0 | 7 | 7     |
| Navy     | 6 | 22 | 7 | 7 | 42    |

|                | Maryland | Navy  |
| -------------- | -------- | ----- |
| First Downs    | 14       | 17    |
| Rushing Yards  | 123      | 131   |
| Passing Yards  | 101      | 161   |
| Pass Att.–Comp. | 24–9    | 19–11 |
| Fumbles Lost   | 3        | 2     |
| Interceptions by | 1      | 4     |
| Penalty Yards  | 70       | 80    |

Navy    TD, Staubach, 2-yard run (kick failed)

Navy    TD, Sai, 2-yard run (Teall pass from Staubach)

Navy    TD, Paskewich, 76-yard interception return (Marlin kick)

Navy    TD, Staubach, 1-yard run (Marlin kick)

Navy    TD, Sjuggerud, 11-yard pass from Staubach (Marlin kick)

Navy    TD, Ounsworth, 8-yard run (Marlin kick)

MD      TD, Hill, 23-yard pass from Shiner (Hill kick)

and, after juggling the ball down the sideline, used his superior speed to obliterate Maryland players' angles, avoiding four separate tackles on his way to a scintillating 76-yard touchdown.

In all, Shiner would throw four interceptions while his team fumbled three other times. Early in the third quarter, with his team safely ahead 35–0, Staubach was removed from the game to a rousing cheer. Unbeknownst to opponents or media, Staubach had hurt his knee, putting the following week's game against Duke in jeopardy. Nevertheless, he had played enough to impress.

"There isn't much hope of an answer in college ball against a man who thinks and fakes like Eddie LeBaron, runs like old Tommy

Harmon, and passes as accurately as Sammy Baugh," claimed the *Washington Post*'s Bus Ham.

As far as Maryland coach Nugent was concerned, "Navy is the best team in college football, and Staubach is the best quarterback I've seen anywhere."

Navy completely dominated its intrastate rival. In the following day's paper, Bob Serling of UPI found the bright side of Maryland's trip to Annapolis: "The Maryland band put on a great show at halftime with their fine music and intricate maneuvers."

While Navy was dictating the fate of the Maryland Terrapins in the Crab Bowl, President Kennedy was exercising compassion as he spent the day giving pardon to a fifty-five-pound turkey, Tom Turkey, who wore a sign around his neck that read, "Good Eating, Mr. President."

Regarding the Midshipmen's fate, prior to the game the Navy athletic department had released the qualifications that must be met in order for the Naval Academy to accept a bowl invitation:

1. Navy must have a representative excellent season.
2. The players must want to go and face giving up part of the Christmas holiday leave and possibly some time from their studies.
3. Officials at the State Department and Naval Academy must feel it is in the interest of the Navy for them to play.
4. The team must beat Army.

Following the Maryland game, bowl officials visited with Navy brass regarding the team's future. In the president's future, after Thanksgiving dinner with his family in Hyannisport, was the Army–Navy game in Philadelphia on November 30.

# CHAPTER 18

# President Kennedy and the Color Barrier

CIVIL RIGHTS WAS AN ISSUE THAT ENVELOPED THE ENTIRE COUNTRY in the early 1960s. Throughout his presidency, John F. Kennedy challenged those who rebuked change and tolerance for all people. While Darryl Hill was effectively the Jackie Robinson of both Navy and Atlantic Coast Conference football, in Washington, D.C., the owner of the NFL's Redskins remained steadfast in the belief that maintaining an all-white team was his right. George Preston Marshall refused to draft or sign black players, and when asked when he would sign his first black player, Marshall retorted, "We'll start signing Negroes when the Harlem Globetrotters start signing whites."

President Kennedy recognized that sports were interwoven with American society, and he could not accept a spirit of intolerance within such a high-profile national entity. The president's staff looked to leverage its power to compel Marshall to integrate the Redskins by exploiting its quasi-partnership with the team. In 1961, the Redskins signed a thirty-year lease with the city of Washington to play their home games at the newly constructed District of Columbia Stadium (later called RFK Stadium). The facility was funded with city monies, thus the team was ultimately dependent upon the government to play its home games in the city. To force integration, the Kennedy administration threatened to void the lease unless the Redskins agreed to select a black player in the coming draft.

Hoping to mend any differences that the White House might have with the league, NFL commissioner Pete Rozelle wrote to his former University of San Francisco classmate and now Kennedy press secretary, Pierre Salinger:

Pete Rozelle to Pierre Salinger,

The next time you have a swimming pool conference with the President, I would appreciate it if you would learn his feelings on the following:

1. Attending the Washington Stadium Opening for the Redskins

2. Being presented with a Gold League pass

[Interior Secretary] Udall accepted the commitment [George] Marshall made to draft a Negro player next December and I do not feel that this is a major problem now. Perhaps we could talk on the phone after you have had a chance to discuss it with him.

Stay loose.

Regards,

Pete Rozelle

Commissioner

That December, the Redskins drafted African-American running back Ernie Davis with the number one pick in the draft. When Davis was in New York in early December to accept the Heisman Trophy (the first African American to win the award), President Kennedy, who was also in New York, sought out the Syracuse University running back to gauge his intentions. When they finally met at the Waldorf Astoria Hotel, the president asked, "What are your future plans, Ernie?" Davis' answer was noncommittal, "I play in the Liberty Bowl at Philadelphia on December 16, Sir. After that I haven't made my mind up."

Davis, who was also drafted into the American Football League by Buffalo and entertained offers from Canadian teams, was well acquainted with the beliefs of the Redskins owner and immediately made his intentions known: "I won't play for that S.O.B." Davis was eventually traded to the Cleveland Browns.

President Kennedy's mission was to move the country forward in more ways than one. The proactive stance that the Kennedy administration assumed with regard to the Redskins was a good example of this ideal. The president was serving as a custodian for American change, and he saw sports as a model of how society should function. By connecting issues to sports, he provided a metaphor to which people could relate. Kennedy believed that sports and their prominent characters could help galvanize the nation.

Kennedy's contributions to both sports and society inspired legendary Army coach Earl Blaik and administrators from the National Football Foundation and the College Hall of Fame to select the president for the foundation's Gold Medal award in 1961. Kennedy greatly respected Blaik and his ability to coach and lead others, compiling a 121–33–10 record at Army that included two national championships. It was during the College Hall of Fame dinner that the two leaders would form a friendship based on mutual respect. Two years later, when the black churches in Birmingham, Alabama, were fire-bombed, the president called upon Blaik to investigate, assess, and arbitrate. When Blaik returned, he shared with the president that one of the most prevalent signs he saw in the South read, "Kennedy for King, Goldwater for President," in reference to the president's support of Martin Luther King Jr.

In the South, progress was proving painful, and race and football were interwoven elements. At the University of Mississippi, the football program became the rallying cry for segregation. Under the leadership of John Vaught, Ole Miss football was the finest program in the nation. After back-to-back national championships in 1959 and 1960, the team lost to Billy Cannon's LSU team in 1961, though

Ole Miss still finished fifth in the polls, recording a nine-win season and earning an invitation to the Cotton Bowl.

In 1962, Ole Miss came into the season ranked sixth in the nation. The University of Kentucky Wildcats traveled to Jackson, Mississippi, to play Vaught's powerhouse football team. The Rebel football program was in the midst of its greatest era and thus stirring great passion across the state, but for this Friday night football event with Kentucky, the game was secondary to the maelstrom that had engulfed the Ole Miss campus and the state of Mississippi. All eyes were focused on African-American James Meredith, who with the support of the White House intended to earn an education at the all-white University of Mississippi. His admission was ordered through federal courts and had the backing of President Kennedy, who continued to advocate for civil rights throughout the country. Despite the court orders to integrate, the school continued to reject Meredith's attempts to enter and register for school.

On the football field that night, the band led the team out of the locker room playing "I Wish I Was Born in Dixie," stirring the passions of 41,000 who waved their Rebel flags with vigor and determined purpose. The country watched as memories of the Old South were rekindled. A statement was being made to all those who were determined to compel the sovereign state of Mississippi to comply with national standards in adherence with federal law. This statement of purpose was further articulated as the crowd members stated their wishes to the president in the form of postcards that were handed out before the game, later signed and forwarded to the White House. The cards read, "Concentrate on Castro and Cuba and leave our fine state alone." In all, three hundred thousand postcards were handed out, and many of those were mailed to Washington.

Prior to arriving at the game, Mississippi Governor Ross Barnett, son of a Confederate solider, segregationist, and Ole Miss grad, had finally acquiesced to the pressure of the presence of federal troops and the White House and agreed with Attorney General Robert Kennedy to allow James Meredith to attend the state school. At the game, the passion and pomp of the crowd stirred within and caused his heart to veto his mind's prior decision. Governor Barnett then addressed the crowd from the field at halftime: "I love Mississippi. I love her people. I love our customs."

Three simple lines were enough to light the fire of hate and social unrest. Amid the blanket of Rebel flags that waved from side to side in the bleachers, a frenzied crowd was now inspired to sustain the status quo. After the game, Barnett called Attorney General Kennedy and rescinded his pledge to allow Meredith to attend Ole Miss. In response, President Kennedy sent the 101st and 82nd airborne to the campus to ensure that Meredith was afforded his rights, as promised to him in the Constitution of the United States. Governor Barnett responded by lowering the Rebel flags on the statehouse and stating, "There has been an invasion of our state resulting in bloodshed of our citizens."

The impasse led to violence, social unrest, and even death. Over twelve thousand troops were sent to Oxford, Mississippi, where tear gas would envelop the Ole Miss campus, turning the learning institution into a battleground of federal versus state power; segregationist versus those who wished to integrate; status quo versus progress. On the Monday following Ole Miss's 14–0 win over Kentucky, Meredith officially became a student at the school. Riots and fighting led to two deaths, forty-eight soldiers were injured, and twenty-eight federal marshals were shot and wounded.

A year later, in November 1963, just weeks before President Kennedy was to travel to Texas, the University of Texas announced that it would also be allowing blacks the opportunity to participate in varsity athletics in the coming year. Just three years earlier, the Texas team made Syracuse's African-American Ernie Davis a target of racial slurs and violent hits in the 1960 Cotton Bowl game in which Davis would be named MVP in the Syracuse victory. The school recognized change was inevitable, and at the same time it was increasing its pool of talent that could be drawn upon.

Though the school was determined to allow blacks to play varsity sports, Texas officials would not allow the black players access to the athletic dorms. Texas, however, would be the first team in the Southwest Conference to allow blacks to play.

Progress was slow, but it was progress, bringing a sense of gratification to the president. When he was told of the Texas compromise, his statement succinctly summarized his feelings at the time: "Giving the Negro a chance at a fair life is my responsibility as president." President Kennedy found each report of integration hopeful, pleased that equal opportunity was slowly becoming a reality and that sports were leading the way.

# CHAPTER 19

# Duke vs. Navy, 1963

ON VETERANS' DAY 1963, PRESIDENT KENNEDY APPEARED at Arlington Cemetery to lay flowers at the Tomb of the Unknowns. It was his third appearance at the cemetery in the past eight months. He was accompanied by his two-year-old son, John. Prior to the wreath laying was a twenty-one-gun salute followed by the sounding of "Taps" by Sergeant Keith Clark, who played at all significant Arlington Cemetery events.

The president's original schedule only called for him to lay the wreath, but he decided to attend ceremonies at the amphitheatre and listen to Commandant of the Marine Corps General David Shoup speak about the special sacrifice that those who serve the country make for freedom. Shoup was a Medal of Honor recipient, Kennedy a Purple Heart recipient. "[The president] has expressed for all Americans past and present [his] deep gratitude to those who have made great sacrifices so that we can be here today, physically and mentally free."

Later that week, the president and wife Jacqueline received the elite drum and bagpipe band the Black Watch (Royal Highland Regiment) at the White House. The band's origin dates back to 1727 and King George II, and its motto reads, "No One Provokes Me with Impunity." The president quipped, "I think that is a very good motto for some of the rest of us."

Following the performance on the White House lawn, which was Jacqueline's first appearance in public since her son Patrick had died after his birth in August, press secretary Pierre Salinger announced that the president's wife would join her husband on a Texas political junket from November 20 to 22, 1963.

In Annapolis, the team prepared for a potent Duke team, and Navy coach Wayne Hardin was worried. Not only had Navy failed to beat Duke during his entire nine-year tenure as assistant and head coach at the academy, but also the team historically did not play well in the contest prior to the Army–Navy game. Too often, his team looked ahead.

At the Boat House following practice and dinner, the team was introduced to Duke in the form of film and chalkboard. The Blue Devils' most potent weapon was Jay Wilkinson, the son of the great Oklahoma football coach, Bud Wilkinson. Coach Belichick called Wilkinson a "cutback artist who runs like a jack rabbit finding daylight." During the season, the Duke halfback had touchdowns of 73 yards, 69 yards, 67 yards, and 45 yards, among others. In Duke's previous game against Wake Forest, Wilkinson out-dueled the Demon Deacons' all-American back, Brian Picolo, scoring three touchdowns. The senior was heavily recruited by Navy (though unsuccessfully) after his father announced that he preferred that his son not play for him or any of his opponents. Duke also had a scrambling quarterback, Scotty Glacken, from Maryland who was only five-foot-ten but was extremely effective when he utilized his lead receiver, Stan Crisson, who led Duke with 6 touchdowns and 36 receptions.

Hardin warned his players not to look past Duke and reminded them that the 1960 Navy team led by Heisman Trophy winner Joe Bellino had its national title hopes ruined by Duke in that year's Oyster Bowl by an embarrassing score of 30–9. Furthering the coach's angst was quarterback Roger Staubach's knee, which still ached from the Maryland game and would force him to wear a brace. Rumors swirled as to the extent of Staubach's injury.

Coach Hardin attended the weekly gathering of the Touchdown Club, where he was to speak to the attendees after they were addressed by navy brass. The lead speaker was Admiral David L. McDonald, chief of U.S. Navy operations. When he stood at the rostrum, he told the crowd that when he was at the Naval Academy, the Midshipmen never beat Army, and the fact that Navy had won four straight didn't mean they should feel empathy but instead no sympathy. The crowd clapped wildly in agreement with the admiral's sentiment, as they did after Secretary of the Navy Red Fay and Superintendent Rear Admiral Charles C. Kirkpatrick ended their speeches with a hearty, "Beat Army!"

As far as Hardin was concerned, this was exactly the sentiment that the Navy coach was chasing down, the type of spirit he was worried might permeate the mindset of all those in the Navy family. Hardin was petrified that his team might look past Duke. As he rose to speak, his blazing red hair was accentuated by his reddening face. Although it was simply a luncheon, Hardin was going to chastise the speakers and crowd to relay his message loud and clear, saying,

> You people in the audience who root for Navy want us to beat Army. But it is truly an obsession with us. At the Academy we preach "Beat Army" 365 days a year. I'm not forgetting that Duke is one of the top teams in the country. This week we're going to look at one of the greatest halfbacks in the country in Duke's Jay Wilkinson. We have never yet played an outstanding game before the Army–Navy contest.

Coach Hardin's Navy squad arrived in Durham duly warned of the potential for disaster.

❨ ❨ ❨

A sellout crowd at Duke Stadium amid perfect skies was ready for the second-ranked Navy team. Duke maintained a 10-game winning streak at home. Prior to the game, efforts by the Blue Devil fans to abscond with the Navy mascot were successfully fended off by midshipmen in the crowd, just as they had done before the West Virginia game.

Duke won the coin toss and elected to receive the opening kickoff. The initial drive was repelled by Navy. It would be the only drive in the first half that didn't produce a score.

Navy would have four possessions in the first half and score 31 points, while Duke would tally 25. Staubach, knee brace and all, would run for a scintillating 95 yards in the first half on runs where he scrambled, ducked, cut, and jumped. The points came fast and furious for both squads.

- 7–0 Navy: Two weeks earlier at Notre Dame, Navy had used the same option, successfully pitching the ball. From the 4-yard line, Staubach ran the option but this time faked the pitch twice, drawing the defenders to the halfback and allowing him to walk into the end zone.
- 7–6 Navy: Duke received the kickoff and marched down the field, leading to a Biff Bracy 3-yard run. Navy's Nick Markoff blocked the extra point.
- 14–6 Navy: The Midshipmen drove 72 yards, highlighted by a 44-yard run by Staubach, who after being manhandled in the backfield escaped to the amazement of even the Duke fans. Johnny Sai finished the drive off from the 1-yard line. The elusive run by Staubach and multiple other magical plays roused Jack Germino of the *Herald Sun* to pen a column the next day with the headline, "Duke 'Almost' Had Their Man!"
- 14–12 Navy: Duke went 70 yards on 11 plays capped off by a Glacken 5-yard run. The 2-point attempt failed.

- 17–12 Navy: Fred Marlin kicked a 31-yard field goal after a 27-yard run by Staubach.
- 19–17 Duke: Crisson scored on an 11-yard pass from Glacken; the drive was greatly aided by a long pass-interference call.
- 24–19 Navy: Nick Markoff ran for 5 yards, capping off a five-play, 68-yard drive. The feature play was a spectacular 30-yard catch by Neil Henderson, which Nick Herbert of the *Raleigh News & Observer* described as follows: "End Neil Henderson, running at full speed, had to leap far forward to get his fingertips on the ball. He held on as he fell to the ground. It was as spectacular a catch as you will see anywhere."
- 31–19 Navy: Navy end Dave Sjuggerud read the screen play; fought through two blockers, stepped in front of the intended receiver, and intercepted a Scotty Glacken pass on the flat. Sjuggerud ran 36 yards for the score to give Navy its second touchdowns in forty seconds. Hardin would later say, "It was one of the greatest jobs I have ever seen of a boy knowing what was going on. He had the play figured out in his head as soon as Duke lined up. He was determined to get the ball."
- 31–25 Navy: In the last two minutes of the half, Duke drove the length of the field, culminating in a Jay Wilkinson 1-yard run with two seconds remaining.

By the end of the first half, both Navy and Duke had earned 13 first downs. The final three touchdowns were scored in a 2:48 span. It was exactly what Coach Hardin had worried about all week: being on the road, in the midst of a shootout against a talented Duke team.

As they entered the locker room, Hardin gathered the coaching staff in a side room and instructed them not to talk to the team. He wanted his players to reflect on their effort collectively, without the interference of the coaches. In the back room, the coaches made adjustments on defense and decided to follow the Duke man in motion and on third down rush the quarterback, leaving the flat open. As Navy made adjustments at the half so did Duke, who decided not to stunt but instead to match up man to man with the Navy offense. Duke coach Bill Murray realized what eight other coaches had discovered too late: Staubach thrives when teams pressure him.

Toward the end of intermission, Navy coach Hardin led the coaches out into the locker room and stood in front of his players, who knew by his silence that he was not pleased. "Do you really think you can score 62 points?" he asked his team, sternly. "Because if you don't, then you better start playing defense."

And defense they played. Throughout the second half the Navy team was under siege. What was a shootout in the first half turned into a scoreless war that featured what Navy players would later describe as the hardest hitting they ever experienced. The two teams, said Navy lineman Al Krekich, were "in the trenches, beating the shit out of each other!"

Seven times in the second half, the Duke offense ventured into Navy territory. The last four drives started on the Navy 38-, 39-, 47-, and 44-yard lines, but in all four Duke would fail to make a first down.

With just over two minutes to play in the game and Navy clinging to a 31–25 lead, Duke punter Rod Stewart dropped a kick deep in Midshipmen territory, which his teammates downed on the 5-yard line. If Duke could hold them and force Navy to punt, Wilkinson, the best return man in the country, would be waiting to win the game. On first down, Navy ran for 2 yards, setting up second down and 8 yards to go. From the sideline the call came in to run the "27 off 36 tackle" play, which called for the ball to be handed off to halfback Johnny Sai.

Sai was a senior halfback and a three-year starter. Along with playing football, he was a top East Coast sprinter on the track team, with a personal best of 9.7 seconds in the 100-yard dash. Sai came to the Academy by way of Oakdale, California, just outside of Oakland. His parents were dairy farmers and had limited resources. He was appointed to the Naval Academy by his local congressman, and when he traveled to Annapolis to serve his plebe orientation, it was the first time he had been on a plane.

With quick feet that allowed him to slide through holes, he frustrated defenders with what Coach Hardin called "Hula-Hoop hips," preventing defenders from squaring him up. Built in compact form, he measured five-foot-eight and 183 pounds, which led some to call him Squatty Johnny; others called him Rags because his Midshipmen uniform always seemed to look disheveled when he walked across campus, shirt tail flapping and pants wrinkled. Army coach Paul Dietzel called him a "squirting type of runner who seems to float past tacklers."

As a sophomore, Sai led the team in rushing with 472 yards only to suffer from mononucleosis in his junior year and run for just 302 yards. To this point in his senior season, highlights included a spectacular 47-yard run against West Virginia and a game-changing 54-yard catch against Michigan at the end of the first half. But this was his moment, as Sai would describe in his own words, the ultimate team play:

> The play was 27 off 36. We were in split backs, Pat Donnelly on the right and [me] on the left. Pat crossed in front of me and took a fake from Roger, and ran to the left side pretending he had the ball and then sealed off the right defensive end. He [Staubach] then handed the ball off to me and faked a roll-out to the left. The fake to Pat caused the Duke safety to come up and tackle Pat and so he was nowhere to be found when I got upfield. Right end Dave Sjuggerud blocked down on the left defensive end driving him well inside and opening a big hole. Right tackle Jim Freeman blocked the left inside linebacker

and drove him to the ground (a de-cleater, as we call it). He ended up face to face with the line backer while lying on top of him. Right guard Alex Krekich blocked the left defensive tackle keeping him from going outside to the hole as well as keeping him from penetrating and blowing up the play. Center Tom Lynch blocked the right defensive tackle and the same as Alex kept him from getting to the hole and penetrating. Left guard Fred Marlin pulled to the right and kicked out the left outside line backer giving me a great hole between his block and Dave Sjuggerud's block. Left tackle Pat Philbin cut off the right inside line backer and kept him from pursuing to the hole. Left end Jim Soupy Campbell ran across the formation to the right and got to the hole about the same time as I did. I had to stutter step to miss him but he got between me and the left cornerback who was coming up to tackle me in the hole. Flanker Ed [Skip] Orr was the split left and was supposed to block the right cornerback. But the right cornerback was Biff Bracy who was a former South Carolina 100-yard dash champion. I just ran my path to the hole after taking the hand off from Rog and saw nothing but green grass after getting through the hole. When I got to the 25-, 30-yard line the thought crossed my mind that coach would kill me if I got caught, so I went from running back to sprinter and managed to outrun Biff Bracy.

In my experience of eight years of playing and thirty years of coaching, it was the best executed play that I have ever seen. Everybody did their job just as it was drawn up on the chalkboard.

This was the essence of Navy football—men, coaches, and players working together for one goal.

After breaking through the hole and into the open, Sai noted to himself that he had never been caught from behind before, and he wouldn't this time. By the time he made it to the 50-yard line,

## #2 U.S. Naval Academy (8-1)
## @ Duke University (5-3-1)

Duke Stadium . Durham, North Carolina
November 16, 1963 . 2:30 p.m. kickoff . Attendance 41,000

| | 1 | 2 | 3 | 4 | Final |
|---|---|---|---|---|---|
| Navy | 14 | 17 | 0 | 7 | 38 |
| Duke | 6 | 19 | 0 | 0 | 25 |

| | Navy | Duke |
|---|---|---|
| First Downs | 19 | 16 |
| Rushing Yards | 308 | 177 |
| Passing Yards | 122 | 116 |
| Pass Att.–Comp. | 14–7 | 17–9 |
| Fumbles Lost | 2 | 1 |
| Interceptions by | 1 | 1 |
| Penalty Yards | 56 | 3 |

Navy — TD, Staubach, 5-yard run (Marlin kick)

Duke — TD, Bracey, 3-yard run (kick blocked by Markoff)

Navy — TD, Sai, 1-yard run (Marlin kick)

Duke — TD, Glacken, 5-yard run (pass failed)

Navy — FG, Marlin, 31 yards

Duke — TD, Crisson, 11-yard pass from Glacken (kick)

Navy — TD, Markoff, 5-yard run (Marlin kick)

Navy — TD, Sjuggerud, 36 yard interception return (Marlin kick)

Duke — TD, Wilkinson, 1-yard run (kick failed)

Navy — TD, Sai, 93-yard run (Marlin kick)

Bracy had taken advantage of his angle and closed within 2 yards. At that moment both sprinters morphed from football players into track competitors, stride for stride, racing down the sideline with 41,000 fans cheering them on. It wasn't until the 5-yard line that Sai knew he would score and secure victory for Navy. The 93-yard touchdown was the longest in Navy history.

When he made it to the sideline, Coach Hardin needled him that he was dogging it, allowing that defender to stay with him for so long. Sai was too tired to converse and made his way directly to the bench, where no Navy player ever sat. From the sideline, Hardin yelled over, "Hey, Sai, the game's not over."

Navy would carry the day, beating the spirited Duke team 38–25. The two teams combined for 723 yards of offense, 506 of them in the first half. Bob Hoffman of the *High Point Enterprise* called Staubach's performance "probably one of the greatest individual deeds by a gridder in this state in many a day."

After the game Hardin told his team there was no time to rest; Army was next, and there would be no underestimation of Army.

At the post-game press conference, he puffed on a cigar while relishing the win and answering questions. "I think both coaches started thinking a little more about defense in the second half," Hardin said. "It was a wide-open offensive first half. I don't think I can remember a game as wild as this in the first half."

When asked about the prospect of a bowl game, he dismissed the very notion of looking ahead. His focus was on the Cadets of West Point. "As for bowl talk, we will have nothing to say until after the Army game. Nothing exists until we beat Army."

At West Point, the volume of mail arriving for Army coach Paul Dietzel was increasing dramatically by the day, many of the envelopes sporting an Annapolis postmark. Earlier in the year, the Naval Academy had pencils made with "Drive for Five" printed on them. Many of the 4,100 Naval Academy brigade members had sealed their pencils in envelopes, with the ultimate destination of Coach Dietzel's West Point desk.

Preparation for the annual Army–Navy rivalry game were now underway, from West Point to Annapolis to the White House.

Back in August, General James Lampert, secretary to the army chief of staff, had sent an invitation to President Kennedy to attend the Army–Navy game on the Saturday after Thanksgiving. Always excited to attend the special game, the president dictated the following reply:

Dear Jim,

The President has asked me to reply to your kind invitation to the football game on November 30 between the Military Academy and the Naval Academy. Barring unforeseen incidents, he plans to be there and we will begin to work with your representatives on the seating in the box.

Signed,

CV Clifton

Major General US Army Military Aide to the President

Prior to the Army–Navy game, the president was busy carrying out his duties as commander in chief. On November 19, three days after the Duke–Navy contest, he was in Tampa, Florida, to speak at the local National Guard armory. In *Ultimate Sacrifice*, authors Lamar Waldron and Thom Hartmann describe a plot to kill the president while he rode in his motorcade in Tampa. Assassins were said to be situated in a high-rise building along the parade route, similar to what had happened in Chicago a few weeks earlier.

# CHAPTER 20

# Dallas, November 1963

THE KENNEDY ADMINISTRATION REALIZED that in order to achieve full impact of its policies and leadership, a second term in the White House was imperative. Unquestionably, President Kennedy had resurrected a spirit of community and introduced a feeling of inclusion among the nation's citizens. However, the president and his administration were keenly aware that there was work to be done to ensure re-election. One needed only to look at Texas to see a state unconvinced that Kennedy was the right man for the forthcoming four years.

Understanding the potential impact of the state's vote in the 1964 election, a four-city tour through Texas for late November 1963 was arranged by the administration. On November 21, the president and first lady arrived in Texas. During stops in San Antonio and Houston, they were welcomed by enthusiastic crowds. Upon each arrival, Jacqueline Kennedy was presented yellow roses in honor of the famous Texas folk song, "The Yellow Rose of Texas." Everywhere she went, the crowds swooned at the sight of her.

When she appeared at a Fort Worth breakfast, the band, at the request of the president, played "The Eyes of Texas Are Upon You." All in attendance stood and cheered . When the president stood behind the podium to deliver his speech he first commented on his wife's popularity. "I introduced myself in Paris by saying that I was the man that

accompanied Mrs. Kennedy to Paris," he said. "I'm getting somewhat that same sensation as I travel around Texas." He paused as the
crowd laughed and his wife shyly smiled. He then added, "Nobody
wonders what Lyndon and I wear."

Following breakfast, the Kennedys boarded Air Force One and
flew to Love Field in Dallas, where they touched down at 12:37 in the
afternoon under a blue sky and were greeted warmly by the crowd.
Before getting into the presidential limousine, President Kennedy
and the first lady greeted those who came to the airport by shaking hands and saying hello. After the warm welcome, the president
entered the car and took his customary place in the back right seat,
while the first lady sat on his left. The host and hostess for the trip,
Governor John Connally and his wife, Nellie, sat in the jump seats
directly in front of the Kennedys. Behind the departing presidential limousine, Secret Service agents trailed. The limo was known to
them as SS-100-X.

SS-100-X weighed 7,822 pounds and was customized by the
company Hess & Eisenhardt. The car had three separate roofs that
included a metal top, a retractable bubble top for viewing, and a
convertible roof. None of the three were in place on this day, since
the president's people wanted to maximize the connection between
the Kennedys and the people of Dallas. The car was divided into
two sections, with a glass partition that could provide separation.
Each section possessed its own temperature control and radio. The
car contained two jump seats and a back bench that could seat three
comfortably. The car also had special compartments to allow for
storage of weapons, fire extinguishers, and first-aid kits.

The president's limousine was followed by eleven vehicles.
The second vehicle, known as *Halfback*, contained Secret Service
agents Emory Roberts, John Ready, William McIntyre, Paul Landis,
and George Hickey, as well as the president's staff and friends Ken
O'Donnell and Dave Powers. Behind *Halfback*, the car called *Varsity* carried Vice President Lyndon B. Johnson, his wife, Lady Bird,

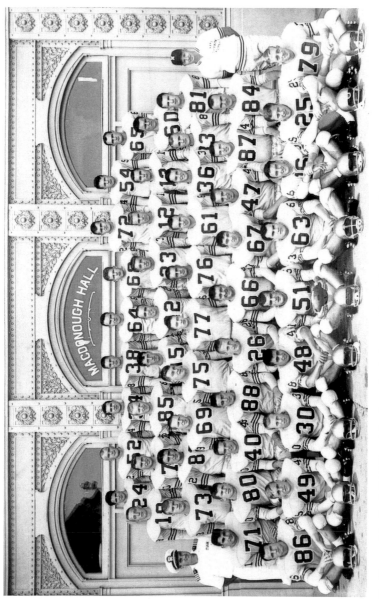

The "team of destiny": 1963 Naval Academy football team. *United States Naval Academy*

The star of the 1963 team, quarterback Roger Staubach would go on to win the Heisman Trophy and earn induction in the College Football Hall of Fame. *Bruce Bennett Studios/Getty Images*

Team captain Tom Lynch was the heart of the Navy defense in 1963 and heart and soul of the entire team. *United States Naval Academy*

Al Krekich was a key cog on Navy's massive front line, an aggressive blocker who kept opposing defenses frustrated in their vain pursuit of Staubach. *United States Naval Academy*

Fullback Nick Markoff's main claims to fame were catching the longest reception in the history of the Army–Navy game (a 65-yard toss from Staubach in the 1962 game) and allegedly kicking a cheerleader during a game with SMU. *United States Naval Academy*

Roger Staubach prepares to throw a pass against the Southern Methodist University Mustangs in October 1963. Although the Midshipmen gained 462 yards of offense compared to 290 for the Mustangs, SMU handed Navy its first and only loss of the regular season—thanks in no small part to some questionable refereeing. *Naval Academy Athletic Association Sports Information Department*

On October 26, 1963, Navy knocked off the number-three-ranked Pitt Panthers by a 24–12 score, helping assert the Midshipmen's place among the college football elite. Roger Staubach (number 12) and fullback Pat Donnelly (number 38) both ran for touchdowns in the game's fourth quarter. *Naval Academy Athletic Association Sports Information Department*

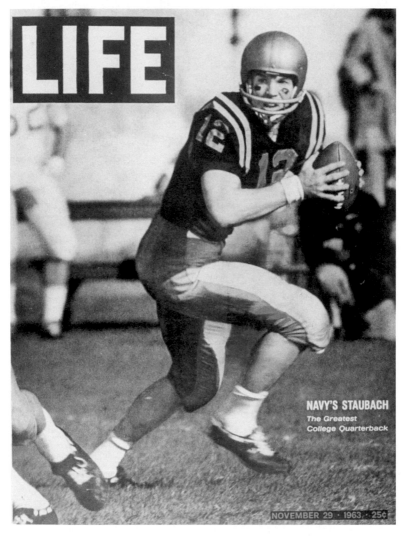

NAVY'S STAUBACH
*The Greatest
College Quarterback*

NOVEMBER 29 · 1963 · 25¢

*Life* magazine was all set to feature Roger Staubach on the cover of its
November 29, 1963, issue. Unfortunately, the tragic events of November 22
pushed Staubach off the cover as the nation struggled to come to grips with
the assassination of a beloved president. *Herb Scharfman/Time & Life Pictures/
Getty Images*

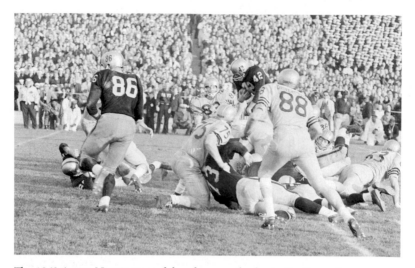

The 1963 Army–Navy game—delayed two weeks due to the Kennedy assassination—was an emotional event for both sides, and it came to a dramatic end. After Army's Ken Waldrop (number 42) was stopped by the Navy defense on the 2-yard line on third down, the Cadets failed to get off a final play before time ran out, leaving them 2 yards and 6 points down as the buzzer sounded. *AP Images*

Quarterback Roger Staubach and fullback Pat Donnelly enjoy the post-game celebration following Navy's fifth consecutive win over the Army Cadets. It was a cathartic moment for many of the Midshipmen after the difficult days of late November 1963. *Naval Academy Athletic Association Sports Information Department*

Roger Staubach capped off a memorable season in 1963 by becoming only the second Navy football player in history to win a Heisman Trophy. (The first was Joe Bellino in 1960.) Staubach would go on to a legendary pro career after leaving the Navy. *Jacob Harris/ AP Images*

Coach Wayne Hardin and his star quarterback Roger Staubach together built a formidable football team in 1963. Although they fell short of a national championship, the second ranking and 9–2 record at season's end proved that it was indeed a team of destiny. *United States Naval Academy*

Staubach puts up a valiant effort here to complete a pass during the
Cotton Bowl game on January 1, 1964, but the number-one-ranked
Texas Longhorns proved to be too much for the Midshipmen. The
Longhorns defense held Navy to a total of –14 yards rushing in
the 28–6 game. *George Silk/Time & Life Pictures/Getty Images*

Coach Hardin, in his trademark fedora, confers with Texas coach
Darrell Royal prior to the Cotton Bowl on New Year's Day 1964.
Hardin posted a record of 38–22–1 in six years as head coach—but
no wins were as big as the five straight against Army from 1959 to
1963. *Herb Scharfman/Time & Life Pictures/Getty Images*

rival Texas politician Senator Ralph Yarborough, and Secret Service agent Rufus Youngblood.

The destination for the president's motorcade was the Dallas Trade Mart, which was located ten miles from Love Field. Along the route, the president and his wife were cheered with great enthusiasm. Twice during the drive, Kennedy ordered his car stopped—once to greet schoolchildren and a second time to share a hello with nuns. Traveling straight down Main Street, the car turned right on Houston Street. From the jump seat in front, Nellie Connally turned to the president and boasted, "You can't say Dallas doesn't love you today." The president smiled as the motorcade made a slow left turn onto Elm Street, decreasing the car's speed to eleven miles per hour as it passed the front of the Texas School Book Depository.

In almost slow motion, as the car descended into Dealey Square, there was a loud cracking noise. Governor Connally immediately recognized it as a volley from a rifle. The president raised both elbows out and put his hands to his throat. In the trail car, agent Glen Bennett yelled, "He's hit!" First Lady Jacqueline Kennedy turned toward her husband and placed her white-gloved hands on him with concern. Instantly, a second shot rang out, and agent George Hickey noticed the president's hair blow in the air as the bullet passed, narrowly missing the distressed president. The bullet struck Connally, entering his back, ricocheting through him, and exiting the front.

The third shot caused a sound of such horror that those within earshot would never escape that echo of death. Striking the president in the head, the wound showered the occupants of the car in blood and brain matter, including Governor Connally, who lay prone on his wife's lap, bleeding profusely.

The first lady climbed out of her seat and onto the car's trunk, her pink wool suit covered in blood. Crawling on all fours, Jacqueline was seemingly desperate to make her husband whole again. Jumping onto the back of the car and urging Jacqueline back was agent Clint

Hill, who had sprinted from the trail car. With a toe on the step he catapulted himself onto the trunk just before driver Bill Greer raced under the triple overpass bridge ahead.

Once on the back of the car, Hill draped himself across the back, serving as a shield for the car's occupants. Looking back at the agents in the trail car, he shook his head "no" at them to indicate the president's fatal state. The first lady kept repeating, "I love you, Jack."

Governor Connally, who was seriously wounded, was yelling, "They're going to kill us all!" while the president's wife wailed, "They've killed my husband. I've got his brain in my hands. They've shot his head off." The country would never be the same.

Along the way to Parkland Hospital, the speeding limousine passed the Trade Mart, where the president had been scheduled to appear, including the following sentiments in his speech: "That we may achieve in our time and for all time the ancient vision of 'peace on earth, and good will toward men.' That must always be our goal, and the righteousness of our cause must always underlie our strength."

Instead of giving his speech, President John F. Kennedy lay fatally wounded in the presidential limousine. When the cars came to a skidding halt outside Parkland Hospital, Agent Emory Roberts leaped from the second car, ran up to the president's vehicle, and pleaded with the first lady, "Let us get the president." The first lady sat calmly in the back seat with her husband cradled in her lap and simply said, "No need." Roberts realized that John F. Kennedy was dead. He turned and gathered a team of agents and surrounded Vice President Lyndon Johnson, whisking him and his wife into a secure room in the hospital.

Twenty minutes later, the fallen president was pronounced dead inside Parkland Hospital, at approximately one o'clock in the afternoon.

John F. Kennedy entered the world privileged but was drawn to serve, not reap. A Navy hero, leader of the free world, a husband

and father of two, he would leave the world not on his own terms but instead a victim of violence.

In the closing paragraphs of his Pulitzer Prize–winning book *Profiles of Courage*, Kennedy wrote prophetically of the dangers of being a man of unwavering principle:

> The courage of life is often a less dramatic spectacle than the courage of a final moment; but it is no less a magnificent mixture of triumph and tragedy. A man does what he must—in spite of personal consequences, in spite of obstacles and dangers and pressures, and that is the basis of all human mortality.

# CHAPTER 21

# A Riderless Nation

JUST MINUTES AFTER PRESIDENT JOHN F. KENNEDY WAS SHOT, Walter Cronkite appeared on televisions in living rooms across the country. The trusted voice of America announced, "From Dallas, Texas, the flash, apparently official: President Kennedy died at 1:00 p.m. Central Standard Time, 2:00 Eastern Standard Time, some thirty-eight minutes ago."

His voice trailed off as the emotion of the moment overcame him, revealing a vulnerability never before seen or heard from the usually stoic CBS anchorman. In his right hand he held his black-rimmed glasses before placing them back on, as if he couldn't believe what he had read.

The news of the president's death greatly unsettled the country. In New York City, the New York Stock Exchange called for the emergency suspension of trading at 2:07 EST. Within the twenty-six minutes from the time it was announced that the president had been shot and the exchange's closing, the market had lost $11 billion in value.

The citizens of the country were unsure of the assassin's ultimate intention. Tensions with Russia and Cuba led many to wonder if the president's killing was part of an overall plan to attack the United States. As a result, the country and its military were placed on high alert. Borders separating the United States and Canada and the United States and Mexico were closed. All departing flights throughout the country were grounded. And military personnel were recalled from leaves domestically and internationally.

Naval Academy students were between classes when whispers of the president's assassination began to spread quickly. When the members of the brigade settled in their seats for their next classes, ashen-faced professors excused the students so everyone could began to grasp the tragedy that had unfolded.

The Navy football players made their way to the locker room to come together with their brothers. As the players sat in front of their lockers, unsure if they would have practice, Coach Wayne Hardin walked in with red eyes and a heavy heart. It was he to whom the president gave a hearty thumbs up after the Midshipmen defeated Army last year. It was Coach Hardin who received a letter of thanks from the White House for the signed football presented to the commander in chief at Quonset Point. It was Hardin who had promised the president that, in the upcoming season's Army–Navy game, Navy would put on a performance worthy of his great office.

Hardin announced to his players that the president was dead. With broken voice, he asked the team to join him in a prayer. As a team they had done everything together. They had survived double sessions underneath the hot Annapolis sun; they had stayed late and run extra plays after the coaches had released them from their duties. And now as a team they knelt on the cement floor and said a prayer for their fallen friend and the country he represented.

Players were excused and subsequently spread across the campus in search of answers. Captain Tom Lynch led a contingent of players, including Skip Orr and Roger Staubach, to the chapel; others went back to their rooms to listen to the radio or gathered in their company room, where the lone television was located.

Superintendent Rear Admiral Charles C. Kirkpatrick—who had sat with the president at the last two Army–Navy games and the previous summer at the White House had assured him that the Navy quarterback would be returning this autumn—released a comment to the press:

"The death of President Kennedy is a terrible shock and represents a great personal loss to each of us at the Naval Academy remembering the president's deep interest for the midshipmen during his visit last summer. We are all left with the knowledge that we have lost a great man and a firm friend."

The flag was lowered to half-mast on the campus, and the chapel was open for Catholic devotions Friday night and protestant services Saturday afternoon. On Saturday, the Naval Academy saluted President John F. Kennedy by firing into the empty sky every half hour from eight in the morning to sundown.

The Pentagon announced a one-month mourning period for all military and federal institutions. This meant that the Army–Navy game was placed on hold. "We all feel we have been hit in the pit of our stomach," Coach Hardin said. "We have no inkling on playing the game."

On the Sunday after the president's death, Press Secretary Pierre Salinger was walking through the White House en route to a meeting with now-President Johnson when he came upon Kennedy's former office. "The door to the President's office was ajar and I glanced inside," Salinger recounts in his book *With Kennedy*. "All of JFK's personal possessions had been taken away during the night—the rocking chair, the ship models, the marine paintings, the portraits of Caroline and John."

Kennedy's connection to the Navy and the Naval Academy had been on display in the Oval Office throughout his presidency. On his desk sat the coconut that he gave to the Solomon Island natives back in 1943 to help save his crew. On the walls hung two paintings that were loaned to the president from the United State Naval Academy Museum collection. The paintings, titled "In Action" and "Dropping Astern," depicted the USS *Constitution* in sea battle.

On Saturday, November 23, an upholsterer from Cape Cod worked for nine straight hours on the East Room to recapture the likeness of the room as it appeared in 1865, as Lincoln lay in death. Portraits of George and Martha Washington adorned the walls while black drapes were hung on the windows and around the crystal chandelier to match pictures of Lincoln's wake that were found at the National Archives. At the base of the mahogany coffin was draped an American flag, and a yellow candle stood at each corner of the casket while an arrangement of white lilies sat at the base of the coffin.

That same morning, the first Catholic mass ever celebrated in the White House was conducted. Later in the day while family, friends, and foreign dignitaries arrived at local airports, Robert Kennedy, Robert McNamara, and later Jacqueline Kennedy chose from three separate potential gravesites at Arlington Cemetery. In the end, they selected the site at the base of the Robert E. Lee mansion, which aligned directly with the American flag and the Lincoln Memorial. At the airport, a portable lounge was constructed to accommodate the royalty and world leaders who would arrive throughout the day.

At the Naval Academy, a single volley from a rifle continued to be fired on each half hour. The flags were flown at half-mast. Signs of cheer for the Army–Navy game were taken down and removed from windows, while the war paint that covered the statue of Tecumseh was cleaned.

In Washington, the president's body was brought to the Capitol to lie in state on Sunday. The coffin was transported by the same black caisson, or old weapons cart, that had been used two decades before to carry the body of Franklin Roosevelt to his funeral. The caisson was drawn by six white horses as drums pounded out a cadence of one hundred beats a minute. Behind the caisson, limousines carried family, friends, and President Johnson and Lady Bird Johnson.

When the caisson arrived at the Capitol, it came to a stop. The families and dignitaries exited their cars and stood at attention at the base of the steps while "Hail to the Chief" was played. For the first time, the former first lady was brought to tears in public. The 1,300-pound casket was then drawn from the caisson and carried up the thirty-six Capitol steps by the honor guard, the oldest military unit in the United States. The casket was placed beneath the rotunda, and the nation's citizens lined up throughout the day to view their fallen leader.

In January 1961, the Naval Academy Catholic Choir had traveled to Washington, D.C., to participate in President Kennedy's inauguration. It was a joyous occasion and a lifetime thrill for the members of the ensemble. Almost three years later, they would again journey to the nation's capital to sing, this time not in celebration but instead to take part in the tragic sendoff of their friend and commander in chief. At the request of the first lady, the choir was asked to sing "Londonderry Air" to the tune of "Danny Boy" as well as the Navy song "Eternal Father Strong to Save," which was sung every Sunday at the 9:00 a.m. mass at the Naval Academy chapel. Among those in the choir were football players Dennis Connolly and Mike Chumer, who looked forward to the opportunity to say goodbye as well as contribute on a day of such sad but historical significance.

The viewing of the president's casket at the Capitol ceased at 10:00 a.m. on Monday, November 25, after thousands had come to pay their respects.

In Annapolis, the Naval Academy Catholic Choir boarded a bus early that morning. The members of the choir did not know where they would be performing the songs they were asked to sing, but the ensemble was determined to perform well in honor of the fallen president. When they arrived in the capital city, they were informed that they would sing on the White House lawn as the procession carried the president's body to his funeral.

Suited in their dress blues, the members of the choir arrived on the chilly morning and took their places on the lawn facing the north entrance of the White House. After the family returned from the Capitol Building with the president's body, a procession began to form at the door.

After standing in place for hours awaiting their moment to sing, the members of the choir could see Jacqueline Kennedy, in black veil and dress, appear at the front of the procession, a stark contrast to the vibrant and beautiful woman whom football players Dennis Connolly and Mike Chumer had seen at Quonset Point or sitting next to her husband on the viewing stand during the inauguration festivities.

The former first lady was supported on each side by brothers-in-law Robert and Ted Kennedy. Kennedy's cabinet and friends followed behind the family, and then a long line of foreign dignitaries. The parade included 220 representatives from ninety-two countries, including eight heads of state, ten prime ministers, and forty state governors. The most prominent figure was the massive Charles de Gaulle of France, who himself had survived three assassination attempts and thus had nine Secret Service agents assigned to him; President Lyndon B. Johnson had eight.

As the procession continued to form, the choir conductor raised his arms, and the ensemble sang the somber Irish melody of "Londonderry Air" with serene beauty. Many in the procession would turn to face the singers as the notes guided the dignitaries toward the North Gate. As the parade of hundreds continued to pour from the White House door, the choir lifted into the Navy hymn of "Eternal Father Strong to Save," which it had sung just three years earlier to the president, rather than for the president.

At the conclusion of the serenade, the procession proceeded on foot through the streets of Washington to St. Matthew's Cathedral, led by the bagpipers of the Black Watch Royal Highland Regiment, who played "Brown Haired Maiden." When the procession arrived at the church, Mrs. Kennedy and the others were greeted by Cardinal Cushing of Boston, who had officiated at the wedding of John F. Kennedy and Jacqueline Lee Bouvier; baptized Caroline and John Jr.; and given the spiritual invocation at the president's inauguration. Cardinal Cushing cried on the steps of the church at the end of the proceedings.

The rest of the country paused from 12:00 p.m. to 12:05 p.m. in observance. Traffic stopped, Western Union ceased, and a bugler played "Taps" in Times Square. In England, the lights of Piccadilly Square were extinguished. At the Seabrook, New Hampshire, fire station, the flag of the PT 109, which was lent by Kennedy shipmate William Johnston, flew at half-mast. For the first time, the flag on the USS *Arizona* was lowered. On the aircraft carrier USS *Franklin D. Roosevelt*, a proclamation was read to the crew: "We of the USS *Franklin D. Roosevelt* have a more personal sorrow at his death not only because he was our commander in chief but also because he served courageously as well in the Navy during World War II. His concern, his interest, and his actions toward the Navy show he knew what only one who has served in the Navy knows, what the words 'a good shipmate' mean." A wreath of flowers was tossed into the Atlantic Ocean that Kennedy loved so much. A twenty-one-gun salute followed.

The funeral mass elicited countless tears. Luigi Vena sang "Ave Maria," a song he'd sung ten years prior at the Kennedys' wedding. Seated in the right front row with Jacqueline Kennedy and her two children were President Kennedy's mother, Rose, and brother, Robert. Across the aisle sat President Johnson along with former presidents Eisenhower and Truman. John Jr., who was celebrating his third birthday, walked from the pew and motioned toward the casket, announcing for all within earshot, "My daddy is in there." Later, John Jr. would stand on the steps of the church and salute his father's casket and caisson as it passed.

The president was laid to rest at Arlington National Cemetery Monday, November 25, 1963.

Beneath the shadows of a falling November sun, an honor guard carried the casket the final steps as the Air Force Pipers played "Mist Covered Mountain." The head of the casket was placed at the top of the grave to face out toward the Lincoln Memorial and the Potomac River. The Irish Guard that had performed for the president during his trip to his ancestral home the previous summer coordinated a drill maneuver. A parade of fifty jets, one for each state, flew in groupings of three, in V formation. The last group only had two planes to signify the fallen commander in chief. The jets were followed by Air Force One, flown by the president's pilot, Colonel James Swindal.

"Let the soul and all the souls of the faithful departed rest in peace," Cardinal Cushing said. In the distance, cannons fired, followed by three rounds of fire from a twenty-one-gun salute. At the conclusion, Keith Clark, the same musician who had played two weeks previous, turned his bugle toward Mrs. Kennedy and played "Taps." Jacqueline accepted the flag from the casket and then lit the eternal flame, which she had wanted for her husband's final resting site.

Later that night, Jacqueline Kennedy returned to the grave with fresh flowers, for an opportunity to say a private goodbye to her husband and the nation's president, John F. Kennedy.

# CHAPTER 22

# March On

BY TUESDAY MORNING, THE COUNTRY WAS STILL attempting to answer questions without answers. For four days, people sat in front of their televisions or by their radios trying to make sense of a time that was unprecedented in American history. People were mentally, physically, and spiritually exhausted, frozen in a state of vulnerability. Despite the pain, people had to return to work, classes at the Naval Academy resumed, and Caroline Kennedy went back to school.

In just five days, Army was scheduled to host Navy in the annual rivalry game, but the status of the game was unknown heading into Tuesday. A statement released by an Army publicist said, "It's a matter of coordination between the institutions of the Army, Navy, and Defense Department in Washington D.C. We're all in a state of shock over this terrible tragedy."

The members of the Kennedy family intervened and asked that the game be played. They understood how much the game and the service academies had meant to President Kennedy. They also understood that the country was desperate for an opportunity to release the emotion of recent days. This game would allow them that chance. At the request of the Kennedy family, the Pentagon released the following statement on Tuesday morning:

The secretary of the Army and the secretary-designate of the Navy decided today that the Army–Navy football game will be postponed one week in deference to the memory of President Kennedy. Consideration was given to cancellation of the game. However, President Kennedy's family requested that the game be played. The game will be dedicated to his memory.

☾ ☾ ☾

With the game officially on, the players reported to practice. Normally the team would dress in the locker room, climb the knotted rope that hung outside the practice facility to gain entrance, and then meet on the field. But instead of meeting on the field as they usually did, the Navy team was asked to gather in the locker room. When the players arrived, it was announced that Roger Staubach was the official winner of the Heisman Trophy. He was the second Midshipman to win the award (after Joe Bellino) and the fourth service academy player—Army's Doc Blanchard and Pete Dawkins being the other two. He was the fourth non-senior to win the award, joining Army's Blanchard, 1945; SMU's Doak Walker, 1948; and Ohio State's Vic Janowicz, 1950. Upon the announcement, the players gave their star quarterback a huge cheer and then proceeded to carry him into the shower, where he was doused in a celebration. A cake was rolled out, and the team smiled for the first time since Friday afternoon.

Some would say that it was unfair to name Staubach the winner of the most coveted award in college football when he still had one game remaining in the season. But not Navy coach Wayne Hardin, whose fondness for Staubach (who he thought might be president one day) was encapsulated by this statement: "He reminds me of Wyatt Earp. He's done things that should not be done on the football field. I've seen Unitas, I've seen most of the top players in this day and age, and Staubach is as good or better than any of them."

The Staubach Heisman campaign was the invention of Hardin and was carried out to perfection by Navy publicist Budd Thalman. Every week, Thalman forwarded quotes and stats that encapsulated the quarterback's brilliance under the title "Everything Coming Up Roger." His publicity methods also included driving weekly to New York City to interact with the giants of sports journalism and forwarding documentation to his massive mailing list. The *Modesto Bee* called Staubach the "most publicized quarterback."

This effort was aided to no small degree by the fact that Staubach was the best player in the country, period. Navy's national schedule of the previous two years had allowed him to showcase his skills to a wide range of media members in all corners of the country. In 1962, Staubach had received an award for his performance against the University of Southern California Trojans. In 1963, he led the Midshipmen to victories over Midwestern powerhouses Notre Dame and Michigan in front of national television audiences. He had rallied his team against SMU despite playing with only one arm and dominated Duke with his running, throwing, and overall leadership. And he helped Navy to numerous victories over eastern powers, including Pittsburgh and Maryland.

In the end, Staubach won the voting in every region for the 1963 Heisman Trophy.

## 1963 Heisman Trophy Voting

| Player, School, Position | 1st | 2nd | 3rd | Total |
| --- | --- | --- | --- | --- |
| Roger Staubach, Navy, QB | 517 | 132 | 45 | 1,860 |
| Billy Lothridge, Georgia Tech, QB | 65 | 119 | 71 | 504 |
| Sherman Lewis, Michigan State, RB | 53 | 80 | 50 | 369 |
| Don Trull, Baylor, QB | 20 | 68 | 57 | 253 |
| Scott Appleton, Texas, T | 27 | 33 | 47 | 194 |
| Dick Butkus, Illinois, C/LB | 10 | 49 | 44 | 172 |
| Jimmy Sidle, Auburn, QB | 11 | 28 | 34 | 123 |
| Terry Isaacson, Air Force, RB | 17 | 20 | 13 | 104 |
| Jay Wilkinson, Duke, RB | 3 | 20 | 35 | 84 |
| George Mira, Miami (FL), QB | 6 | 16 | 30 | 80 |

The trophy presentation took place in New York City at the Downtown Athletic Club. Roger was joined by his parents, Bob and Betty; his girlfriend and future wife, Marianne; team captain, Tom Lynch; Superintendent Rear Admiral Charles C. Kirkpatrick; Coach Wayne Hardin; and Budd Thalman.

Staubach, always humble, told the media that he wished he could break the trophy into forty-four pieces so everyone on the team could share in the award. "I owe [it] to everyone—my grade school coach, my coaches in high school and junior college, Coach Hardin, and of course my teammates."

Bob Staubach said, "God only gave us one child. But he sure gave us a good one."

The quarterback told reporters that the Heisman Trophy was something he would treasure all his life. "I don't want to let anyone down."

During their stay in New York, a limousine was made available for family and friends. The family also went to see the Tony Award–winning play *How to Succeed in Business Without Really Trying*. As Roger waited outside with Marianne in his Naval Academy blue uniform, patrons entering the theatre started handing him their theatre tickets, thinking he was an usher. Marianne turned to him and said, "That will keep things in perspective. You just won the Heisman Trophy and people think you're an usher."

Later during his stay in New York, Staubach was a guest on the *Ed Sullivan Show*. When he was introduced by Sullivan, he placed his hand under his chin and wiggled his fingers. After the show, Thalman asked him, "What the hell was that finger thing you did out there?" Staubach laughed and said, "I told the team I would wave to them on the show."

While in New York, Staubach learned that he had been drafted by the Dallas Cowboys in the tenth round of the NFL draft. He was also drafted by the Kansas City Chiefs of the American Football League. Questions immediately arose about his future football plans, but the Heisman quarterback was careful to answer that he would consider such opportunities at the conclusion of his years of service required following graduation.

Prior to President Kennedy's death, *Life* magazine had committed to a cover story on Roger Staubach. Coach Hardin had granted the magazine full liberties to conduct the interview, much to the dismay of the regular press. The Staubach issue had gone to press and was released to portions of the public before being recalled so that *Life* could run a Kennedy tribute issue in its place. The magazine had outbid *Time* magazine and United Press International for the rights to Abraham Zapruder's now-iconic film of the Kennedy assassination. Pictures of the significant slides from the film were published in the November 26, 1963, issue of *Life* magazine.

A Staubach cover photo had also been planned for that week's issue of *Sports Illustrated*, and high-level discussions were held to determine whether to replace the cover with one featuring the fallen commander in chief. Editor-in-chief Henry Luce, who was also the president of the *Time* empire, wanted to make sure that Staubach was worthy of the cover during a week of such important history. Turning to his ace college football writer Dan Jenkins, Luce demanded, "Are you sure that Staubach is going to win the Heisman?" Without hesitation Jenkins replied, "You can bet on it." Luce then turned to the magazine's editor Andre Laguerre and ordered, "Go with it!"

On Thanksgiving Day, Staubach and the rest of the Navy team gathered at the Boat House and watched the Texas Longhorns come from behind to beat Texas A&M, 15–13, completing their first undefeated season since 1920. Five of Texas' last six victories had been by five points or less. Navy assistant coach Steve Bellichick attended the game and returned confident in his team's ability to beat the Longhorns, if they were to meet in a postseason bowl. But first they had to prepare for archrival Army.

# CHAPTER 23

# Army vs. Navy, 1963

DURING HIS DAYS AT WEST POINT, PRESIDENT DWIGHT EISENHOWER TOOK great pride in being an Army football player. The fact that his football career was cut short by injuries did not diminish his passion for the Army team. For years he had been the team's number one booster, often calling Army coaches Earl Blaik or Paul Dietzel for updates or to make suggestions. The fact that President Kennedy was a passionate fan of Navy football meant that the thirty-fourth and thirty-fifth presidents of the United States held opposing positions on the service academy football teams. The two men even wagered on the 1963 Army–Navy game, before Kennedy's death.

The normal high jinks that traditionally surround the Army–Navy game were tempered on both campuses given recent events, although that didn't mean the intensity of the rivalry game would be moderated. The game had great ramifications for both teams beyond the first priority of realizing victory against a brother service academy. In victory, the winning team would be invited to the Cotton Bowl and earn a check of $200,000 for its school. Despite the fact that Texas had already been named national champion, the Longhorns opponent would play the game to claim its right to the title. If Army were to win and play in the Cotton Bowl, it would be the team's first postseason contest in the long and rich history of the program.

In Philadelphia at the annual sports banquet prior to the big game, it was reported in newspapers that Navy assistant athletic director Rip Miller, when speaking to the audience, asked in a mocking tone, "What's the name of that Army quarterback?" He then added, "While you're at it, give me the name of the Army halfback, too."

At West Point, Army coach Dietzel found nineteen copies of the article reporting the snub sitting on his desk. He would carry one in his pocket, willing to share with anyone who would listen how Navy was disrespecting his team. While meeting with the press at West Point, Dietzel noted that Staubach was a great talent. "No one has stopped Staubach cold," Dietzel said. "He's gonna do something spectacular in every game he plays. But there is no reason to get panicky. Just remember this: The Cadets have never surrendered to a foe yet!"

Dietzel was also sure to praise his own quarterback, junior Rollie Stichweh, calling him "as fine an athlete as I've ever coached."

Carl "Rollie" Stichweh was a star baseball, basketball, and football player at Mineola High School in Long Island, New York. He initially was interested in attending Princeton College to play basketball but decided on West Point. He was a quarterback in high school but played only defense as a sophomore at Army.

In the 1962 game against Navy, his coach called Stichweh the best defensive player on the field. But that wasn't good enough for him. On the bus ride back to New York after the devastating loss, Stichweh informed the coaches that he would like to play quarterback in the coming year. Nine games later, the six-foot-tall quarterback with the golden crew cut had led his team to a 7–2 record and was prepared to upset the second-ranked team in the country, Navy.

During a walk before the Navy game, Stichweh and Coach Dietzel talked about the game and the coach's expectations. Dietzel also shared with the quarterback that some of the Navy brass were having trouble remembering his name or how to pronounce it. Dietzel then pledged to his quarterback, "Tomorrow, after the game, they *will* remember your name."

Throughout the buildup to the game, the Navy coaches were called upon to provide sound bites or evidence of their teams' readiness. Coach Hardin noted that Army had a nice team but that his team had bigger aspirations. "We have a lot of respect for Army," he said, "but we think we are the number one team in the country, and we want to prove it."

In the last practice before departing Annapolis, the Navy team was running through drills on the practice field when a fantastic sound emanated toward them, growing louder and louder with each passing second. From out of the sky, an F-4 Phantom II jet zoomed in, just five hundred feet off the ground, seeming to fly directly at them. When the plane reached the practice field, the pilot placed the jet in upthrust and flew directly vertical. The heat from the engines could be felt on the players' faces as the pilot then completed a victory roll in his plane, prompting the players to roar in appreciation.

Later, at the relatively subdued but hearty pep rally in front of Bancroft Hall, a bonfire bounced shadows off the players as they marched to the stage. When Tom Lynch took the microphone, the crowd went quiet. "There's one more thing to do," he said, "and we're going to do it tomorrow afternoon." The players then boarded two buses for the ride to Philadelphia. As the team pulled away, the brigade chanted "Drive for Five."

Just off the courtyard in Annapolis, an empty grave was dug for Navy's next victim, the Cadets of Army. Academy superiors were not pleased with the open grave on campus, for both moribund and safety reasons, but they let it remain.

❨ ❨ ❨

On the morning of the game, the Naval Academy Brigade boarded one hundred buses for the trip to Philadelphia. The procession was led by police escort and trailed by transports called "drag buses," which carried the midshipmen's dates. The men arrived at the stadium and conducted their march on at 11:45 a.m., ninety minutes before game time. They were followed onto the field by the cadets of West Point, who were the home team.

In the bowels of the stadium the players from both teams sat or stood nervously in their respective locker rooms preparing for the biggest game of their lives. The stadium, which was built in 1926, did not possess modern conveniences. The setting in the cold cement holding cell was more appropriate for Roman times, where gladiators' success or failure meant life or death. Players sat on benches in front of their lockers, nervously tapping their feet, rocking back and forth, or visiting the open bathrooms, where the sounds of vomiting would echo off bathroom stalls and resound throughout the room. The tension was palpable, not only from the players but from coaches and fans alike. Prior to the game, Army coach Dietzel was heard to say, "Emotion so high it can be cut in chunks."

Prior to taking the field, Cotton Bowl representatives visited each locker room to remind the teams what was at stake. A bowl appearance could earn a school more than $200,000, but more importantly it would validate the success of the season. It had been rumored that President Johnson had urged college football officials to invite the winner of the Army–Navy game to play his state school, the University of Texas, in Dallas, which was still suffering from the glares of the country following the president's death.

The stipend for the Army–Navy game would be more than $500,000 for each team.

Throughout the stadium it was impossible to escape the pain of recent days. In the president's box, which was situated in the middle of the bleachers per Kennedy's request in 1962, black rosettes were hung with American banners. Occupying the seats for this game were not leaders of state but instead children of a local orphanage who were hosted by Cyrus Vance, the secretary of the army, in accordance with the Kennedy family's wishes. Around the top of the massive concrete stadium, the thirty-six flags were set at half mast. The end zones had the names Army and Navy stenciled in white, while in front of the H-shaped wooden white goalposts there were faded tracings of a football, drawn with lime, that encircled the initials *JFK*. Workers had been instructed to erase the reference to the fallen president, but the three letters refused to fade.

When the Pentagon finally acquiesced to the Kennedy family's request that the game be played, the teams and fans never fully anticipated what the game would represent to the nation. For two weeks, America had walked in a daze, unable to make sense of the senseless. On November 22, a piece of the country's spirit had also died. The flame of opportunity and hope that had blazed so bright had now been replaced by a cloud of uncertainty. When the Army and Navy teams took the field on this day, there was a tangible emotional release of sadness. On the field and in the stands it was finally acceptable to run and clap and feel emotion again. From the moment Army appeared in its dark shirts and gold pants and Navy sprinted onto the field with its gold shirts that read "Drive for Five" on the back, a spark of electricity was ignited, one that would surge for the next three hours.

Prior to kickoff, an assembly of two hundred cadets and midshipmen marched together to midfield. The bands of both schools then played "America the Beautiful." Standing in front of the assembly, cadet Richard Chilcoat, who just last year had sent President Kennedy a letter asking him to grant "immunity" if Army had won, now stood in front of the 102,000 fans, teams, and a national television audience and announced, "The cadets and the midshipmen dedicate this game to the memory of our late commander in chief, John Fitzgerald Kennedy." Standing next to him, midshipman Walter Kesler then asked for a moment of silence. Not a sound was heard from the 102,000 fans who filled the cement benches and lined the field in makeshift bleachers.

Following the moment of reflection, the two bands joined together to play "The Star-Spangled Banner." At the conclusion, the two captains joined with head official Barney Finn at midfield for what was yet another sad reminder of the country's loss. From the moment Tom Lynch and Dick Nowak had been named captains of their respective teams, they had looked forward to the traditional coin toss with the commander in chief. But now they stood at midfield reminded again of the void the nation felt. What was intended to be a lifetime memory turned out to be a sad remembrance.

Lynch won the toss for Navy, and it was time to play football. Army came into the game convinced it could beat the second-ranked team in the country. The Cadets would play with a chip on their shoulder, desperate to show the nation that the incessant talk about Navy was misplaced.

Navy scout John Hopkins called Army's defense one of the best in the country. In nine games, Army had only allowed 10 touchdowns. Coach Dietzel had learned from the 1962 game that blitzing Roger Staubach only provided him opportunities. In his book, *Call Me Coach*, Dietzel wrote, "the first year we played, I knew how good Roger Staubach was and I made up my mind that we were not going to give him a chance to throw the ball. We decided to put pressure on him with all kinds of blitzes and rushes. That turned out to be a serious mistake." For the 1963 contest, he amended his defense to contain the quarterback and to disguise blitzes. The strategy worked, as Navy was forced to punt after failing to move the ball on its first possession. Army had delivered a message.

Army recovered the punt on its own 35-yard line and marched down the field. Led by the running of the quarterback, Stichweh, who accounted for 40 of the 65 yards on the drive, Army would strike first on a 10-yard scrambling run by Stichweh, who leapt into the air desperate to reach the end zone. In midair he crossed the goal line at the same time that Navy defenders Skip Orr and Johnny Sai dove at the Army quarterback, turning him inside out. Stichweh landed in the end zone on his back for a touchdown. This reckless disregard for his personal well-being shown by the Army quarterback would be a theme throughout the day.

Navy tied the score in the second quarter on a Pat Donnelly 1-yard touchdown run. The big play on the drive was a fourth-down screen pass to Johnny Sai for 27 yards, down to the Army 11-yard line, that kept the drive alive.

At halftime the score was 7–7, but Army had outplayed the Midshipmen on both sides of the ball. The intermission allowed the teams to make adjustments while the crowd was serenaded by respectful patriotic music.

Army returned to the field encouraged by its superior first-half performance. As the players ran from the locker room to their bench, the cadets in the crowd streamed from the bleachers onto the field and formed a corridor for the players to parade through and receive encouragement from classmates. On the other side, Navy's bench area was empty; the team was still in the locker room. When Navy finally arrived, with the excuse that someone's watch was off, the Midshipmen were assessed a 15-yard penalty.

In the third quarter, a Donnelly 1-yard touchdown was the lone scoring play, giving Navy its first lead of the game, 14–7. The key plays on the drive were quick-hit handoffs to Donnelly right up the middle of the Army defense.

Navy would score again early in the fourth quarter. Following two back-to-back roughing penalties on the Cadets, Donnelly would score for the third time in the game, running 20 yards, bouncing the run outside to the left where he raced down the sideline, breaking tackles and seemingly putting Navy securely ahead 21–7. Navy had made the better halftime adjustments, it appeared.

Prior to the game, Coach Hardin went out of his way to promote Donnelly as one of the top players in the country who didn't receive the proper attention because of the great season his quarterback was having. On this day, Donnelly was noticed by all, as his three scores had tied him with Joe Bellino for most touchdowns ever scored in an Army–Navy game.

With the scoreboard reading 21–7, the sun was falling in the December sky, and the Midshipmen were fulfilling the motto on the back of their shirts, "Drive for Five." Everyone, though, knew there was no quitting for Army. Prior to the game, Staubach was acutely aware of the resilience and talent of the Army team, and he that knew to beat them would take a full-game effort. In an interview when accepting the Heisman Trophy, he said of the big game, "We better beat 'em. We'll have to knock them over to beat them."

Army was wavering but was not yet fallen. With 10:32 left in the game, the Cadets knew they would have a chance if they could just mount a charge. And that's just what they did.

Throughout the game, Army had controlled the pace. The Cadets knew leading up to kickoff that if they could control the ball and keep Staubach off the field they would have a chance to win. Consequently, the tension-filled game seemed to be played in slow motion. To accomplish this strategy, Army stalled and delayed at every chance. After each scrum, players would lie on piles or be slow to get up. In huddles they would maximize the allotted time, making Navy wait and grow impatient. For the entire game, Navy had only five possessions from which the team scored three touchdowns.

Navy kicked off after its third touchdown to Ken Waldrop, who proceeded to return the ball to the Navy 48-yard line. On runs from Stichweh, Waldrop, and Ray Paske, the Cadets moved the ball to the 1-yard line, at which time Stichweh carried the ball into the end zone for a roll-out touchdown. In the crowd, the Cadets fans grew in confidence while Navy fans grew worried.

People watching the game on television were confused. After watching Stichweh roll right and plunge into the end zone for a 1-yard touchdown, they saw him do exactly the same thing again. Immediately, the CBS phone lines were inundated with phone calls to confirm whether Army had scored again. What the fans would find out was that twenty-nine-year-old CBS producer Tony Verna of Philadelphia had just introduced instant replay. Because of the solemn mood surrounding the game, CBS had decided it would be inappropriate to promote the new technology prior to or during the game. Thus Verna had no choice but to just run the replay while play-by-play announcer Lindsey Nelson warned the television audience.

Verna had hoped that the first replay would capture an amazing piece of Staubach magic. Up until the Stichweh run, though, the rewind machine had failed to function seven different times.

In a piece written by Army sports information director Bob Beretta for the publication *Army Football: 100 Years*, Nelson recalled the pioneering moment in television:

> Tony [Verna], Jim [Simpson], Terry [Brennan], and I were riding down Broad Street on our way to the game when Tony told us that he had a gadget he might want to get on today, but that I would have to explain to the audience what it was. He had devised a means of playing back tape immediately, with no delay for editing. "If you use it, you'll have to explain it was a playback of what had happened, because it will confuse the audience." Well Army had the ball on the navy two, and the Army quarterback was a fellow by the name of Rollie Stichweh. As the players were coming out of their huddle, Verna said to me in the Telex, "Ok we're going to go with it on this play." So Stichweh rolled out and dove into the end zone for a touchdown and I said, "Now folks, don't be confused, Army has scored only one touchdown, what you are about to see is a replay."

Following a successful two-point conversion scored by a scrambling Stichweh, Army trailed Navy 21–15 with 6:19 remaining in the game. A renewed energy enveloped the stadium as the people in the crowd lifted from their seats in anticipation of a possible onside kick.

On the left hash mark moving right to left, Army kicker Dick Heydt teed up the ball. As he approached, he stutter-stepped and aimed his foot at the top half of the ball. When the toe of his cleat made contact, the ball dove into the ground and bounced diagonally across the field. The ball bounced, bounced again, and then bounced a third time. When it landed, Stichweh was there to cradle the ball for the Cadets on the Navy 49-yard line.

Army players leaped in the air in excitement while Navy players stood in disbelief. Army now had a chance to win the game. In the crowd, Army fans started to chant over and over again, "SMU and Army too. SMU and Army too." The noise level had ascended from a buzz that had permeated throughout the game to a noise level that one player said resembled a "New York train station at rush hour." The players were unable to communicate or hear the signals from the quarterback.

With still over six minutes to play, Army methodically moved the ball, stopping to huddle, continuing to move at the slow pace that had been preprogrammed in the players' minds throughout their preparation for the game. With the ball moving slowly down the field, the scoreboard now showed three minutes remaining. On the Navy sideline, Coach Hardin called over Staubach to discuss the course of action if Army scored. "If they score, you'll still be able to use all our plays." Then with only two minutes left, Hardin turned to Staubach and said, "Roger, you're going to have to use the two-minute drill when you get out there."

With just over one minute left, Army had moved the ball to the Navy 7-yard line and had a first down. The crowd was now in a frenzy. All 102,000 people were on their feet. Many had worked their way from the bleachers down to field level. With each play, more and more fans crossed over the track that encircled the stadium and lined the field. Army was driving into the south end zone, where the Naval Academy brigade happened to be seated. The noise was deafening. On the Navy sideline, Hardin asked his quarterback, who still stood next to him, "Do we have a one-minute drill?"

On the first two plays, the Cadets had inched the ball toward the end zone. On third down, Army called for a sweep to the right side for Ken Waldrop. On the snap, the ball was pitched to the Army halfback, who for a split-second could see a path to the end zone. But as quick as the hole had opened it closed when linebacker Pat Donnelly and tackle Jim Freeman converged on the ball carrier, tackling him on the 2-yard line. Freeman began to roll off the top of the pile when he noticed the seconds ticking away on the scoreboard and decided to roll back on the pile.

In the stands, Coach Dietzel's wife looked at the clock and began to fret that time was escaping. Sitting with her was her husband's close friend Ara Parseghian, with whom he had played at Miami University of Ohio and who now was head coach at Northwestern. Parseghian tried to calm the coach's wife by telling her that there was enough time.

With less than ten seconds to play, Army stood over the ball, poised to take the lead. A year before, in a *Sports Illustrated* article, Dietzel had said, "You can learn more character on the 2-yard line than you can anywhere in life." The ball now sat on the 2-yard line.

Army made its way to the line of scrimmage, the noise now buzzing in the ears of players and officials alike. The Navy defenders anticipated that either Stichweh or Waldrop would carry the ball to the right and thus had slanted in that direction. Army had called for a run off the right side.

On the last three plays, Navy's defense had dug in and called upon the same spirit that had pushed them to this very moment. It was for this crossroads in time that they climbed the rope before practice; that they held two-a-days beneath the hot August sun in Annapolis; that they stayed on the practice field at the direction of their captain long after their coaches had released them. It was for this moment that the 1963 Navy football team had prepared. Now the players would call upon their brotherhood of love and respect and care for one another, and refuse to break.

Stichweh stepped forward and placed his hands down to receive the ball.

Eleven players on offense and eleven players on defense stood poised, all crowded around the line of scrimmage. It was football in its most raw and genuine state. It was a return to the roots of the game, when men would line up eye to eye with the sole intention of imposing their will upon the other team. It is as if the two teams had returned to the Plain at West Point back in 1890, when they first fought on the gridiron hoping to bring glory to their schools.

Hardin turned to Staubach and informed him that he would only have one play to work with. Staubach didn't hear him. Instead he turned to the Mother of God, in the form of a Hail Mary, to intercede.

Stichweh barked out his signals, but they weren't being heard. Again he tried, but team captain Nowak turned to him and signaled that he couldn't hear. Desperate for help, the quarterback appealed to the head official to intercede with the frantic crowd.

The official acknowledged the Cadets' difficulty and stopped the clock. The Army players were aware that time had been halted and assumed that the clock would restart upon the snap of the ball, thus they again took their time at the line of scrimmage. Instead, the official restarted the clock once he felt the Cadets had been given ample time to regroup.

Standing behind the defensive line, Navy linebacker Lynch kept one eye on Stichweh and one on the clock. For him the seconds were like drips of water, each second seemed to extend beyond its allotted period. The ball lay in the center's hands. Suddenly, a shadow started to bounce along the goal line like a buoy moving up and down in the troughs and crests of the Severn River. The shadow was cast by referee Ray Barbuti, who began to blow his whistle, which pierced the din that had overwhelmed the field. Simultaneously, Lynch pointed upward to the sky to alert someone, anyone, that the clock had reached 0:00. A

## #2 U.S. Naval Academy (9–1)
## @ U.S. Military Academy (7–3)
Municipal Stadium . Philadelphia, Pennsylvania

December 7, 1963 . 1:30 p.m. kickoff . Attendance 102,000

|      | 1 | 2 | 3 | 4 | Final |
|------|---|---|---|---|-------|
| Navy | 0 | 7 | 7 | 7 | 21 |
| Army | 7 | 0 | 0 | 8 | 15 |

|                   | Navy | Army |
|-------------------|------|------|
| First Downs       | 17   | 16   |
| Rushing Yards     | 176  | 248  |
| Passing Yards     | 113  | 25   |
| Pass Att.–Comp.   | 12-7 | 7-4  |
| Fumbles Lost      | 2    | 1    |
| Interceptions by  | 1    | 0    |
| Penalty Yards     | 45   | 45   |

Army   TD, Stichweh, 10-yard run (Heyet kick)

Navy   TD, Donnelly, 3-yard run (Marlin kick)

Navy   TD, Donnelly, 1-yard run (Marlin kick)

Navy   TD, Donnelly, 20-yard run (Marlin kick)

Army   TD, Stichweh, 5-yard run (Stichweh run)

physically exhausted Stichweh, who had played almost the entire game on offense and defense, turned to official Finn to intervene but to no avail. From the side, Barbuti yelled as he waved his arms back and forth over his head, "That's it, boys."

Army center Lee Grasfeder heard but couldn't believe it. With the ball in his hands, he stood up and placed the ball behind his back. Breaking through the line, Lynch knocked the ball out of the center's hands onto the ground. As it lay there, Finn reached for the ball to pick it up, but Lynch beat him to it. Lynch held the ball in both hands and raised it to the sky. It was over. Navy had done it.

The improbable finish brought on memories of the 1946 Army–Navy game. That Army team, led by one of the great backfields in college football history in Doc Blanchard and Glenn Davis, had won 28 games in a row leading up to the game against Navy and were the heavy favorites. With time ticking off the clock and the Cadets leading 21–18, Navy was driving deep into Army territory. With just seconds remaining on the clock, a Midshipmen runner struggled to the sidelines, diving out of bounds at the 3-yard line to stop the clock. Strangely, the clock continued to tick. Because crowds had streamed down from the bleachers and bordered the sidelines, officials couldn't determine whether the Midshipmen player had made it out of bounds, so the clock was allowed to run to 0:00, bringing fans onto the field and ending the game. Navy coach Tom Hamilton later addressed why he didn't kick a field goal and earn his team an upset tie: "A tie is like kissing your sister."

On this day, there was no agony for Navy. Supporters of the Midshipmen swarmed the field. The wooden goalposts were toppled over as the Navy players jumped and hugged and breathed sighs of relief. Beneath their feet, the initials JFK were a reminder of their number one fan. The Army players didn't move. With hands on hips they were frozen in a state of shock until eventually the reality of the devastating loss sunk in. Slowly, they worked their way to the locker room. The Navy players understood their pain. Skip Orr sought out his Long Island neighbor, Stichweh, and congratulated him on a magnificent game. Some players walked over to Dick Nowak, whom they knew from a visit to the Naval Academy, but they backed off to give him his space when they saw him spike his helmet, which then jumped twenty feet into the air.

Following the game, George Minot of the *Washington Post* wrote, "The sands of time ran out on the brave old Army team today as the Cadets were poised on the 2 yard line." Dan Jenkins of *Sports Illustrated* wrote of the last drive, "Waldrop, Ray Paske, and Stichweh moved Army surely but with agonizing deliberation toward the goal. . . . Army's ultimate downfall therefore was its own in-diligence."

In the press box, Texas coach Darryl Royal, who had traveled to Philadelphia to scout his team's next opponent, couldn't believe the intensity of what he just saw. "I'll tell you one thing," he said. "Nobody's backing off down there. They're trying to maim each other." He would later say about the backfield, "I had no idea Staubach was that quick. You've got to be under control when you rush him. He loves to come out of there, doesn't he? That Staubach is the fastest thing I ever did see, and those backs can run like all get out."

Navy had only six plays in the fourth quarter to Army's twenty-four. In all, Navy had five possessions, three of which resulted in touchdowns.

In the Navy locker room Cotton Bowl chairman Felix McKnight spoke with Superintendent Rear Admiral Charles C. Kirkpatrick and Coach Hardin, inviting the Navy team to play in the January 1, 1964, Cotton Bowl against the University of Texas. Coach Hardin then turned to his jubilant players and asked, "Men we've been invited to the Cotton Bowl. Do you want to go?" The Navy players yelled yes, and Hardin turned to McKnight and offered, "Good, we've got a game."

Standing in front of their lockers, players hugged, smiled, and exhaled. It had been a difficult two weeks. Coach Hardin, holding the game ball in his hands, got his jubilant team to tone it down so he could say a few words. "You would have made the president proud of you today," Hardin said. "You played a game of great pride. In honor of him, I would like to dedicate this ball in his name and give it to the Kennedy family if they'll have it." The players cheered in agreement.

The mood in the Army locker room was beyond subdued. Some players sat on the benches in front of their lockers almost catatonic, while others kicked barrels, threw their helmets, and punched walls. Many of the players were brought to tears. News media would be kept out of the locker room for thirty minutes as the players and coaches tried to compose themselves. Coach Dietzel wondered why they wouldn't just allow the game to be settled on the field, but the point was moot. The game was over. As Navy had played with great honor, so had Army. It was exactly what made the game so special. It was the honesty of the effort, an illustration of the essence of sports.

In the midst of the excitement and pain, both coaches broke away from their teams to field a phone call from President Lyndon Johnson, who congratulated the coaches on the effort.

It was Coach Hardin's fifth straight victory over Army, a feat never before accomplished in the rivalry. In the locker room he commented, "We didn't play our best game against Army, and Army was tremendous, superb in every respect. Nevertheless, we won and I still think these boys of mine are the best of the country."

Controversy reigned for days after the game. Coach Dietzel stated it was ultimately his fault for not knowing the rules but pointed out that in a similar situation at Penn State earlier in the year, officials didn't start the clock until the ball was snapped when play had been stopped. He still felt that Army should be allowed the opportunity to run the last play. Official Barney Finn said, "I could have stopped the clock until today and the crowd of 102,000 would still be screaming."

When Navy returned to Annapolis, the four thousand midshipmen brigade was ready in front of Bancroft Hall. Several jumped on top of the buses and surfed them. One by one the players emerged from the doorway and were swarmed by their classmates. A makeshift rally was held, which allowed coaches and players to ring the Japanese Bell twenty-one times and then address the brigade. When Tom Lynch took the microphone, he assured those present who was the winner. "There's no doubt it was a moral victory for Army," said the team captain, "but I have yet to see one of those in the record books." He reminded everyone that the score would always be Navy 21, Army 15.

Hardin added, "The clock didn't beat Army. This Navy team beat Army." A wild cheer ensued, and he continued, "If Army got one more play, the score would still have been 21–15."

A week after the great victory, an envelope showed up in the mailbox of Navy captain Tom Lynch. When he opened it, he found a silver dollar. Accompanying the coin was a letter from Secretary of the Army Cyrus Vance.

9 December 1963
Dear Midshipman Lynch,

I am forwarding the coin which the late President Kennedy would have used and would have presented to you had he made the toss of the coin at the Army–Navy football game this year. Please accept this memento of a memorable football game.

With best wishes,

Sincerely,

Cyrus R. Vance

Secretary of the Army

Tom Lynch would treasure the coin, and the victory, for the rest of his life.

# CHAPTER 24

# Deep in the Heart of Texas

IN JOHN F. KENNEDY'S PULITZER PRIZE-WINNING BOOK *Profiles in Courage*, one of his favorite case studies was about Texan Sam Houston. At the conclusion of the chapter on Houston, Kennedy wrote eloquently of the politician, who preferred to step down from political office rather than to have his beloved state of Texas torn apart. "I am stricken down," Houston told the politicians of his state, "because I will not yield those principles which I have fought for . . . the severest pang is that the blow comes in the name of the state of Texas." Two centuries later, Texas was again at a crossroads as the eyes of the nation were upon them.

The city felt collective guilt. When ambulance driver Aubrey Rike was placing President Kennedy's body in the casket at Parkland Hospital, he said to himself, "Now I'm sorry I live in Dallas. I was born and raised here, but now I'm ashamed."

Dallas mayor Earle Cabell asked each person of the city to "search his heart to determine if through intemperance, word, or deed, he might have contributed in some fashion to the movement of this mind across the brink of insanity. . . . Dallas is on its knees and it is going to take a lot of forgiveness before this city can again straighten up and hold its head up high."

The nation glared at the city of Dallas with great contempt. Cabell received thousands of telegrams articulating disdain for the city, which held a tight conservative political ideology, with many outspoken against Kennedy's policies.

In some minds, Dallas was somehow complicit with Lee Harvey Oswald in assassinating the president, and the people of the city were incompetent and crooked. The death of Lee Harvey Oswald infuriated those who wished that justice would be properly served. Former Texas governor Goodwin Knight further fueled this opinion when, after Oswald's death, he said, "This is the crime of the century, yet because of the carelessness of these officials in Dallas, the American people will now forever be denied the whole truth of the assassination." Governor Connally was so concerned with the competence of the Dallas Police Department that he had them removed as his guard at Parkland Hospital, replacing them with the Texas Highway Patrol.

Reporter Michael McLane of the *New York Times* wrote, "The citizens of Dallas are surely engaging in the greatest spiritual self-examination any American community has undergone in this century."

Within this spirit of reflection and embarrassment, many from Dallas, and Texas in general, felt it imperative that the city find a way to shed a healthier light upon itself. One natural stage for this was the upcoming Cotton Bowl, which would be on national television on New Year's Day. The top-ranked team in the country and flagship team of the state, the University of Texas Longhorns, had already accepted an invitation to the Cotton Bowl. Now, all they needed was an opponent, one that would project interest and enthusiasm and put the great state of Texas under a truly positive national spotlight. The Navy Midshipmen were a perfect fit for all these needs, a season-long viable contender for a national championship as well as a team that had a significant national following. All eyes would once again be on Dallas, Texas, but this time for a much more positive reason. So it was that Navy was invited to battle the Texas Longhorns on New Year's Day, 1963.

Presented with the opportunity, the initial response from Navy players, on the field and off, was hesitant. Some of them hadn't been home since the summer and preferred to enjoy the holiday vacation at home with their families, rather than wearing pads and helmet to play a Texas team that had already been crowned national champions. The team's miserable experience in Texas in October was still in the minds of the Midshipmen. And certainly, the recent events involving President Kennedy in Dallas only confirmed the notion the players had of the city.

There wasn't much question that the team was suffering from a malaise since the death of Kennedy. The long layoff leading up to the Army game had resulted in a sub-par performance, which Coach Wayne Hardin noted. "Flat and complacent for the most important game you'll ever play," Hardin told them. "Don't ever lose sight of your main objective. If you get overconfident, do it some other week. Don't do it against Army!"

Midshipmen, though, soldier on. The nation needed the Naval Academy in Dallas. Dallas needed the Naval Academy in Dallas. President Lyndon B. Johnson wanted the Naval Academy in Dallas.

William Wallace of the *New York Times* wrote, "It has been suggested that the Navy was very nearly obligated to accept a Cotton Bowl bid invitation because a refusal would hurt the feelings of the grief stricken citizens of Dallas."

It was game on, Texas–Navy in the 1963 Cotton Bowl, live from Dallas, Texas.

# CHAPTER 25

# Texas vs. Navy, 1964 Cotton Bowl

WITH A SEMESTER BREAK BOTH HIGHLY ANTICIPATED AND MUCH DESERVED, the Navy Midshipmen were permitted to travel home. However, their break would end on Christmas Day. Before departing the Naval Academy for break, each was handed a plane ticket that would get him from his hometown to Dallas for the 1964 Cotton Bowl to play the top-ranked Texas Longhorns.

When the Midshipmen arrived in Dallas, they were greeted at the airport warmly by co-eds in Stetson hats who welcomed the players and provided each a care package to remember his visit. The players were then shuttled to the hotel, which would serve as a virtual prison for the next seven days. In 1960, Coach Wayne Hardin felt that the Navy team, led by Joe Bellino, that traveled to Miami for the Orange Bowl had been content simply to have qualified for a postseason bowl game. As a result, the team had not put forth its best effort and was dominated by the University of Missouri. This time around, Hardin was determined that the trip be focused on one thing and one thing only: the bowl game.

Hardin was also concerned that his team had gotten out of shape over the break. "You know how it is when mom prepares their favorite fattening dish," he said. "A player isn't going to offend her by turning it down." So, on the first day in Dallas, Hardin held a double practice session at the Dallas Cowboys practice facility.

At night, Naval Academy staff restricted the players' freedom to make sure their focus didn't waver. Events were organized for the players, including a trip to a rodeo and viewings of the films *It's a Mad, Mad, Mad, Mad World* and *Around the World in Eighty Days.*

The event that most caught the players' fancy was a visit from the attractive drill team known as the Kilgore College Rangerettes. The Rangerettes were a famous marching team composed of beautiful, statuesque co-eds whose one purpose at Kilgore College was to keep the fans happy at halftime. Interestingly, it was during this gathering that the players were reminded of their team's relative undersized stature: Almost every Rangerette was bigger than them, which led to the question, if the girls in Texas are that big, what was the Texas football team going to look like on New Year's Day?

During the week of preparation, the team took time off from drills and practices to travel by bus to Dealey Square, where President Kennedy was assassinated. They walked up the back stairs of the Dallas School Book Depository and stood at the window where Lee Harvey Oswald reportedly fired the fatal shots. From that perch, their minds replayed the events of that day over and over again.

Suddenly the spirit that usually possessed men of such an age reverted back to the melancholy that had enveloped the team and the nation for the last month. The visit to the tragic site had served as a reminder of the horror of November 22 and offered little closure. In their white Naval Academy uniforms, the team descended the stairs of the book depository and marched down the sidewalk, coming to a stop parallel to where President Kennedy had lost his life and the Midshipmen lost their biggest fan. With the grassy knoll on their right, the team knelt on the sidewalk and said a prayer.

Not long after the visit, Coach Hardin would be infuriated with their lack of enthusiasm during practice. "If it wasn't our worst practice of the year, it was our second," a disgusted Hardin told reporters. "I guess it was our worst. I hope it was a case of too much turkey. Our passing was off; our running was off. And our defense was off. And we had no spirit." He continued:

When a midshipman is at the academy he always knows where he is going, where he has to be, and what he is going to do. How much time he will practice and study and when he will go to bed. So when he gets five days off he doesn't seem to know what to do with himself. It takes some work to get the discipline back.

In Dallas and across the country the game was being touted as a dream match-up, many saying it was one the most anticipated bowl games ever. Tickets were in such demand that a lottery had to be organized for the final 25,000 tickets. The game was to be played in Cotton Bowl Stadium, where Navy had suffered its only loss that season. Navy receiver Skip Orr reminded everyone that this was a different time and a different city now.

Texas Longhorn coach Darryl Royal decided to take over control of the defense for his team's bowl preparation. Royal was a firm, quiet, Christian coach who—despite having originally resided on the other side of the Red River, where he played football at Oklahoma and was the backfield partner of legendary Sooner coach Bud Wilkinson—fit right in with his southern drawl in Austin, Texas.

Royal was a no-nonsense coach who demanded that his players listen, tuck in their shirts, and perform. He didn't yell or swear but still managed to hold the respect and attention of his players. If a player missed a class, he would find himself on the cut list, which would result in the player running the bleachers of the football stadium at 5:00 a.m. the next day. Royal was a perfectionist who cared about his team and its ability to function as a unit, as instructed. When later in the week Hardin debated with officials about what shirts the teams should wear, Royal simply said, "I don't think what color shirt we wear will make a difference in the game."

Royal's compassionate side was evident when he took time out of the week's preparation to present Texas Governor John Connally, a Longhorn alumnus, with a football signed by the team. Connally was still recovering from wounds suffered in the November 22 motorcade.

Throughout the week of practices, Coach Royal stressed one thing to his defense: "Contain Roger Staubach!" If a player allowed the scout quarterback to get outside of him, practice would stop, and they would do it over and over again until they realized the key to the game. Texas would go with a ten-man line that focused on the quarterback.

The *Washington Post*'s George Minot, who visited the Texas practice, took note of another point of emphasis that had surprised him, which he wrote about in his pre-game column: The Texas team was working on throwing the ball. When asked about this apparent change in approach from run and option run, Royal denied that the team was contemplating a more aggressive offensive game plan. "We're braver throwing the ball in practice than in a game," Royal said.

The Navy team had watched Texas play two games during the season. After Navy's game versus SMU, the players had stayed overnight in Dallas to be spectators at the following day's Texas–Oklahoma game, and on Thanksgiving Day the team watched Texas on television at the Naval Academy Boat House. In both games the Longhorns threw infrequently, at best, and thus the Navy team, scouts, and coaches anticipated an offense focused on the run. Texas averaged eight pass attempts a game and had only thrown two touchdown passes the entire season, none in the last six games.

Texas' run-first offense had led many to criticize the national champions, that their slow pace merely lulled opponents and fans alike into defeat. The lack of respect from the nation led to a chip on the shoulders of the Longhorn players. In their locker room, an article written by Pittsburgh sportswriter Myron Cope was taped to the wall that called Texas a "Cheese Champion" who would be a "Patsy for Navy."

By the end of the week, the Navy team had had enough of Dallas and the hotel in which they were sequestered. The hard practices and long season had led to some injuries, the most significant being a hamstring strain to fullback and linebacker Pat Donnelly. Reporting for the Associated Press, Mike Rathet wrote an article with the headline, "Middies Donnelly Sustains Leg Injury." In the article Rathet quoted Coach

Hardin as saying, "He went down like a shot. He is going to start the game but we won't know what he is going to be able to do until the game starts." The Longhorns would take note. It was a game between the two best teams in the country, and every edge would help.

❨ ❨ ❨

On New Year's Day, the Texas skies were sunny and pleasant with temperatures in the high forties. Across the country, televisions were tuned in, including the television of a family in the north that had a lot invested in this match-up: the Kennedys. The Navy players had no idea that they were playing anything more than a big football game. However, with the living rooms of families in forty-nine states full of people tuned in, this was much more than a big football game. Many were looking for Navy, which represented the nation, to achieve revenge against a team from the state where its leader was unjustly taken away.

Cotton Bowl Stadium was draped in American flag bunting and filled top to bottom. The midshipmen and Naval Academy personnel who had traveled to the game greeted their heroes as they raced onto the field in their gold pants and white shirts. Texas followed in their burnt-orange shirts, to a rousing ovation from the predominantly Longhorn crowd. Navy took the field with confidence. Their only concern for the Midshipmen was the injury to Pat Donnelly's leg, but before the game, he was able to maneuver sufficiently to attempt to play. It was the Cotton Bowl, after all.

One person was missing from the stadium, though. Originally, President Lyndon Johnson planned to attend the game, and the Dallas Police Department committed three policemen to patrol the stadium twenty-four hours a day for the week leading up to the game. However, reports of a potential bomb being planted in the stadium led him to watch the game at home with friends.

Prior to the game, Navy scouts had set an immediate benchmark: prevent Texas from scoring on its first drive. "The first quarter will tell the story," defensive coach Rick Forzano explained at a pre-game press conference. "If we can stop them on their first drive we will win. If we can't—I don't know." During the season, Texas had scored on the first drive in eight of eleven games. Over the last eight games, Texas had scored seven times on its opening drive. This early lead allowed the Longhorns to control the ball on offense and put the game in the hands of their defense to hold the lead. Shirley Povich of the *Washington Post* wrote that "the first ten minutes are as important as the next fifty minutes" in that year's Cotton Bowl game.

The game would be a competition between the Midshipmen's exciting offense and the awesome defense of the Longhorns. The Texas team had allowed an average of only 6.5 points a game by its opponents. The defense was anchored by a 239-pound tackle, all-American Scott Appleton. Coach Royal said that Appleton "doesn't pay attention to anyone who doesn't have the ball." Also on the line was team captain David McWilliams and young stud Tommy Nobis.

Before the coin toss and the national anthem, Hardin was interviewed as he walked from the locker room. The interview was connected to both the CBS feed and the public address system at the stadium. It was during the question-and-answer segment that the man in the green fedora and suit coat would restate the intention of his team, which was to prove who the number one team in the country was. In the crowd, the Texas crowd booed and the Longhorn players took note. When it was Coach Royal's turn to share his thoughts on the game he simply answered in his best drawl, "We're ready to play."

Following the national anthem, Texas captains Scott Appleton, Tommy Ford, and David McWilliams walked from their sideline like three Texas gunfighters, and stopping at midfield, they stood across from Navy captain Tom Lynch. Texas won the coin toss and elected to receive the football. After the kick, the Longhorns offense was led onto the field by its crew-cut-topped quarterback, Duke Carlisle. Carlisle, known for his ability to run and operate the "split T" formation, was a superb athlete but was not known for his passing ability. All week Navy coaches stressed to the players the importance of stopping the run.

Texas, though, came to the line of scrimmage on its first possession and elected to pass. The ball was on the team's own 42-yard line when Carlisle situated himself behind center. Behind him, his running backs were split. When he took the snap from his center he stepped to his left and faked a handoff to his running back. The stacked defense flowed left, reacting to the offense and the running back who carried out the play action. Carlisle then pivoted back to the right and found Navy end Dave Sjuggerud charging at him from the back side. Carlisle cocked his arm and released the ball, somehow threading the ball between the outstretched hands of number 81 on Navy. On the right flat, the Longhorns' fastest runner, halfback Phil Harris, had circled out of the backfield where he found himself, as designed, isolated with Navy linebacker Pat Donnelly. Donnelly, with wrapped leg and constricted muscle, pushed off on the Cotton Bowl turf while tracking the trajectory and speed of the ball. As the ball arrived he dove through the air, but his leg didn't respond. The ball, instead of being deflected or intercepted, floated over Donnelly's outstretched hands and neatly over the left shoulder of Harris into the halfback's waiting hands. Since the play originally moved left, the right side of the field was devoid of defenders. Harris, with the ball under his right arm, sped down the right sideline while the Texas crowd rose to its feet. When the ball carrier arrived at the Navy 25-yard line defensive specialist Bob Sutton arrived at an angle but not with momentum. The Texas back turned his shoulders toward the middle of the field and wrong-footed Sutton, thus opening up the sideline. Harris ran into the end zone where the name Navy was stenciled in the grass, giving Texas a precious 7–0 lead in the first three minutes of the game.

It was exactly what the Navy coaches had feared. Texas had scored on its first possession, which had been the first ingredient the Longhorns had used in their recipe for victory throughout the season. The men in burnt orange were now allowed to play their game and work with a lead as opposed to chasing their opponent.

Two possessions later, with Texas still ahead by seven early in the second quarter, the Texas coaches would again call for the throw-back pass and again isolate their speedy Harris on the injured Donnelly. As he had been the previous time, Donnelly was in perfect position, but again his legs wouldn't respond as requested. He leaped to intercept the under-thrown ball but was only able to get a hand on it, deflecting the ball into the air where it fell into the arms of Harris, who then raced 63 yards for a touchdown. Texas lineman Staley Faulkner watched his speedy teammate run into the end zone, then he turned to the Navy lineman who stood near him and asked, "Who do you think is number one?"

Texas had thrown two touchdown passes in the first half, matching its total for touchdown passes for the entire season. The Longhorns were now positioned to control pace and to apply their talents on the defensive side, which could focus on Navy's passing game. Appleton, Nobis, and McWilliams were now allowed to set their hands in the turf and attack Staubach. Texas scored again in the second quarter and once more in the third.

At his ranch in Texas, President Johnson lost interest in the one-sided game and decided to call his friend Harry Jersig, the owner of the Lone Star Brewing Company, and invite him and his wife to join them for some eggnog. While on the phone, the president asked Jersig how he was spending his New Year's Day. "I'm up here just seeing Texas beating the heck out of Navy," Jersig said. "Sure are," Johnson replied. "You should be ashamed of the way you're treating those Navy boys. I'm their commander in chief."

The president later called Jacqueline Kennedy to discuss the game and ask her about her trip to Florida and whether John Jr. was enjoying the truck that Johnson had bought him for Christmas. The rest of the Kennedy family sat in front of their television, not pleased by the outcome of the game. Neither was much of the country. Navy's major accomplishment to this point was managing to avoid a shutout, thanks to a Roger Staubach roll right to the pylon from the 2-yard line.

In the closing seconds of the game with the outcome long determined, the Texas team had again driven the ball down the field and had first and goal on the 1-yard line. The sun had already set on the stadium—and the game. In the end zone, the Navy defense huddled and looked at each other—no words needed to be said. Each had been trained and disciplined never to quit, never to give up. Here, on the 1-yard line in a 28–6 rout, the character of a midshipman manifested itself. The team would not allow Texas to score.

Eleven men set their hands into the worn chalk of the goal line and dug their feet into the torn turf of the end zone. Each man would be accountable for his own assignment. They would stand shoulder to shoulder, determined not to let one another down. Jim "the Snorter" Ounsworth; the hard-hitting Tom "the Rat" Holden; Edward "Skip" Orr, who started the season fourth on the depth chart only to go on to write his name in the Cotton Bowl record book with nine receptions; Bob Wittenberg; Jim "Soupy" Campbell, a senior playing the last plays of his football career; Bruce Kenton; Gary Kellner, who had come up so big in the Notre Dame game with two touchdowns; Kip Paskewich, the sprinter who had scored twice at West Virginia, setting a tone for the entire year; John "the Radish" Connolly, who had sat in the Notre Dame locker room appreciating the opportunity that would bring him to such places; Dick Earnest, who had returned from a broken arm suffered only two months earlier; and Charlie Durepo, who would stand taller than all on this last stand of the 1963 season.

On the sideline, Coach Hardin paced with green hat in place and face still crimson with the zest of a competitor who demanded and expected so much from his players, and they responded by giving every inch of their souls.

On the other side of the ball, eleven orange shirts broke their huddle and lined up across from the Navy wall. They would snap the ball four times, and four times the Navy shipmates would refuse to budge. Orr and Durepo and Kellner took turns standing up runners and allowed teammates to swarm, crawl, and scratch to the ball. At the conclusion of the downs, the ball still sat on the one-inch line and would move no further. There was no cheering or back slapping. They all knew in their hearts they had never quit; they never surrendered. They were midshipmen to the core.

According to many reports, Texas coach Darryl Royal had spent time between the Army game and the Cotton Bowl speaking with friend and Army coach Paul Dietzel about the Navy team. Army had scouted each of the Midshipmen games during the 1963 season and reportedly had broken the code of Navy's defensive signals. Staubach, in his book *Time Enough to Win*, wrote of the Texas defense, which seemed to beat Navy to the spot all game. "Stories cropped up years later that Texas had our defensive signals which accounted for their offensive success," the quarterback wrote. "Supposedly, Army was responsible. Army scouts all Navy games and vice versa. Army was supposed to have figured out our signals and given them to Texas. I'd say there was a chance that happened."

Such speculation was held by many in the Navy camp, as Texas spent the afternoon harassing and chasing Staubach across the field. The Longhorns would sack the Heisman winner five times for losses that would stretch back 55 yards. And though the Navy quarterback would set a Cotton Bowl record of completions (21) and yards (228), and receiver Skip Orr would set a record for pass receptions (9), it wasn't nearly enough. Navy rushed for minus 14 yards, never able to play its game. When Staubach was asked who Texas' best defender was, he said, "Well they all had me down at one time or another and I didn't catch their numbers."

"Texas did everything a champion is supposed to do," Coach Hardin said after the game. "We thought we were better and we expected to win the national championship away from Texas, but we just weren't good enough."

## #2 U.S. Naval Academy (9–2)
## @ #1 University of Texas (11–0)
Cotton Bowl Stadium . Dallas, Texas

January 1, 1964 . 1:45 p.m. kickoff (CST) . Attendance 75,531

|       | 1  | 2  | 3 | 4 | Final |
|-------|----|----|---|---|-------|
| Navy  | 0  | 0  | 0 | 6 | 6     |
| Texas | 7  | 14 | 7 | 0 | 28    |

| | | Navy | Texas |
|---|---|---|---|
| First Downs | | 16 | 18 |
| Rushing Yards | | –14 | 168 |
| Passing Yards | | 227 | 234 |
| Pass Att.–Comp. | | 34–22 | 21–8 |
| Fumbles Lost | | 2 | 1 |
| Interceptions by | | 1 | 1 |
| Penalty Yards | | 35 | 72 |

Texas  TD, Harris, 58-yard pass
from Carlisle (Crosby kick)

Texas  TD, Harris, 63-yard pass
from Carlisle (Crosby kick)

Texas  TD, Carlisle, 9-yard run
(Crosby kick)

Texas  TD, Phillipp, 2-yard run (Crosby kick)

Navy  TD, Staubach, 2-yard run (pass failed)

After the game while in the locker room, Texas coach Royal fielded a phone call from President Johnson. "It's a real honor to have you as a citizen of our state," Johnson said to Royal. "You've brought it dear glory and reflected great credit. Tell all your boys I'm mighty proud of each one of them. They reflect great glory and great pride in our state, and we are all so proud of their patriotism and manhood and sportsmanship. We know you spent a lot of hours, and it was reflected today. Our buttons are bursting."

Johnson also called Hardin while he and his team were still in the locker room. "Coach, Lyndon Johnson. Just wanted to call and let you know that I was thinking of you and its not who wins or loses but the way you play the game. You should be mighty proud of yourself and your boys."

On this day, Texas was the better team. The hopes of a storybook ending were not to be. Injuries, collaborating opposing coaches, and a team that never truly recovered from the events of November 22 all combined to hurt the Midshipmen's chances at victory.

This group of undersized, overachieving football players finally departed Dallas, a city where their lives had been so negatively affected during the previous two months. They were the second-ranked team in the country. They had brought great pride to the brigade and all those connected to the Naval Academy. Still, it would be a long plane ride home.

# CHAPTER 26

# Annapolis, January 1964

COACH HARDIN AND HIS WIFE PULLED THEIR CAR UP to the Naval Academy campus, where Tom Lynch and Roger Staubach waited on the chapel steps. A Maryland blizzard blanketed the night and covered the streets. The Hardins, Heisman-winner Staubach, and team captain Lynch had been invited to attend a dinner to honor the retirement of Marine Commandant General David Monroe Shoup. General Shoup was known to be a favorite of President Kennedy's, despite the fact that the commandant had held an opinion different from the president's during the Cuban Missile Crisis back in October 1962.

The party was hosted by Navy football fan and Under Secretary of the Navy, Red Fay. Also present at the party were Dean Markum of President Kennedy's staff; Robert Kennedy and his wife, Ethel; and Ted Kennedy and his wife, Joan. It was the first time all the Kennedys had been together since the president's funeral, and emotions were still raw. At the dinner, there were three tables to accommodate the thirty guests, with assigned seats to allow those who hadn't met to become acquainted.

Staubach was assigned a seat next to Ethel Kennedy, whom he was happy to meet. After introductory pleasantries, Ethel proceeded to castigate the Heisman winner for losing to Texas. For four months he had scrambled, dodged, and avoided the fastest and biggest football players in the country, but there was no escaping the wrath of Ethel. "You went down there to play the Cotton Bowl and you were representing the navy and the country," she told him. She spoke of how important the football team had been to her brother in law, the president. It was less than two months since the assassination, and the death of President Kennedy still weighed heavily on the family.

Later in the night, all who were present were required to perform or say a few words, as was tradition at a Kennedy event. Coach Hardin sang "Show Me the Way to Go Home." Tom Lynch told a story regarding the long streak of Navy football captains who were unable to finish the season because of injury, which led his mother to deduce, "The team must select a guy they don't like to be captain."

When Staubach rose to speak, the conversation with Ethel was still ringing in his ears. He assumed her displeasure was shared by many at the party, so he didn't sing a song or tell a story but instead apologized to all present for not winning the Cotton Bowl.

At the end of the dinner party, Hardin was walking to the door when Robert Kennedy approached him. Robert, who had traveled to watch Navy play in Michigan and attended the home game against Pittsburgh, was a legitimate fan of the team. As he approached Hardin, it was apparent that the attorney general's demeanor had changed. He pointed his index finger at the coach and tersely said, "I thought you knew how important that game was to my family."

The Navy contingent returned to Annapolis honored to have been invited and in the company of such worthy individuals, but at the same time they were bothered by the understanding that they had let so many people down.

Later that month, the same members of the Navy football program were invited to the twenty-ninth annual football awards dinner of the Washington Touchdown Club. Coach Hardin was presented with the Coach of the Year Award, while Staubach received the award for most outstanding college back. During the quarterback's acceptance speech, he reminded the crowd that Navy was 9–0 within the other forty-nine states, thus Texas should never have been annexed.

Also on this night, the Navy team was presented with the College Team of the Year Award. The selection of Navy had been made prior to the Cotton Bowl, which made acceptance of the award somewhat awkward in light of the team's loss in Dallas. Tom Lynch accepted the award for the team, while Hardin was asked to speak about the validity of the award. The red-headed coach proceeded to draw upon the experience of his friend President Kennedy. He told the audience of 1,600 guests that back in 1960 some said that John F. Kennedy should give up the presidency because of questions surrounding the election. "Well, he didn't," Hardin said simply. "And I'm not giving this up either. Thank you."

The night ended with a tribute to President Kennedy, who was presented posthumously with the Mr. Sam trophy, named in honor or Sam Rayburn, the previous speaker of the house. The honor was annually presented to the politician who contributes most to sports. Accepting the award on behalf of the future Kennedy Library was Massachusetts governor and past winner of the Touchdown Club's Knute Rockne Award for best lineman, Endicott Peabody.

As custodian of the award, Governor Peabody told the audience, "The Mr. Sam award will serve as a symbol of something we all admired so much in John Fitzgerald Kennedy—his enthusiastic love of sports, his dedication to the vigorous life, his unflagging interest in the health and fitness of all his fellow citizens, but, most particularly, of the youth."

# Epilogue

FROM THE MOMENT JOHN F. KENNEDY WAS ELECTED PRESIDENT in 1960 to the 1964 Touchdown Club awards dinner, the commander in chief and the team from Annapolis were interwoven. The team and the president shared a mutual admiration.

In the prime of his life, the thirty-fifth president of the United States was prepared to lead the nation to a new frontier of inclusion and participation. He asked that the citizens of the United States become partners in the process by investing their time and resources while assuring them that their efforts would yield Americans a greater nation.

The forty-four young men of the 1963 Navy football team believed in his ideals and were prepared to follow their commander in chief. Many of them marched in his inauguration parade, and all suffered through his painful death.

The Navy 1963 football team ranks among the great college football teams of all time. Led by a charismatic captain in Tom Lynch and one of the finest players ever to play college football in Roger Staubach, it was, in the words of Coach Wayne Hardin's butcher, a "team of destiny."

Following the suspenseful game against Army to close out the 1963 regular-season schedule, Lynch spoke of the spirit that had consumed the team throughout the year. "All season," he said, "we've had a kind of motto that the way to really accomplish something worthwhile is to fight your way through tough spots. So when we found ourselves down there with defeat staring us in the face, I think that all of us subconsciously thought about this thing we have believed all along. It's kind of what we had in the back of our minds and it helped us throw ourselves in there and hold Army."

Lynch's leadership and the special quality of the individuals on the team under his direction were also addressed by quarterback Staubach in a post-game locker-room interview following a 1963 victory. "This is the closest bunch of guys and the closest team in the world," Staubach said. "Tom Lynch—our captain, and one of the best in the world—talks to us twice a week. We play games one at a time and we want to win them all. We just don't have any letdown on this club."

The Navy men were driven to prove wrong anyone who questioned the depth of their will. It was this drive to push beyond their means that roused President Kennedy to cheer and served to propel the 1963 team to greatness.

Football, however, didn't define these men. Instead, the sport and the 1963 season would serve as one spectacular chapter in the story of their lives. Twenty-three of forty-four players were on the superintendent's list for top grades. The majority of them played other sports. Pat Donnelly and Jim Campbell were all-American lacrosse players; Roger Staubach impressed baseball scouts by hitting .421 as a sophomore; Tom Lynch twice won the brigade's heavyweight boxing championship; Kip Paskewich and Johnny Sai were great sprinters; and Bob Teall was a tennis player.

The men of the 1963 Navy football team graduated from the Naval Academy and then set sail in defense of their country. Three members of the football program—Tom Holden, Doug McCarty, and Mike Burns—perished in the name of defending freedom and democracy. In the Memorial Hall wing of Bancroft Hall, the names of these three warriors were added to a list of other brave men of the Naval Academy who sacrificed all. Above their names are the following words:

With immortal valor and the price of their lives, these proved
their love of country and their loyalty to the high traditions of

their alma mater by inscribing with their own blood the narrative of their own deeds above. On and underneath the seven seas, they have set the course. They silently stand watch wherever Navy ships ply the waters of the globe.

Five members of the 1963 Navy football program later rose to the rank of admiral, including Lynch, who eventually returned to the Naval Academy to serve as superintendent of the institution that he loved. He drew upon the wonderful spirit of Superintendent Rear Admiral Charles Kirkpatrick, who had mentored Lynch and his classmates throughout that glorious season.

In 1961, Coach Hardin said of his position as Navy football coach, "They give you a pretty good salary and treat you fine as long as you beat Army. It's the top job. I wouldn't want to coach anywhere else." Two years later, as friction increased with the administration, Hardin warned himself before the 1963 game with Army, *I know if I don't win this game, they'll be after my scalp. So I don't intend to get into that mix if I can help it.* One year later, his 1964 team lost to Rollie Stichweh and the Cadets. Stichweh, who played like a warrior in the losing effort in 1963, was carried off the field on the shoulders of Cadets in a story of athletic redemption.

Coach Hardin was fired after the game. His next stop was Temple University, where he would lead that football program to its greatest days.

In 1964, Municipal Stadium in Philadelphia was renamed John F. Kennedy (J.F.K.) Stadium in honor of the man who twice traveled to the arena to serve witness to the best of a generation as they waged battle upon the gridiron. Almost thirty years later, the stadium was condemned and eventually demolished.

Amid the dust of the once-proud stadium, the echoes of past glory still reverberate through the Philadelphia sky. It was there that gladiators once played the sport with such passion that those who came to witness were overwhelmed by the magnitude of the event. It was on that field in 1963 that men played the game with deep sincerity. It was on that field that forty-four men from the Naval Academy honored the memory of their friend and commander in chief.

After the stadium's razing, Tom Lynch went to retrieve bricks from the rubble. He collected forty-four and had the bricks engraved with the names of his teammates and the years they participated in the Army game. He then presented one to each of his Navy brothers. The spirit of those bricks brought the inanimate objects to life, letting them serve as tangible reminders of those wonderful days.

It would be aboard this journey of nostalgia that they would sit in the Boat House once more watching game films; they would stand with great pride at a pep rally as Superintendent Rear Admiral Charles C. Kirkpatrick inspired the brigade with his eternal motto, "You can do anything you set your mind to do"; they would run back onto the practice field with helmet in hand and with a world in front of them; they would smile as they remembered moments of comradeship on planes and buses or in the locker room. And, of course, they would allow themselves the pleasure of traveling back in time to those immortal Saturdays of autumn 1963, when the Navy team left its mark on both the campus of the Naval Academy and the sport of college football itself.

The bricks would sit on desks at work or in offices at home, reminding each member of this special fraternity that he was part of something genuine and special. Forever, the lifeblood of this brotherhood would eternally link the team members together—always ready to block; always ready to stand watch; always ready to provide a shoulder as they grew older but did not separate. It was forty-four men who were fused together to form a team of destiny, forever destined to be a team. Forty-four men who would never give up the ship. A collection of men who know what being a good shipmate means, on the field, at sea, and in life, as did their biggest fan and fellow navy brother, John F. Kennedy.

# Afterword

by Roger Staubach and Admiral Tom Lynch

ALMOST FIFTY YEARS AGO, THE NAVY FOOTBALL TEAM and the entire Naval Academy Brigade of Midshipmen shared in a magical season that still lives in our hearts. In the autumn of 1963, a collection of men joined together to assert the power of teamwork on the football field. As members of that team, we wore the uniform with pride, driven to represent and honor our classmates, alumni, and navy personnel around the world with whom we felt a profound bond.

The football team and the brigade as a whole were led by our dynamic superintendent, Rear Admiral Charles Kirkpatrick, who pushed all midshipmen to believe they were capable of anything they set their minds to. Our superior football coach, Wayne Hardin, challenged us to be the best team we could be and, along with his staff, put us in position to win each and every Saturday.

When we took the field in Morgantown, West Virginia, for the opening game of the 1963 season, we did so with great anticipation, yet with little idea of what the season would hold. When it was over, the memories of a golden season were forever engraved in our hearts.

The football team of the Naval Academy consisted of a collection of men that to this day remain as close and committed to each other as the first day we donned the gold helmets of Navy. On the football field we blocked and tackled and ran for one another. It was a friendship formed on the gridiron that has never wavered.

The year 1963 was also one in which the nation was devastated by the tragic death of President John F. Kennedy. The Navy football team had a special relationship with the commander in chief, and the players were personally affected by his loss. Many of us were honored to have had the opportunity to march in his inauguration parade in January 1961. A year and a half later, the president visited the team at our summer football camp at Quonset Point in Rhode Island. We felt a kinship with President Kennedy. A navy hero himself, he was leading the country on a course of great promise and hope.

As the president marched down the line for inspection in the twilight of that late August evening in 1962, he took the time to say a personal word to each player, asking our names and where we were from. He was a man who represented the essence of leadership. We pledged to him that day to play a game worthy of the president when we would meet Army later that year, a game that President Kennedy planned to attend, as he had the 1961 contest between the service academies.

We defeated Army on December 1, 1962, just as the Midshipmen had done the year before and the two years before that. As we prepared to face our rivals again in 1963 with the chance for a fifth straight victory, the president said he was looking forward to watching the two great teams compete again. Unfortunately, the president's assassination just over a week prior to the game's scheduled date cast a pall over the academy and the entire nation. The game was rescheduled for a week later, and we dedicated the game in his honor.

In *The President's Team*, Michael Connelly captures the essence of the 1963 Navy football team and the world around it. This chronicle brings back both warm memories of that golden season and great sadness at the loss of our president.

# The 1963 Navy Midshipman Football Team: Where Are They Now?

### Bruce Abel, Class of 1964, quarterback

Following graduation, Bruce Abel remained to coach the plebe team, along with Jim Campbell, Dave Sjuggerud, Steve Moore, Bob Orlosky, Alex Kreckich, Tom Lynch, and Charlie Durepo. Abel flew a P-3 in antisubmarine/anti–surface warfare for six years of active duty, retiring from the reserves in 1990. He spent much of his civilian career in the commercial nuclear power industry with Westinghouse and then worked for a large drugstore chain, providing corporations with prescription drug programs for their employees. Retired in 2004, he now lives in Atlanta where his two children and four grandchildren also live. His wife of forty-two years passed away in 2007.

### James Angel, Class of 1966, defensive back

James Angel spent his navy career on a guided-missile destroyer as a gunnery officer. He completed a master's degree in exercise science at the University of Alabama and earned a Ph.D. in exercise physiology and nutrition from the University of Tennessee. Angel joined the faculty of Liberty University as a member of the Health Science and Kinesiology Department before accepting the chair position in the Exercise Science and Sports Medicine Department at Samford University in Birmingham, Alabama. Angel has also traveled to Cuba, China, and North

Korea to assist in delivering humanitarian aid. He has been married to his wife, Linda, for forty-one years.

### Bruce Bickel, Class of 1966, quarterback

After fulfilling his service obligation, for which he was highly decorated for bravery and was seriously wounded in Vietnam, Bruce Bickel served as vice president of ministry with the Fellowship of Christian Athletes. He then attended a seminary and received his master of divinity and doctor of theology degrees, after which he served as the senior pastor of churches in Kansas City, Kansas, and Chicago, Illinois. Currently, Bickel is a senior vice president and managing director for PNC Financial Services Corporation in Pittsburgh, Pennsylvania. He is also the founder and president of the Transformational Leadership Group, a character-based leadership training consulting group.

### Jim Breland, Georgia Tech Class of 1966, end

Following the 1963 season, Breland transferred to Georgia Tech, where he was named all-American and was later voted into the Georgia Tech Hall of Fame. He earned his undergraduate and master's degree in Civil Engineering while serving in the Naval Reserves. Breland worked as senior vice president and a board member of the engineering firm Post, Buckley, Schuh & Jernigan in Atlanta. He and his wife, Emily, reside in Hilton Head, South Carolina, and have one son.

### Michael "Wimpy" Burns, Class of 1964, tackle

Known as Wimpy to his teammates, Michael Burns went to flight training school after graduation. He flew helicopters and was assigned to Quonset Point. Burns died in active duty when his helicopter malfunctioned over the Atlantic Ocean.

### Ron Buschbom, Class of 1966, tackle

Ron Buschbom graduated as a first lieutenant in the United States Marine Corps and went to Quantico for five months of basic training for officers. Buschbom was recruited (involuntarily) for the Quantico Marine football team, was fairly seriously injured, and received a disability retirement. He used his veterans benefits to obtain a master's degree in business administration and a law degree. Buschbom ran his own firm for seventeen years and now runs the Ft. Myers office of the largest insurance defense firm in Florida.

### James "Soupy" Campbell, Class of 1964, end

James Campbell, whom Coach Steve Belichick called the "greatest athlete he ever coached," was a decorated fighter pilot who flew over two hundred missions in Vietnam. He retired as commander and then flew for Eastern Airlines before designing golf courses. His brother Bill, who played football at Columbia University, was awarded the College Football Hall of Fame Medal Gold Medal and is considered an honorary member of the Navy football team. James Campbell died in 2006.

### Mike Chumer, Class of 1964, tackle

As a Marine Corps officer, Mike Chumer served in systems analysis and design at the Marine Corps Automated Services Center in Okinawa, Japan. He consulted with the Chinese Marines on development of large mainframe and communication systems. He also assisted the Marine Corps in designing satellite-based battlefield information systems. Chumer earned his Ph.D. from Rutgers University in communications and information science. He is currently on the faculty at the New Jersey Institute of Technology and the State of New Jersey's Preparedness College. He also provides guidance on various dimensions of Homeland Security emergency management. Chumer participates in Highland's Forum, a Department of Defense think tank that advises the assistant secretary of defense on networks and information integration.

### Dennis Connolly, Class of 1964, tackle

Following graduation, Dennis Connolly went into naval aviation. He flew A6 planes from the aircraft carriers USS *Kitty Hawk* and USS

*Independence* in Vietnam as well as completing a tour in the Mediterranean. His combat decorations include twelve Air Medals, a Navy Commendation, and Navy Achievement Medals. Connolly left the navy in 1972 with the rank of lieutenant commander and then flew with United Airlines. He received his MBA from Loyola College in Baltimore in 1979 and began a career in commercial real estate development. He is currently senior vice president with the American Operations Corporation and has four children and two grandchildren.

### John "the Radish" Connolly, Class of 1966, guard

Jack Connolly attended naval flight school where he was designated a naval aviator. He deployed on the carrier USS *Intrepid* during the Vietnam conflict and then on the USS *Roosevelt* in the Mediterranean. He coached in the Navy football program, serving as head junior-varsity coach and head lightweight football coach, as a naval officer before being discharged in 1974. Connolly earned a law degree from the University of Baltimore and was admitted to the Maryland and Massachusetts bar. He practices law in Falmouth, Massachusetts, where he also served three terms on the school committee.

### Dick Curley, Class of 1964, center/linebacker

Ensign Dick Curley served on the USS *Oklahoma City* as a deck officer and then USS *Holder* in Norfolk as Operations Officer, followed by one year tour in-country Vietnam before becoming Exec on USS *Leonard F. Mason*. Then he was off to the first of three tours in Washington, D.C., before becoming Commander of the Fleet Training Group in Pearl Harbor; this completed a little less than twenty-five years of enjoyable service. Upon retirement Curley joined a small company working with the FAA as Program Manager introducing the then new air traffic control system, preceding full-time assistant professor at the University of Mary Washington for six years.

### Pat Donnelly, Class of 1965, fullback/linebacker

Pat Donnelly played in the College All-Star game against the Chicago Bears before deploying to Vietnam with the Seabees. He completed graduate school at Cambridge University in England as a Churchill Scholar and then earned an MSCE at MIT. He spent twenty-four years on active duty with many foreign assignments in Europe and East Asia. He also served two tours at the Naval Academy, first as an instructor in the Engineering Department and an assistant football coach under George Welsh, then as comptroller.

After retiring from active duty, Donnelly became the vice president of engineering with classmate Bob Gosnell's development company. He joined Jones, Lang, LaSalle (formerly the Staubach Company) as vice president for design and construction management. Donnelly married his wife, Missy, after returning from his second Vietnam deployment and has had two sons, both associated with the navy, and a daughter.

### Charles Durepo, Class of 1964, tackle

Charles Durepo's first naval assignment was as coach for the plebe football team, after which he completed navy flight training. In 1966 he was assigned to the USS *Jenkins* out of Pearl Harbor and deployed to Vietnam in 1967–1968. A final tour at Johnston Island completed his five-year Navy career. Durepo married Susan Busik, the daughter of director of athletics Bill Busik, on November 22, 1964. They have a son and two daughters.

### Richard Earnest, Class of 1964, halfback

Richard Earnest flew F4 Phantoms for ten years and served three tours in Vietnam, flying 320 missions that resulted in twenty-one air medals and the Distinguished Flying Cross. He received a master's degree in management from the Naval Postgraduate School in Monterey, California, and entered the high-tech business world in 1973. Over a period of thirty years, he ran six different computer software companies, including two public companies. He has been the mayor of Del Mar, California, and he ran for U.S. Congress in 2004. He is currently running a small start-up company in the energy storage market for electric vehicles. He is married to Jackee, and they have two children and one grandchild.

### James Freeman, Class of 1965, tackle

James Freeman worked in the Navy Supply Corps for twenty years, serving two tours in Vietnam. He retired in September 1985 from the NPGS Monterey Comptrollers Office and taught math at Monterey High School for the next fifteen years. He then retired again to his hometown of Denison, Texas, where he plays golf and travels.

### Wayne Hanson, Class of 1965, halfback

Following graduation, Wayne Hanson flew P-3 airplanes for ten years. He left active duty in 1971 and flew commercially with two airlines (Eastern and United). He retired in December 2002 at the age of sixty and lives with his wife, Margaret, in Evergreen, Colorado. His three children and four grandchildren also live nearby.

### Eugene "Gino" Hardman, Class of 1966, guard/linebacker

Gino Hardman served two tours of duty in Vietnam as a United States Marine, the second as provost marshall of Danang. He retired after ten years at the rank of captain. From 1976 to 1987, Hardman worked for Deak International, a company dealing in the foreign exchange of precious metals. He started the Hardman Academy of Tennis and then took a position at New Mexico Military Institute in the athletic department, which evolved to a role as director of the McBride Museum at the institute. Hardman and his wife, Elaine, have been married for thirty-eight years and have one son.

### Neil Henderson, Class of 1965, end

Neil Henderson served on nuclear-powered missile submarines for five years and later earned an MBA from Dartmouth College. He spent twenty years at Norton Abrasives in Worcester, Massachusetts, and served as the senior vice president of Worldwide Bonded Abrasives until the company was sold. He became the CEO of American Optical Company until it was sold in 1997. He is now retired and has dabbled in real estate development in California and Utah. Henderson has been married to the former June Whitt for forty-five years and counting. They have two sons and three grandchildren.

### Bill Higgins, Class of 1966, end

Bill Higgins coached plebe football and boxing at the U.S. Naval Academy as head of midshipman services and officer inspector of uniforms. He served as an FBI agent before returning to the Naval Reserve and then entering the real estate brokerage field.

In 1990 Higgins volunteered for active duty in Desert Storm and served as the deputy assistant chief of staff for the U.S. Navy's Logistics Support Force during Desert Shield and Desert Storm in Bahrain, working for Bob Sutton. Higgins retired in 1996 from the U.S. Naval Ready Reserve, where he was assigned to the Defense Logistics Agency as the officer in charge of REEFEX, the largest artificial reef program in U.S. history. He is currently commander of the Southern Command for the New York Naval Militia, which includes New York City. He is married to Barbara Corcoran and has six children and two grandchildren.

### Thomas "the Rat" Holden, Class of 1964, guard

Thomas Holden joined the Marines and held the rank of first lieutenant. He received a Purple Heart and a Silver Star for selflessly saving a company in distress in Vietnam. He died in battle a hero, earning a second Purple Heart and Silver Star posthumously.

### Joe Ince, Class of 1964, halfback/punter

Joe Ince served six years on active duty as a submarine officer on both diesel and nuclear submarines, making three deterrent patrols on a ballistic missile sub. As a civilian he earned an MBA at Harvard then returned to his hometown of Houston and was in the investment management business for thirty years. He is now in full-time ministry work with the Christian Union. Ince married the former Susan Haden and has three children and two grandchildren.

### Duncan Ingraham, Class of 1966, halfback

Duncan Ingraham served as a plebe football coach; engineer on the destroyer *Harlan R. Dickson*; and then flag lieutenant at COM-NAVBASE, Newport, Rhode Island. He received his MBA from the University of Rhode Island and began work in the financial, insurance, and real estate business. He is married to Jeannie, and they have two children and four grandchildren.

### Douglas Katz, Class of 1965, halfback

After several sea assignments, Douglas Katz commanded the USS *Deyo* and then the USS *New Jersey*, providing pre-Olympics presence off the coast of Korea in 1988 and representing the United States at the Australian Bicentennial Naval Salute. Katz assumed command of Cruiser-Destroyer Group Two in November 1990, leading the *America* battle group during Operation Desert Storm. He was then redeployed aboard the USS *America* and became the first Desert Storm battle group commander to return to the Gulf after the war. He was promoted to vice admiral commanding the U.S. Naval Forces Central Command and the Middle East Force prior to its re-designation as the U.S. Fifth Fleet. Katz assumed command of the Naval Surface Force U.S. Atlantic Fleet in September 1994. He has received numerous decorations for his service. He and his wife, Sharon, have two children.

### Gary Kellner, Class of 1964, end

Gary Kellner attended flight school in Pensacola, Florida, where he received his wings. He went on to do advanced training in F-8 Crusaders and was assigned to first squadron (VC-10) in Gitmo for hot-pad duty. He was reassigned to VF-51 and was deployed to Vietnam on the USS *Bon Homme Richard*. Kellner then served in the candidate guidance office at the Naval Academy before returning to the fleet with VF-191 and deploying to the West Pacific on board the USS *Oriskany*. He assumed duty as weapons officer on the USS *Midway*, which was forward deployed in Japan. His last tour of duty was to the staff of

ComNavAirPac as the weapons officer. After settling in the Dallas–Ft. Worth area, Kellner worked as a property tax consultant for an additional twenty-three years. His family includes a son, a daughter, a son-in-law, and two beautiful granddaughters.

### Andy Kish, Class of 1965, fullback

Andy Kish went to flight school in Pensacola, Florida, but never obtained wings due to a vision disqualification. He served on surface ships, including a one-year tour in Vietnam as the executive officer stationed at the Naval Support Activity area in Da Nang, RVN. He retired from the navy in 1971 and then worked for Nestle for thirty-two years, rising to the position of senior vice president. He and his wife, Diane, have two daughters and four grandchildren and live in Tucson, Arizona.

### Lawrence Kocisko, Class of 1965, guard

Larry Kocisko took a turn as assistant plebe coach before completing naval flight training to fly P-3 Orions. He served as a patrol plane commander and a maintenance officer. He also flew commercial planes (for Delta Airlines) before he retired in 2002. He is married to Jeanne, and they have four children, eight grandchildren, and seventy foster children.

### Al Krekich, Class of 1964, guard

Al Krekich's first "sea tour" was on the USS *Warrington* in Newport, Rhode Island, followed by a one-year tour in Vietnam as the officer in charge of a swift boat. From Vietnam it was back to Newport for training and a tour of duty on another destroyer, the USS *Davis*. Subsequent sea assignments included command of the frigate USS *Ainsworth* and the cruiser USS *Belknap*.

Krekich was promoted to rear admiral and reassigned to the Joint Staff in the Pentagon, working in the strategy and policy section. Following tours that included an assignment as commander of Cruiser-Destroyer Group Two in Charleston, South Carolina, he returned to the Pentagon as the navy's director of surface warfare. Promoted to vice admiral with three stars, he was assigned to San Diego as commander of surface forces for the Pacific Fleet.

Krekich joined the private sector as president and general manager of the Norfolk Shipbuilding and Dry-dock Company (now United States Marine Repair). He remains active with three nonprofit ventures and a consulting role with a national mutual fund. He and his wife, Bobbi, have two sons.

### Thomas Lynch, Class of 1964, center/linebacker

Thomas Lynch received his Master of Science degree from George Washington University and then completed a thirty-one-year career of naval service, retiring with the rank of rear admiral. His naval service roles included chief of U.S. Navy legislative affairs, commander of the *Eisenhower* battle group during Operation Desert Shield, superintendent of the U.S. Naval Academy (1991–1994), and director of the U.S. Navy staff in the Pentagon (1994–1995). Lynch joined Jones, Lang, LaSalle (formerly the Staubach Company) after six years as senior vice president at Safeguard Scientifics Inc. He is currently a partner with the Musser Group; chair of the Naval Academy's Athletic and Scholarship Foundation; serves on the USO World Board and the boards of the Catholic Leadership Institute, Infologix, and Telkonet boards. Lynch married his high school sweetheart, Kathy, and they have been married for forty-four years and have three children and ten grandchildren.

### James Maginn, Class of 1964, tackle

James Maginn was deployed on the USS *Walke* and then served two tours of duty in Vietnam, the second as commander of a squadron of twelve PT boats. After retirement from active duty in 1969, he remained in the reserves for fifteen years and ascended to rank of captain. He later entered the banking industry and participated in several joint ventures related to real estate development. Maginn is currently president and CEO of the Watts Companies.

He and his wife, Andrea, have been married for forty years and have two children and two grandchildren. They live in Manhattan Beach, California.

### Nick Markoff, Class of 1964, fullback

Nick Markoff served eight years on active duty, completing cruises as an F-8 Crusader pilot and an A-7 Corsair II pilot. He left active duty and spent the next twenty years in the Naval Reserves, retiring as a captain. Inspired by his past coaches and his father, Markoff pursued a career teaching, coaching football and wrestling (among other sports), serving as athletic director, and working with youth. He has been married to wife Mary for over forty-two years and has five children and eighteen grandchildren.

### Frederick Marlin, Class of 1965, guard/kicker

Frederick Marlin was commissioned into the Navy Supply Corps in 1965. His naval career included four years at the Subic Bay Naval Base in the Philippines working at the naval supply depot and the ship repair facility. This was followed by a tour as comptroller at the Naval Academy. After twenty years of active duty, he retired from the navy and taught math and coached football for a high school in Orlando, Florida. He married Sue, an Army nurse, and has three children and seven grandchildren. The entire family resides in Orlando.

### Douglas McCarty, Class of 1965, end

After graduation, Douglas McCarty became a flight instructor for the U.S. Navy in Pensacola, Florida, where he later died during flight training. He was married to Barbara, with whom he had two daughters.

### Ed Merino, Class of 1965, end

After leaving the Naval Academy, Ed Merino went into business. After thirty years of experience as CEO, board member, and board chairman, he founded Office of the Chairman, for which he serves as a boardroom coach, guiding executives to discover their ultimate success. Merino married wife Robyn in 1965, and they have two children together, as well as one granddaughter.

### Richard Merritt, Class of 1964, tackle

Richard Merritt flew P-3s in two different squadrons, VP-10 and VP-26, out of Brunswick, Maine, hunting Russian subs. He served one tour in Southeast Asia doing radar picket in the Gulf of Tonkin. Merritt resigned from active duty in 1970 and worked for Eastern Airlines as a pilot until 1989. He received a law degree in 1981 and currently practices law in New York and Florida.

### Steve Moore, Class of 1964, halfback

Commissioned to the Supply Corp as ensign, Steve Moore was assigned to USS *Nantahala* patrolling to the Atlantic Ocean and Caribbean and Mediterranean Seas. He attended submarine school in Groton, Connecticut, and was assigned to the USS *Sam Houston* in defense of the Atlantic. He later joined the Nuclear Support Division. In 1975, Moore moved to New England and joined the dot-com industry.

He is married to his "lifelong love," Judy, with whom he has three sons, Steve Jr., Andy, and Matt. Reflecting on his current life, Moore said, "This phase of our lives has a golden hue, gilded by the marriages of our three sons, the birth of our five grandsons, the warm renewal of past friendships, and the steadfast brotherhood of the Navy team of 1963."

### Fred Moosally, Class of 1966, tackle

Appointed president of Lockheed Martin Maritime Systems & Sensors (MS2) in October 2002, Fred Moosally's career spans forty years of service to industry and the military. His twenty-four-year career with the U.S. Navy included command positions aboard a guided-missile destroyer and a battleship. In 2005 he was awarded the Navy League's Admiral Chester W. Nimitz Award for exemplary leadership in the maritime defense industry.

### Phil Norton, Class of 1966, end

As a member of the supply corps, Phil Norton deployed on the USS *Pickaway*, which was stationed in San Diego before going to Vietnam. After retiring from the navy, Norton worked for Memorex and then started the Systems Leasing Corporation, which was sold to Pacific Corp. He next started the business ePlus. Norton has been married to Pat for forty-three years, and they have three boys and grandchildren.

### Bob Orlosky, Class of 1964, halfback

Bob Orlosky coached the plebe team and taught physical education. He spent twenty years as a carrier-based aviator and staff officer. He also worked for Coopers & Lybrand and Affiliated Computer Systems. Orlosky is currently employed by the FAA leading a team that acquires and validates air traffic controller and technician training. He married Betty Kuharik on Thanksgiving Day, 1965, and they have two sons and four grandchildren.

### Edward "Skip" Orr, Class of 1965, halfback/safety

Skip Orr was an assistant plebe football coach at the academy and flew P-3 planes, in which he completed a Southeast Asia tour and earned an Air Medal and several other unit/squadron medals. Orr flew commercial planes for Eastern Airlines for eighteen years and became senior vice president for the Staubach Company, serving in that role for nineteen years. He has been married for forty-three years and has four children and five grandchildren.

### Jim "Snorter" Ounsworth, Class of 1964, fullback

Jim Ounsworth graduated in 1966 from the U.S. Navy Nuclear Power School and in 1975 from the University of Virginia School of Law. He served as an officer on a destroyer deployed in Vietnam and then entered the submarine service as chief engineer of a missile submarine. Ounsworth later became a partner in the law firm of Pepper Hamilton before being hired as chief legal counsel and a member of the investment committee of Safeguard Scientifics, a successful venture capital company in the 1990s. He lives part-time in Philadelphia and part-time in Paris working from time to time as a legal and venture capital consultant.

### Kip Paskewich, Class of 1965, halfback

Kip Paskewich served four years on various deployments as a line officer in a destroyer and working in amphibious tactical air control. He began his civilian career in 1969 with several companies specializing in architecture/engineering/construction management and contracting, as well as working as a computer/software integration and consulting contractor. He earned a master's degree in architecture from the University of New Mexico and provided professional services in commercial and government sectors, including at various Department of Energy research and development laboratories and military facilities. He designed and then personally constructed Barbara's and his passive solar home in the East Mountains of Albuquerque, where they raised their two children.

### Patrick Philbin, Class of 1965, tackle

Patrick Philbin was assigned to an antisubmarine warfare squadron until 1970 and subsequently flew in the reserves until 1974. He then became a commercial pilot (Eastern, Trump Shuttle, U.S. Air) and received a law degree from St. Johns University. Philbin started his own law firm and was assigned as an arbitrator. Currently, he is the chief of staff for the Domestic Nuclear Detection Office.

### Norm Radtke, Class of 1964, quaterback

Norm Radtke spent three years on the USS *Farragut* in the engineering department and then served as executive officer of the USS *Hickman County* in Vietnam. He was later the officer in charge of the destroyer escort USS *Marsh* in Long Beach, California. During his naval service, Radtke was awarded the National Defense Service Medal, three Bronze Stars on the Vietnam Service Medal, Navy Expeditionary Medal (Vietnam), and several other honors. Radtke went to the University of

Michigan Medical School and did a residency in ophthalmology at the University of Florida. Since 1983, he has been the director of the Retina Vitreous Research Center in Louisville, Kentucky, and an adjunct professor in the department of psychological and brain sciences at the University of Louisville. He has been married for thirty-seven years to his wife, Chris Tina, who is an artist. They have two grown children and one grandchild.

## Mike Riley, Class of 1965, guard
A navy pilot (lieutenant) in Vietnam, Mike Riley resigned after five years and then became a Delta Airlines pilot for thirty-three years. He is retired and living in Florida with his wife, Marie, three daughters, and five grandchildren.

## Steve Roesinger, Class of 1964, end
Commissioned in the supply corps upon graduation because of his bad eyes, Steve Roesinger spent two years on a tanker in the South China Sea until he was stationed in Saigon, Vietnam, then to Da Nang. Roesinger went to Loyola in downtown Chicago to improve his Russian, then took two semesters of MBA work at night at Northwestern, after which he spent a summer in Russian school at Middlebury College before starting his MBA at Harvard. He moved to Denver and began his commercial real estate career, continuing as a partner at the Frederick Ross Company. He was married in 1979 and has three children.

## John "Rags" Sai, Class of 1964, halfback
John Sai served for two years on the USS *Midway*, which included a nine-month deployment to the Tonkin Gulf where he flew missions over North Vietnam. He got married and subsequently reported to the USS *Eversole*, a destroyer, for two years with another deployment to the Tonkin Gulf. He was next sent to naval gunfire liaison officer school and survival school and then assigned to the 3rd Marine Division in Dong Ha, Vietnam.

Sai went to the University of California–Berkeley and earned his California teaching credential. He taught math and coached football and track for thirty-four years at three different high schools in central California. He has been retired for five years now and is doing a lot of traveling and working part-time at a local golf course.

### Steve Shrawder, Class of 1966, halfback

Steve Shrawder served aboard the USS *Waldron* for a year and a half, working part of that time with the battleship *New Jersey* engaged in gunfire support in Vietnam. He received orders to report to flight school in Pensacola and played football one last time for the Pensacola Navy Goshawks along with Roger Staubach. He was assigned to Helicopter Combat Support Squadron Four, which had a permanent detachment in Vietnam. He volunteered to go back in 1971–1972.

Shrawder became a special agent with the FBI from 1972 to 1975, after which he returned home to Millersburg, Pennsylvania, where he and his wife had grown up, to raise his family. In Pennsylvania he was employed in the mining industry and in manufacturing while serving on the local board of education. In May 2009, he was inducted into the Pennsylvania Sports Hall of Fame.

### David "Shug" Sjuggerud, Class of 1964, end

Dave Sjuggerud achieved more than 350 carrier landings in deployment during the Vietnam War, flying F-8 Crusaders and F-14 Tomcats. After the war he served in engineering development as a test pilot flying F-4 Phantoms. He retired from service in 1986 with the rank of captain and multiple service medals. In civilian life he worked for McDonnell Douglas. Sjuggerud died in 2008 and is survived by his wife, Jean, and two sons.

### Roger Staubach, Class of 1965, quarterback

Roger Staubach spent four years in the U.S. Navy. Following his service time, he played for the Dallas Cowboys of the NFL from 1969 through

1979. A six-time Pro Bowler, he led the Cowboys to four Super Bowls and two championships. He is a member of the College Football Hall of Fame and the Pro Football Hall of Fame.

In the offseason Staubach started a real estate career and worked at the Henry S. Miller Company. He founded the Staubach Company in 1977, a commercial real estate firm, which merged with Jones, Lang, LaSalle in July 2008. He has been married for more than forty years and has five children and fourteen grandchildren.

### Bob Sutton, Class of 1964, quarterback/defensive back

Rear Admiral Bob Sutton served as a surface warfare officer for thirty-four years, serving on seven ships and commanding two of them. During his 1990–1991 assignment in Operation Desert Shield/ Desert Storm, Admiral Sutton was the forward-deployed logistics commander for the U.S. Navy. He also participated in the repatriation of U.S. and coalition-partner POWs upon signature of the cease-fire agreement. He served as director of the Navy International Programs Office as well.

After he retired from the navy in 1999, Sutton took a position with ITT Industries as director for air surveillance. He is currently the president of BecTech Inc., which provides engineering and acquisition management support primarily to the U.S. Navy in the area of surface ship combat systems.

Sutton serves on the board of directors of the Surface Navy Association, National Capital Council of the Navy League, and National Maritime Heritage Foundation. He is also chairman of the Naval Affairs Committee for the U.S. Navy League. He is married to Rebecca Sutton, CEO of BecTech.

### Steven Szabo, Class of 1965, fullback

Steven Szabo served in the Marine Corps for four years, including thirteen months in Vietnam. He also played football for the Quantico Marines in 1965, 1967, and 1968. Following his discharge, Szabo attended John Hopkins University for a doctorate in applied math. He subsequently coached football for forty-one years in college and the pros, included stints at the University of Michigan (2006) and Ohio State University (1979), both of which played for the national championship. He also coached for the National Football League's New England Patriots when they won the Super Bowl in 2004. Szabo currently works at Eastern Michigan University as associate head coach/linebackers.

### Robert Teall, Class of 1964, halfback

Robert Teall served five years as an officer in the Marine Corps, including combat duty in Vietnam. After his service ended, he earned his law degree and worked in the legal profession in Ohio and North Carolina. Teall married the former Sue Bunck, with whom he had three children and ten grandchildren. He died in 2008 after a long struggle with Alzheimer's.

### Bill Ulrich, Class of 1964, halfback

Bill Ulrich served for twenty years on cruisers and destroyers in the U.S. Pacific Fleet, including a tour in Vietnam as the officer in charge of a Swift boat, participating in Market Time Operations for which he was awarded the Bronze Star with Combat "V" for action against the enemy. His final tour of duty was completed as commanding officer of the USS *Fife* operating in the western Pacific with carrier strike groups. He retired in 1984 and was employed as a senior analyst in computerized, simulated war-gaming exercises for the Fleet. Ulrich has been married to his wife, Karen, for more than forty years and has two children and three grandchildren. The entire Ulrich family currently resides in San Diego, California.

### Robert Wittenberg, Class of 1964, tackle

Robert Wittenberg completed two Vietnam tours and then stayed in the navy for twenty-seven years, during which he had three commands: VA-115 (an A-6 squadron), VA-128 (the A-6 training squadron), and

CVW-1 (a carrier airwing based on the USS *America*). Wittenberg is still flying and training pilots for AirTran Airways.

## Steve Zientak, Class of 1966, guard

Steve Zientak deployed on a destroyer on the East Coast of the United States and the Mediterranean before going in-country in Vietnam for a year with Military Sea Transportation Service, Mekong Delta. He left active service in 1971, secured a law degree in 1976, and then practiced law in Silicon Valley, California, for twenty-five years before retiring. He is still married to his first wife of forty-three years and has two daughters living nearby and five grandchildren.

The author was unable to find the whereabouts of or information about the following individuals:

David Gillespie, Class of 1965, guard

Bruce Kenton, Class of 1965, end

John Mickelson, Class of 1965, end

# Bibliography and Sources

## Books

Boyles, Bob, and Paul Guido. *50 Years of College Football: A History of America's Most Colorful Sport*. New York: Skyhorse Publishing, 2007.

Clary, Jack. *Navy Football: Gridiron Legends and Fighting Heroes*. Annapolis, MD: Naval Institute Press, 1997.

Collier, Peter, and David Horowitz. *The Kennedys: An American Drama*. New York: Summit Books, 1984.

Dietzel, Paul F. *Call Me Coach: A Life in College Football*. Baton Rouge: Louisiana State University Press, 2008.

Halberstam, David. *The Education of a Coach*. New York: Hyperion, 2006.

Kennedy, John F. *Profiles in Courage*. New York: Harper & Brothers, 1956.

Knuckle, Robert. *Black Jack: America's Famous Riderless Horse*. Renfrew, Ontario: General Store Publishing House, 2002.

Leamer, Laurence. *The Kennedy Men: 1901–1963*. New York: William Morrow, 2001.

Martin, Ralph G. *A Hero for Our Time: An Intimate Story of the Kennedy Years*. New York: MacMillan Publishing Co., 1983.

Newseum, Susan Bennett, and Cathy Trost. *President Kennedy Has Been Shot*. Naperville, IL: Source Books Media Fusion, 2004.

O'Brien, Michael. *John F. Kennedy: A Biography*. New York: Thomas Dunne Books, St. Martin's Press, 2005.

Pennington, Bill. *The Heisman: Great American Stories of the Men Who Won*. New York: Harper Entertainment, 2005.

Russo, Gus. *Live by the Sword: The Secret War against Castro and the Death of JFK*. Baltimore: Bancroft Press, 1998.

Salinger, Pierre. *With Kennedy*. Garden City, NY: Doubleday, 1966.

Simmons, Edwin H., and J. Robert Moskin. *The Marines*. Quantico, VA: Hugh Lauter Levin Associates, 1998.

Sorensen, Ted. *Counselor: A Life at the Edge of History*. New York: HarperCollins, 2008.

Staff of the *New York Times*. *Four Days in November, The Original Coverage of the John F. Kennedy Assassination*. New York: St. Martin's Press, 2003.

Staubach, Roger, with Brian St. John and Sam Blair. *First Down, Lifetime to Go*. Waco, TX: A Keyword Book, 1976.

Staubach, Roger, and Frank Luksa. *Time Enough to Win*. New York: Warner Books, Inc., 1981.

Verna, Tony. *Instant Replay, The Day that Changed Sports Forever*. Beverly Hills, CA: Creative Book Publishers International, 2008.

Waldron, Lamar, and Thom Hartmann. *Ultimate Sacrifice: John and Robert Kennedy, the Plan for a Coup in Cuba, and the Murder of JFK*. New York: Basic Books, 2005.

Whittingham, Richard. *Rites of Autumn: The Story of College Football*. New York: The Free Press, 2001.

## Newspapers and Periodicals

Associated Press: Herb Thompson

*Boston Globe*: Herbert Black, Jimmy Breslin, Ray Coffey, James Doyle, Abe Plotkin, Martin Steadman

*Capital* (Annapolis): Hymy Cohen, Fred Geiger, Peter Lisagor

*Charleston Gazette*: A. L. Hardiman

*Chicago Sun Times*: Jerome Holtzman

*Dallas Morning Sun*: Sam Blair, Gary Cartwright, Roy Edwards, Karen Martin

*Durham Herald*: Jack Horner

*Durham Sun*: Hugo Germino

*Fresno Bee*

*Hartford Courant*: Bill Lee

*High Point Enterprise*: Bob Hoffman

*Lima News*: Jim Weeks

*Los Angeles Times*: Shaveneau Glick, Charlie Park

*Modesto Bee*

*New York Newsday*: Greg Logan

*New York Times*: R. W. Apple Jr., David Brinkley, Arthur Daley, Allison Danzig, Gerard Eskevasi, Sydney Gryson, Leonard Koppett, James Sheehan, Michael Strauss, Lincoln Werden, Gordon White, Tom Wicker

*Raleigh News & Observer*: Dick Herbert, Frank Spencer

*South Bend Tribune*: Joe Doyle

*Sports Illustrated*: Walter Bingham, Dan Jenkins, Rex Lardner, Roy Terrell, John Underwood

United Press International: Bryce Miller, Albert Merriman Smith

*Washington Post*: Robert Addie, Will Grimsley, George Minot, John Norris, Shirley Povich, Martie Zad

## Websites

All Sports. "Roger Staubach Career Biography and Statistics." www.allsports.com/players/roger-staubach.

"All Time Records of Navy." football.stassen.com/cgi-bin/records/fetch-team.pl?team=Navy.

American Presidency Project. "John F. Kennedy." www.presidency.ucsb.edu/ws/index.php.

AP Poll Archive. www.appollarchive.com.

Atkinson, Rick. "One Tough Hoss." www.cusa-fans.com/articles/cusa-football-2008/smu-football-mac-white_060408.html.

"Base: Advancing a Post-Military Landscape: Quonset Point Naval Air Station." quonsetpoint.artinruins.com/quonset_main.htm.

"Beano Cook's Top Ten Moments in College Football." www.tonyvernatv.com/links/ESPN.pdf.

Clary, Jack. U.S. Naval Academy Alumni Association & Foundation. "Navy to Play Its 1,200th Football Game Saturday against SMU." https://www.usna.com/SSLPage.aspx?RSS=acad&referrer–&pid=6218.

"Cuban Missile Crisis." www.u-s-history.com/pages/h1736.html.

Department of the Navy: Navy Historical Center. "USS *Constitution* Captures HMS *Guerriere*, 19 August 1812." www.history.navy.mil/photos/events/war1812/atsea/con-guer.htm.

Eyewitness: American Originals from the National Archives. "Fallen Leaders." www.archives.gov/exhibits/eyewitness/flash.php?section=14.

Flanagan, Brian. "The President's Game, Army–Navy, 1890–2005." www.gvsu.edu/hauenstein/index.cfm?id=A34B5ECF-E063-A4F3-B9B3CC70C4B62704.

"Former JFK Secret Service Agent Speaks Out in New Book." April 8, 2008. rfkjrforpresident.com/2008/04/08.

Frank, J. "Ray Barbuti: The Italian American Chariot of Fire, 2003." National Italian American Foundation. findarticles.com/p/articles/mi_qa5518/is_200307/ai_n21340086/?tag=content;col1.

"Funeral Music." www.jfklibrary.org/Historical+Resources/Archives/Reference+Desk/Funeral+Music.htm.

Gelston, Dan. "Army–Navy, Instant Replay: Tony Verna, 45 Years Later." Associated Press. December 5, 2008. www.insidesocal.com/tomhoffarth/archives/2008/12/army-navy-insta.html.

Goldstein, Richard. *New York Times.* "James Swindal, 88, Pilot of Kennedy's Presidential Plane." May 1, 2006. query.nytimes.com/gst/fullpage.html?res=9C0CE5DE113FF932A35756C0A9609C8B63.

Goudie, Chuck. "Former Agent Says Kennedy Assassination Thwarted Weeks before President's Death." WLS-TV. November 27, 2007. abclocal.go.com/wls/story?section=news&id=5778871.

Grady, Sandy. "Another Epic West Virginia Battle." *USA Today.* May 13, 2008. blogs.usatoday.com/oped/2008/05/another-epic-we.html.

Hawkins, Geraldine. "How the Rough Rider Revived Army–Navy Rivalry."
    *All Hands*. December 2008. findarticles.com/p/articles/mi_m0IBQ/is_1101/
    ai_n31127243.

Hett, Karen. "The Day John F. Kennedy Was Assassinated." May 2004. freepages.
    genealogy.rootsweb.ancestry.com/~mccannkin/KendyAssn/kenmems.html.

Howard, Robert. "The Individual Who Tried to Enter Trauma Room 1." August 8,
    2006. educationforum.ipbhost.com/lofiversion/index.php/t7632.html.

"Inside Air Force One." www.theexpress.com/express%20397/features/features2.htm.

Interdonato, Sal. "Army–Navy: From Heated Rivals to Pals." *Times Herald-
    Record*. December 5, 2008. www.recordonline.com/apps/pbcs.dll/
    article?AID=/20081205/SPORTS36/812050364.

JFK Library. "Items in the Oval Office." www.jfklibrary.org/Historical+Resources/
    Archives/Reference+Desk/Items+in+the+Oval+Office.htm.

"JFK Reports and Documents: The Eyewitnesses." www.jfk-online.com/jfkdocs.html.

"John Fitzgerald Kennedy: President of the United States." www.arlingtoncemetery.
    net/jfk.htm.

"John F. Kennedy." The Biography Channel website. www.biography.com/bio4kids.

"John F. Kennedy." encarta.msn.com/encyclopedia_761576731/john_f_kennedy.
    html.

"June 12, 1944: John F. Kennedy Receives Medals." www.history.com/this-day-in-
    history.do?action=Article&id=654.

Magazine of the Week—*Life*, November 29, 1963. www.dtmagazine.com/magazine
    ofweek9212006.html.

National Archives. "The President John F. Kennedy Assassination Records
    Collection." www.archives.gov/research/jfk.

Naval History and Heritage Command. "Report on Loss of PT 109." www.history.
    navy.mil/faqs/faq60-11.htm.

"Navy Coach Legend Steve Belichick Dies at Age 86." November 20, 2005. www.
    patriots.com/news/index.cfm?ac=latestnewsdetail&pid=14002&pcid=47.

*New York Times*. "Charles Kirkpatrick, War Hero Who Led Naval Academy."
    March 16, 1988. www.nytimes.com/1988/03/16/obituaries/charles-kirkpatrick-
    war-hero-who-led-the-naval-academy.html.

NUWC. "Naval History in Rhode Island." December 27, 2004. www.nuwc.navy.mil/
    hq/history/0002.html.

"Orange Bowl 1961." www.mmbolding.com/bowls/Orange_1961.htm.

Order from Chaos. "Army–Navy Football Game." November 29, 2006.
    braveastronaut.blogspot.com/2006/11/army-navy-football-game.html.

Ponton, Anthony. "John F. Kennedy and West Virginia, 1960–1963." April 27, 2004.
    www.marshall.edu/etd/masters/ponton-anthony-2004-ma.pdf.pdf.

Rabble. "Football: 1963 Football Preview." April 26, 2003. army.scout.com/2/107273.
    html.

Reid, Thomas F. "Personal Memoirs of the State Funeral of President John F.
    Kennedy November 22–25, 1963." December 4, 2008. www.freerepublic.com/
    focus/f-news/2143214/posts.

Rios, Delia. "In Mrs. Kennedy's Pink Suit, an Indelible Memory of Public Grief." *Deseret News.* November 22, 2003. www.deseretnews.com/article/1,5143,540034493,00.html.

Sarmah, Satta. "Navy Veteran David Sjuggerud Was Humble about Experiences." U.S. Naval Academy Alumni Association and Foundation. November 30, 2008. https://www.usna.com/SSLPage.aspx?RSS=obits&referrer=&pid=6623.

Sidney, Hugh. "Kennedy Assassination Chronicles." JFK Lancer Productions and Publications. www.jfklancer.com/pdf/Camelot.pdf.

Socci, Bob. "A Look Back at the First Game at Navy–Marine Corps Memorial Stadium." October 5, 2005. www.navysports.com/sports/m-footbl/spec-rel/100505aaf.html.

Steiger, Gus. "Navy vs. Army: 1962." April 10, 2003. navy.scout.com/2/104302.html.

*St. Petersburg Times* Online. "JFK: A Timeline of His Life." www.sptimes.com/News/111199/JFK/timeline.shtml.

Sullivan, Patricia. "William Busik, 85; Dies, Naval Academy Football Star." *Washington Post.* October 22, 2005. www.encyclopedia.com/doc/1P2-72608.html.

"Survey of Historic Sites and Buildings: Kennedy Compound, Massachusetts." www.nps.gov/history/history/online_books/presidents/site30.htm.

Terrell, Roy. "Army, Navy and Joe Bellino." November 28, 1960. vault.sportsillustrated.cnn.com/vault/article/magazine/MAG1072065/3/index.htm.

Thompson, Wright. "Ghosts of Mississippi." sports.espn.go.com/espn/eticket/story?page=mississippi62&num=3.

Underwood, John. "Big Day for 'D.'" January 13, 1964. vault.sportsillustrated.cnn.com/vault/article/magazine/MAG1075541/index.htm.

Underwood, John. "On, Brave Old Army Team." April 29, 1968. vault.sportsillustrated.cnn.com/vault/article/magazine/MAG1081106/index.htm.

*USA Today.* "Army vs. Navy: More than Just a Game." November 25, 2007. www.usaweekend.com/07_issues/071125/071125army-navy-football-game.html.

"Vets Share Story of Old Guard's Most-Public Hour." December 18, 1998. www.arlingtoncemetery.net/jfk-funr.htm.

VFP62.com. "In Memory of Dave Sjuggerud." March 26, 2009. www.vfp62.com/Sjuggerud.html.

"Where is the Honor Guard?" www.ancestrymagazine.com/2008/07/on-the-web.

Worldnetdaily.com. "JFK Assassination Plot Uncovered in Chicago?" November 22, 2007. www.wnd.com/news/article.asp?ARTICLE_ID=58836.

Also, special thanks go to the John F. Kennedy Library, which provided various reference materials including but not limited to the following: President Kennedy speeches; interviews conducted by the library of pertinent individuals related to the president; and school, family, and naval data.

# Index